Education Deform

Bright People Sometimes Say Stupid Things about Education

James M. Kauffman

A SCARECROWEDUCATION BOOK

The Scarecrow Press, Inc.
Lanham, Maryland, and London
2002

A SCARECROWEDUCATION BOOK

Published in the United States of America
by Scarecrow Press, Inc.
A Member of the Rowman & Littlefield Publishing Group
4720 Boston Way
Lanham, Maryland 20706
www.scarecroweducation.com

4 Pleydell Gardens, Folkestone
Kent CT20 2DN, England

British Library Cataloguing in Publication Information Available

Library of Congress Cataloging-in-Publication Data

Kauffman, James M.
  Education deform : bright people sometimes say stupid things about education / James
M. Kauffman.
    p. cm.
"A ScarecrowEducation book."
Includes bibliographical references (p.) and index.
ISBN 0-8108-4316-1 (cloth : alk. paper)
  1. Education—United States—Philosophy. 2. Education—Aims and objectives—United
States. 3. Educational change—United States. I. Title.

LB14.7 .K38 2002
370'.1—dc21

                                                              2002022506

∞™ The paper used in this publication meets the minimum requirements
of American National Standard for Information Sciences—Permanence of Paper for
Printed Library Materials, ANSI/NISO Z39.48-1992.
Manufactured in the United States of America.

Contents

Foreword

Almost all of us have gone to school. Most of us have gone to public schools. This seems to qualify us in our minds as experts on public education. We all seem to have an opinion on how children should be taught, how schools should be run, and how teaching should be improved. There is nothing more public than public education. At the same time, there sometimes seems nothing so hidden as the science of schooling, the field of educational research. It is hidden partly because it is not particularly glamorous or exciting and thus not appealing to the popular press. Year by year, increment by increment, educational research has shown that children best learn to read by direct skill instruction, that what children bring to school by way of family background or home environment is usually more critical to educational success than their school experience, and that children with disabilities are regrettably more likely to have poorer school outcomes despite our best efforts than children without such individual differences.

We would all like to believe the opposite. It is more appealing to think that we can just scatter books around the classroom or just read aloud to children and all will magically become good readers. It is more glamorous to think that six hours of good schooling per day will overcome years of poverty or neglect. It is more exciting to think that we can just ignore individual differences, treat all children the same, and thus make disabilities disappear. These beliefs all make for better stories and thus are more likely to be what we see or hear from the media.

Educational research is also hidden by the fact that it is very often pedantic, unnecessarily obscured by jargon, and prone to faddism. It is often by necessity complex, as is most research in the social or behavioral sciences, in which many variables cannot be controlled as much as we would like. The media have more trouble with such complexity and tend to avoid it. The fact remains, however, that the weight of research evidence still supports the former conclusions. There are of course always exceptions, and we rejoice in these exceptions. Exceptions, however, do not negate the overwhelming weight of evidence.

This is the crux of Jim Kauffman's book. It is in the gap between what we know and what we would like to believe, that even the best of us are drawn to say stupid things about education. The 1990's "All children can learn," the current "Leave no child behind," and my perennial favorite, "Every child will be average or above in academic performance" are but a fraction of these. They are wonderfully evocative, at first hearing. However, as Jim points out, their message not only fails close scrutiny but also obscures solutions to problems.

These statements are nonetheless, as he also illustrates, made by those of us who truly care about improving schools. They are made by those of us who know that the key to improving education is to inspire both the public and school professionals alike to renewed or redirected effort. They are thus statements that, for this very purpose, roll up enormously complex issues into a short sound bite. They are also stunning in their stupidity.

Our wonderfully diverse society has become so timid about personal offense, however, that few have the courage to confront such stupidity. Kauffman's courage in doing so will be seen by some as curmudgeonly at best and intolerant at worst. His dissection of such stupid statements, of misguided postmodernism, of misdirected multiculturalism, and of other such mistakes, however, is not only courageous but in the end constructive. Such analysis in effect lays out essential complexities behind each statement or approach. In doing so it leads to far more thoughtful consideration of solutions. For this, public education owes him a great debt.

Steven R. Forness, Ed.D.
Professor of Psychiatry and Biobehavioral Sciences
School Principal and Chief of Educational Psychology Services
UCLA Neuropsychiatric Hospital

Too much of what is said today about education and its reform is nonsense that shortchanges students and their parents. I have no illusion that what I wrote will stamp out mindless rhetoric about schools and schooling. But, maybe, it will help parents, teachers, administrators, and my colleagues who teach teachers to revisit some ideas they've heard or talked about. If this book helps anyone make more sense in thinking and talking about education, then I'll have achieved my primary objective.

Statements that don't make sense have for too long drained all hope out of public schooling and sapped even much of the hope from private schools. I think we can regenerate the hope that public and private education can actually be improved, but only if we first separate sense from nonsense about important issues. We can do better in our thinking about education and schooling. We must do so for the sake of our children and, ultimately, for our own sake and that of our society.

In the first chapter, I explain how stupid statements made by bright people twist education policy and practice. By *stupid* I mean things that don't make sense, that are not logical in the light of what we know. By *bright people* I mean those in positions of influence on education, whose statements and judgments may be expected to affect education policy and practice. They may be elected or appointed or have achieved prominence in their communities in other ways, perhaps through writing, speaking, or business success. They include the people who administer schools and those who train teachers, as well as teachers themselves. By *policy* I mean the laws and rules by which an organization or activity is created, monitored, evaluated, and controlled. This includes the informal rules by which organizations are managed.

In the second chapter, I describe how advertisers, politicians, comedians, and educators use stupid statements artfully. In chapters 3–6, I discuss some of the more common forms of statements that are worthless for improving schools: slogans, self-contradictions, misleading statements, and the simply unintelligible. In the final chapter, I suggest how we might make better sense in talk of education and its reform.

This book is a set of essays about education and its critics. The prologue sets the stage for the chapters; the epilogue is my reflection on what the chapters mean. If the organization of the chapters or essays seems arbitrary, that is because in my mind there is no way to organize statements about education in a way that avoids relatively arbitrary, overlapping categories. Slogans are part of what I call "the art of the stupid," and they deform educational policies. They are also misleading. Self-contradictions and nonsequiturs are often unintelligible, are part of the art of the stupid, and deform educational policy making. "Postmodernism" (the idea that Enlightenment science and rationality are not the best ways to weigh the truth of propositions) is a recurring theme throughout the chapters, as there is no way to separate it entirely into a single category that I have created. I have tried to group my thoughts in ways that make sense to me, but I have not tried to avoid all redundancies. Some points do bear repeating, and I have deliberately allowed the repetition of some statements and ideas in more than one chapter.

Each chapter begins with a quotation that is a point for discussion in that chapter. In each of the first six chapters I have included a vignette that illustrates how questionable statements about education can affect what happens in schools. These vignettes, under the heading *Deformed Education*, are drawn from the actual experiences of teachers, parents, or colleagues. I've changed the names and details to protect people's identities, but the descriptions are of real travesties in education. All the vignettes illustrate multiple issues, so they should not be read as exemplifying only the concept I discuss in a particular essay or chapter.

SOURCES AND CONSEQUENCES OF NONSENSE

It's important to understand how nonsensical statements about education are created and accepted in today's world outside of schools.

Surely, it's possible for someone to make sense about one thing and not to make sense about another. But I think it's important to see how statements about education are embedded in a social context in which stupid statements are made about many things. However, inane statements about education and its reform have dire consequences for kids, parents, taxpayers, and educators. If we are to improve our communication and the education of our children, then we need to recognize ludicrous statements for what they are, regardless of who makes them.

Educators are not the only ones to have made statements about education that are nonsensical or at odds with reliable data. People in all walks of life have done so. In *The Darwin Awards*, Wendy Northcutt observes that there are many failures of common sense in the modern world. I note that these failures of common sense often apply to comments about education. In fact, I think the extent of stupidity about education is captured in a quotation attributed by Northcutt to Albert Einstein: "Only two things are infinite—the universe and human stupidity, and I'm not so sure about the universe."[1]

When apparently well-informed people say things that don't make sense, we wonder why they said them. All of us—myself included— have made such statements about one thing or another, sometimes out of ignorance, more often because we didn't think enough about the issue. Unfortunately, some people who have stopped to think still end up embracing what I think is nonsense. Of course, my objective is to convince you that what they say is nonsensical and that I make sense.

The consequences of preposterous statements about education and its reform are severe, particularly when bright people make such statements. People in positions of authority too often accept them as reasonable, repeat them, and base their actions on them, keeping education in a chronic state of denial of reality and cyclic revision—change that is silly and leads nowhere but back into another go-'round. This cycle of mindless change is not likely to stop unless we are able to tell the difference between statements that are insightful and statements that are not.

Too often, we forget that the adults who make illogical statements about education do not suffer the worst fallout. The students in our schools bear the brunt of adults' words that don't make sense. Many of the adults whose theories and school reform rhetoric provide nothing but high-sounding drivel do not seem to be thinking of actual, flesh-and-blood children when they spin out their nonsense. Their statements reduce children to abstractions or widgets rather than treat them as human beings. Keeping real kids in mind has a way of helping us know the difference between sense and nonsense.

KIDS' UNDERSTANDING OF NONSENSE

Kids don't always recognize sense when they hear it or read it. They don't have "built-in crap detectors," as I've heard some adults suggest. Kids are suckers at least as often as are adults. Michael Shermer, founder of the Skeptics Society, put it this way: "In their early years, children are knowledge junkies, questioning everything in their purview, though exhibiting little skepticism. Most never learn to distinguish between skepticism and credulity."[2] Many cannot distinguish sense from nonsense as adults.

Genius is not required to see that, left to their own devices, children will not automatically learn to discriminate between useful and useless ideas by the time they are adults. Most of us don't expect kids to learn complex mathematical operations or other complex skills on their own, and for good reason. "Children can always tell what's b.s. and what isn't" or other sentences with similar meaning are statements that, ultimately, hurt kids.

Teaching students to discriminate defensible statements from those that won't stand up to careful scrutiny is surely one goal of education. Thus we might expect highly educated people, especially those who study education, to recognize and avoid nonsense in their statements about education and its reform. Unfortunately, people with advanced academic degrees seem about as likely to be suckers for idiotic propositions as are those with little formal education. Still, some people hang onto the notion that education itself is the answer to this problem, that if people are just "educated" about issues—given the information necessary to make a good decision or behave sensibly—they will be rational. That idea hasn't worked yet, and I see no reason to believe that it will preclude stupidity.

GENERAL AND SPECIAL EDUCATION

Reform typically is thought to apply to the entire enterprise of education—general and special. However, special education is often completely ignored in talk of school reform. For example, in *Left*

Back: A Century of Failed School Reforms, Diane Ravitch barely mentions children with learning problems and almost totally ignores the issue of disability. She accuses G. Stanley Hall of demagoguery when he refers to a "great army" of students incapable of benefiting from an academic curriculum.[3] If such school children did not number in the hundreds of thousands in the late nineteenth century, they certainly did in the late twentieth century. Several hundred thousand individuals probably are a "great army."

The particular problems of students who can learn the general education curriculum only with extreme difficulty, if at all, are not routinely taken into account. These are children with disabilities, sometimes referred to as *exceptional children*, a term that may also apply to gifted children. Their omission is a curious one from an administrative standpoint, as special education for children with disabilities is now mandated by federal law and consumes a very substantial portion of the education budget at local and state levels. Their omission is also a scientific faux pas for, as Stephen Jay Gould argues in *Full House*, phenomena can be understood only by taking full *distributions* into account (in Gould's language, the "full house" of what is measured, from lowest or least to highest or most).[4] This means giving attention to the high and low extremes (i.e., right and left tails of mathematical distributions or curves), not just averages or typical cases (i.e., mean, median, or mode). Basing education reform solely on modal or average students or student capabilities is thus both administratively unjustifiable and scientifically indefensible.

Some statements about reforming American education are nonsense primarily because they do not consider the students who are at the margins of ability or performance, whose achievement is way below or way above that of most students their age—exceptional children. For these students at the margins, the consequences of poor thinking about education are particularly disastrous. Special education is thus a prominent part of the discussion in this book.

ACKNOWLEDGMENTS

I owe many people thanks for helping me finish this project. Jeanmarie Bantz, Barbara Bateman, Kathy McGee Benton, Rick Brigham, Liz Campbell, Martha Coutinho, Jean Crockett, Steve Forness, Stu Horsfall,

Sarah Irvine, Jennifer Jakubecy, Tim Konold, Tim Landrum, Carla Manno, Devery Mock, Mark Mostert, Lesley Myers, Susan Osborne, Lynne Perry, Steve Reynolds, Gary Sasso, and Rich Simpson deserve my gratitude for their patient reading of drafts of part or all of the manuscript and helping me express myself better. Their suggestions greatly improved the final product. In no way is any of them responsible for any factual error, absence of discernment, or lack of finesse in my writing.

I acknowledge with gratitude the support of my colleagues in the Curry School of Education at the University of Virginia, particularly Dean David Breneman and Dan Hallahan, chair of the Department of Curriculum, Instruction and Special Education. They kindly granted my academic leave, which made completion of this book possible.

I give special thanks to Patty Pullen, my wife and best friend, a truly gifted and now retired special education teacher. Her tolerant reading and rereading of the manuscript drafts and her kind and steady encouragement were invaluable. She treats me like an old dog—which is to say of her that she treats me with great affection and thoughtfulness. She loves me even though I have trouble learning the things she tries to teach me, and in return I am as loyal to her as a good old dog. Many times during my work on this manuscript she reminded me to stay on the porch if I don't want to run with the big dogs and to stay out of the kitchen if I can't stand the heat. Her admonitions should give me pause, as she's almost always right. I'm afraid I'm off the porch and headed for the kitchen. As she's often told me, I'll have no one to blame but myself if I am bitten or burned. But I know Patty will love me even if I am wounded, regardless of why I may suffer. Makes me glad to be her old dog.

NOTES

1. Northcutt (2000, p. 17); see also Northcutt (2001).
2. Shermer (1997, p. 13).
3. Ravitch (2000, p. 46).
4. Gould (1996a).

Prologue

"Writing commentaries is some kind of a disease of the intellect," wrote the late Nobel Prize–winning physicist Richard Feynman in *The Meaning of It All*.[1] I have written only a set of commentaries — essays, perhaps I should call them. Well, I say to myself, but Feynman said this in his own book of commentaries on science and pseudoscience, and he obviously had no disease of the intellect. In its context, I think his statement means that commentaries are useless for finding out anything *new*. That squares with my understanding and intent. I do not explore any new ideas in my commentaries, nor do I promote any new ones. I only try to bring some coherence to ideas and evidence that have been presented before. And I take some comfort in the fact that scientist Stephen Jay Gould has also been an inveterate writer of essays. No, the fact that I've written some essays doesn't put me in the same intellectual class as Feynman and Gould. It just reassures me that I haven't done something totally crazy. I realize, too, that there is a lot of truth in the ancient observation that there is nothing new under the sun.

Whether I make sense or merely make more off-target statements, and precisely where and how I do either, is for you to judge. I do not think there is only one way of viewing the world or only one correct conclusion about everything. I do know that judging all disagreements with one's own conclusions to be stupid is intellectual arrogance that should be avoided. However, I do think Roger Shattuck had it right in *Candor and Perversion: Literature, Education, and the Arts*:

> A real world of material things, sometimes called nature, exists around us. Nature includes us, and we share it imperfectly with one another through perception, action, memory, language, love, and wonder.
>
> The world scoffs at old ideas. It distrusts new ideas. It loves tricks.[2]

Shattuck's other theses make sense to me, too. I make no apology for assuming that there is a real world out there and that this assumption and its corollaries apply to most of the things we need to know about education. Neither do I apologize for recommending that we attempt to apprehend those realities through what has become known as science or the methods of the Enlightenment. Though smart people may sometimes say stupid things, eventually the day is won by thinking about things in ways associated with Enlightenment science. The world may well scoff at old ideas (many of which are found by each succeeding generation to be sound), distrust new ideas (many of which deserve distrust and are discredited in due course), and adore tricks (including sleights of mind performed under the guise of educational reform). One defense against the cognitive trick is knowledge of history, but that knowledge, like any other, still allows bad choices.

As you read this book, I hope you'll frequently ask yourself questions like these: Have I heard (or read) this or something like it before? What does it mean? Is this nonsense, or what? What is a sensible way of looking at this issue or problem? I hope you'll ask these and other questions not just about the statements I call stupid but about the ones I make, too. One of the big favors we can do for each other, I think, is to point out statements that don't add up, no matter who makes them.

It has occurred to me that some readers will find many of my own statements in this book nonsensical. There are, to be sure, different perspectives on what is stupid and what is not. To me, this does not suggest that nonsense does not exist, simply that it is often mistaken. Readers will judge whether I have mistakenly called erudition empty-headedness and whether any of my own statements are nonsense. To the extent that I have written something senseless, my unwittingness should prompt laughter, whether I have intended to be comedic or not.

A given is that my writing, like that of every other author, will be misunderstood or misrepresented by some. Misunderstanding and misrepresentation go with the territory: writing. Ralph Waldo Emerson wrote that "To be great is to be misunderstood."[3] However, it does not follow logically that to be misunderstood is to be great or to have the potential for greatness. In no way do I mean to suggest that all writing is understandable. Some writing is so bad that it fosters confusion. I hope that my writing cannot be so characterized—that any misunderstanding or misinterpretation is not due primarily to my own shortcomings as a writer.

I realize, too, that my wanting to make sense in a logical, linear way makes me retrograde in the minds of some of my contemporaries and many who are my chronological junior. I want things to make sense in a way that some of my critics consider old-fashioned, old-paradigm, elitist, sexist, racist, and all too Western. I want statements about education and its reform to be logical, to reflect critical thinking using the kind of logic that has been associated with science as it is understood in the Enlightenment tradition—yes, even though some of my colleagues in universities believe that the Enlightenment is horribly outdated, misguided, and primitive, if not evil. Call it male, call it European, call it godless, call it God-inspired, call it oppressive, call it anything you want, but I think that science following the Enlightenment tradition remains the most reliable, useful, practical, and hopeful way of thinking about things. This way of thinking is also, in my judgment, the most egalitarian way of approaching problems.

True, science has its limitations. It cannot answer all questions, although it can answer many. And it answers with probability statements, not the conviction that the ultimate truth has been found. Scientists can be wrong, as Michael Shermer points out. In fact, Shermer notes the observation of Kenneth Feder that "thinker," "writer," "scholar," "charlatan," and "kook" are not mutually exclusive categories.[4]

So, what can be done? In my opinion, it would certainly be wrong to cut off the debate between the defenders of science and its detractors. In America today, everyone has the right to hold personal beliefs and to express them, and I do not want to see that changed. However, those of us who believe that science and reason are our best tools for finding the truth have no duty to be accessories to condemnation of our views. We defenders of Enlightenment science understand that "Our critics actively dislike the Enlightenment and its consequences."[5] Aryeh Neier may be correct in concluding that what is unfolding in the early twenty-first century is a war in which "tribalists and fundamentalists have identified cosmopolitanism and modernity as their archenemy."[6] David Ignatius, too, sees the unfolding conflict as being "about the transition to the modern world."[7] The transition to the modern world began centuries ago and is not yet complete. Simon Winchester wrote of the meaning of the first geological map of England, made in the early nineteenth century by William Smith:

> It is a map whose making signified the beginnings of an era not yet over, that has been marked ever since by the excitement and astonishment of scientific discoveries that allowed human beings to start at last to stagger out from the fogs of religious dogma, and to come to understand something certain about their own origins—and those of the planet they inhabit.[8]

I agree with Gerald Holton that we should not decry the verbal attacks on science and modernism themselves. Nevertheless, those of us who embrace Enlightenment ideas do need to oppose such verbal attacks more directly and forcefully in our own statements.[9] This point and counterpoint is part of the process of forming and perpetuating a culture. In my view, it is a good idea to shore up and perpetuate modern cultures derived from the Enlightenment, including the ideas and methods we call science. Essayist Michael Skube expressed an observation with which I concur: "The values bequeathed the West by the Enlightenment—reason and tolerance, generosity and doubt, most of all the autonomy of the individual conscience—are humanity's best, indeed its only, hope."[10]

Roger Shattuck suggests that we can say it again—say the sensible things, the things that bear repeating (realizing that everything's been said before)—and try to say it better (which means, as Shattuck reminds us, knowing how it's been said before). No one can read everything, and I have read just enough to know how much I haven't. Still, I've tried to say it better, knowing that others have said many of the same things with extraordinary clarity and grace, as has my University of Virginia colleague E. D. Hirsch, Jr., in *The Schools We Need and Why We Don't Have Them.*[11] No doubt, I'll need to try again, just like everyone else. I recall novelist Philip Roth's wry observation in *American Pastoral* that writers are always wrong. The only thing that keeps them going, he suggests, is the perverse illusion that some day they just might get something right.[12]

NOTES

1. Feynman (1998, p. 115).
2. Shattuck (1999, pp. 4–6).
3. Emerson (1983, p. 265).
4. Shermer (1997, p. 173); see also Shermer (2001).
5. Rosovsky (1996, p. 540).
6. Neier (2001, p. A29).
7. Ignatius (2001, p. B7).
8. Winchester (2001, p. xvi).
9. Holton (1996).
10. Skube (2001, p. B4).
11. Hirsch (1996).
12. Roth (1997).

CHAPTER 1

The Deforming Effects of Nonsense

"If I'm honored to be confirmed by the Senate, I will dedicate myself every day to the task of assuring that no child in America will
be left behind."

— Rod Paige, U.S. Secretary of Education nominee

RENEWED HOPE ABOUT EDUCATION REQUIRES
CONFRONTING IGNORANCE AND STUPIDITY

A Bruce Eric Kaplan cartoon shows a couple at a cocktail party, drinks
in hand. The caption: "I was reading somewhere that people are stupid."[1] The statement reveals ignorance and banality without the
speaker's awareness that the statement about stupidity is dim-witted.
The social context depicted in Kaplan's drawing implies that ignorance
and stupidity are pervasive, mundane, dreary features of typical cocktail conversation. The cartoon illustrates with stinging humor the cultural illiteracy that people like E. D. Hirsch, Jr. have described.[2]

Musician Frank Zappa is reputed to have said something like this:
"Physicists tell us that hydrogen is the most common thing in the universe. They are wrong. The most common thing in the universe is ignorance." Ignorance (not knowing) and stupidity (not thinking very well
about what we know) are parts of the human condition, but both must
be resisted in ourselves and in others. Otherwise, why have education?

Many people are neither ignorant nor stupid, yet say things that don't
make much sense. How many ill-informed or nonsensical things must
someone say or do before we conclude that he or she is either ignorant

or stupid? There is no fixed answer to that question, any more than there is a fixed answer to how much doubt is reasonable for a juror in a court case or how much money makes a person rich or how little income makes a person poor. Besides, my topic is not stupid people but bright ones who make thoughtless statements—specifically, untenable statements about education. And education, perhaps more than any other topic in contemporary American life, seems to be awash in such statements.[3]

People of all descriptions make poorly reasoned statements and do inane things: U.S. presidents, presidential candidates (not to mention leaders of this or that nation or political or religious faction), presidents of this and that corporation and other business executives, athletic coaches, university administrators and faculty members, school teachers, unemployed people, laborers, radio talk show hosts, columnists, lawyers—the list could be extended nearly ad infinitum. Usually, these people know better, but sometimes they don't. They may be playing with a full deck, but they seem not to understand trump in the game they are playing. They may be ignorant of the rules of the game or may have temporarily forgotten them. Some seem to have retired early from thinking about certain things, as columnist Richard Cohen has noted.[4]

Bad thinking and ignorance in comments about education and its reform are not recent phenomena. Some of the statements I call stupid are a century old or older; others are of recent vintage. If you study the history of education, then you are very likely to see that such statements about education have a long, distinguished history of carnage—intellectual wreckage and policy disasters, nearly all of which seem to the thinking person to have been entirely avoidable.[5] Historian Steven Gillon has pointed out that rhetoric and reform often have unintended consequences.[6] Still, some negative consequences are utterly predictable. And it is these avoidable catastrophes that should give us pause when we hear statements that don't add up. They should give us as much pause as the action that wins a person a Darwin award—recognition for having permanently removed oneself from the human gene pool by an act of extraordinary stupidity, a distinction to which I return later.[7]

Here's an example of stupidity, ignorance, and irony combined: some educators, and some education reformers, argue against pedagogy—against teaching! From Jean-Jacques Rousseau to John Dewey to some of our contemporaries like Alfie Kohn, we find educators and people who comment on education urging us to assume that children will learn if simply left alone or, at most, provided tasks with minimal instruction in solving them—learn more authentically and thoroughly by experience than by direct instruction. Certain literary figures have suggested the same. Roger Shattuck noted:

> It would appear that these three profoundly different modern authors [Kipling, Proust, Nietzsche] can speak with one voice to issue a stern antipedagogical declaration.
>
> What, then, are we teachers doing in the academy? If we take seriously the lesson against lessons offered to us by these three authors, we should simply abandon our post, whatever it is, in the house of higher [or K–12] education.[8]

Later, Shattuck suggests that an important function of literature and teaching is learning vicariously from *other* people's experience: "we do not have to find out everything for ourselves *from scratch*."[9] Shattuck's observation is a comfort to me, and it is also rather commonsensical. He and many others have noted how knowledge is made and accumulated. True, the tension between the view that no factual truth exists and old-fashioned realism may be a false and silly dichotomy in some respects, as Stephen Jay Gould notes at the end of his essays *The Lying Stones of Marrakech*.[10] Nevertheless, Gould himself observes in many other essays that although "facts" may be hard to pin down and science can make mistakes, the accumulation of reliable knowledge using the methods of Enlightenment science is absolutely essential for the achievement of many good things, including social justice. The choice of a point of view or scale of measurement, Gould suggests, should be determined by one's objectives. I think our objective should be improving the education of children, and in the pursuit of that objective I think old-fashioned realism is indispensable.

But common sense does not seem to have swayed many earlier or contemporary educators and commentators. Reliable research data have not swayed them either. These ideas remain popular: Children learn what they should naturally and effortlessly; they learn best through exploration and by working together in groups; they learn most through "child centered" education in which teachers provide little guidance and avoid direct instruction most or all of the time. The best large-scale comparisons, however, do not confirm the idea that the abandonment of direct teaching is effective pedagogy. In fact, the data show precisely the opposite—that the most effective teaching is more direct, content-oriented, and teacher-controlled.[11]

Yet one of the most popular ideas about education reform today runs something like this: Teachers should get out of the way and let kids learn; empower children to direct their own learning; set students up with problems to solve and watch them figure things out together for themselves; allow kids to teach and learn from each other rather than control the content, pace, and structure of lessons. Hirsch has described how such "progressive" ideas about schooling became de rigueur in schools of education.[12] But, as Hirsch points out, progressive ideas about schools and teaching have become pervasive and well entrenched in the public mind as well. And even freelance writers like Alfie Kohn are now able to attract wide followings by playing to public sympathies with "progressive" educational reforms that Hirsch and others have demonstrated clearly are inimical to equitable education. Kohn—surely a bright guy, although in my opinion misguided—makes his ostensible "case" against rewards in *Punished by Rewards*, against direct instruction in *The Schools Our Children Deserve*, and against standardized testing in *The Case against Standardized Testing*.[13] His proposals would "reform" the schools by a closer adherence to "progressive" methods of instruction and assessment. Ignorance and warped thinking reign in such curdled "reforms," which *de*form education, making a twisted wreck of it. E. D. Hirsch, Jr. has argued persuasively that ideas like Kohn's promise more of the same inequity and failure we have seen from "progressive" methods for nearly a century.[14]

The truly radical reform of education consists not of re-trying the failed "progressive" approaches that have dominated American public education since about 1920 but using the scientific evidence we have and can obtain to put instruction on a sound empirical footing. E. D. Hirsch, Jr. in general education and I in special education have made that argument in previous writings.[15] We and others have noted how education that may be described as more "conservative" or "traditional" better serves the liberal objective of giving poor and minority students a fairer chance to learn in school and achieve a more equitable share of American economic success.[16]

Eventually, ignorance and stupidity suck the hope out of education as surely as they do out of any program to serve the social good. Peter Edelman describes the loss of hope that major social problems such as poverty can be addressed effectively.[17] Beginning in the Reagan era, people became convinced that government is incapable of solving major social problems, that volunteers and entrepreneurs can better serve the poor and those with special needs. Edelman's observations provide a cautionary tale for education, for we are hearing that special education is a failed government program.

It is time for a renewal or rediscovery of hope that education—public and private—can be made better. But the regeneration of optimism depends on our first confronting nonsense about education.

WE ALL MAKE STUPID STATEMENTS, BUT IT IS NOT HELPFUL TO IGNORE THEM

Many of the things said about education and its reform don't add up, don't "compute," don't make sense. In a word, they are stupid, regardless who says them. They represent the opposite of critical thinking. They don't correspond to what we know about how and under what conditions human beings learn specific skills. And yet they are often repeated, even embraced and promoted mindlessly by academics and politicians. This mindless rhetoric has a profoundly negative effect on education. It twists education, warps it, and deforms it into caricature. It cripples educational practice and undermines education's intellectual foundations.

There are those who suggest that rhetoric makes little difference. But the recent history of welfare reform suggests to me that mindless rhetoric is far from harmless. In the Reagan era, rhetoric about welfare began to describe it as a failure and a waste, as an outdated and nefarious program that breeds dependency and low self-esteem, a relic of failed liberal intentions. Certainly, welfare policy was in need of improvement, but that hardly justified the hyperbole about its failure or the new policies that leave many needy people without assistance, especially during economic downturns. Peter Edelman stated with reference to the decimation of welfare, "What I didn't appreciate was the power of the rhetoric and the extent to which it contributed to new negative welfare politics."[18] Nor does what I have observed happening in my own field of special education suggest that witless statements have no appreciable effect. What is being said about special education today—that it does not work, that it is wasteful, that it is a devious way of giving children an inferior education, that it is rife with racial bias and discrimination, that it is separate and therefore unequal—seems likely to lead to its early demise.[19] What educators, freelancers chasing the money, and politicians have claimed incessantly is that "progressive" education will improve the schools. Their rhetoric is now part of public discourse, even though the things they suggest have been tried and found wanting.

The irony in education's deformation at the hands of its ostensible scholars and reformers is considerable. Most of those who urge education's reform refer to students' need to learn critical thinking and problem solving. Yet critical thinking about reform rhetoric leads to the conclusion that many of the proposals and slogans of reformers, perhaps most, are thoughtless and unworkable. You can't teach critical thinking or problem solving in the abstract. You can only think critically or solve problems when there is some content to talk about. The content of education is neglected or, worse, condemned as trivial by too many contemporary educators and critics of education. Consequently, we are left with formless and ineffective education.[20]

Who are the people whose mindless rhetoric deforms education? I name some of them by necessity when I quote them or cite their work, but I could not name them all, nor do I want to. Besides, the point of this book is not to attack people but to weigh ideas. Some of those whose statements are in my opinion mindless and deforming of education are fellow educators, colleagues, even personal friends whom I admire for many reasons. But make no mistake in understanding this: Mindless rhetoric comes from many sources, including politicians, media personalities, school administrators, teachers, and university faculties—from faculties of arts and sciences as well as of education. Our concern should not be so much *who* says something as whether *what* someone says is intelligible, rational, consistent with what we know to be true, and helpful in solving problems. Consequently, in essays where I think particular citations or quotations are not necessary to make my point unequivocally, I have avoided them.

Although I may call statements nonsensical or stupid, I am not thereby calling the people who make them stupid. As I have noted before, bright people who are in positions of influence sometimes say and do really dumb things. In fact, as Wendy Northcutt notes in her book about the Darwin Awards, "the prerequisite to behaving stupidly is to possess intelligence." Besides, all of us have come close to winning a Darwin Award ourselves.[21] People with at least middling intelligence win the Darwin Award by removing themselves permanently from the human gene pool by some act of unusual stupidity. But in this book we are concerned only about the unreasonable things people say, not the tragic nonverbal things they do that may win them a Darwin Award or nomination—peering into a gasoline can using a cigarette lighter as a light source, for example. As Northcutt observed, "Most of us have a basic common sense that eliminates the need for public service announcements such as, WARNING: COFFEE IS HOT! Darwin Award winners do not."[22]

Texas Representative Tom DeLay may have said something truly silly about the teaching of evolution: "Our school systems teach children that they are nothing but glorified apes who evolutionized out of primordial mud."[23] An incredibly silly statement, perhaps, but Tom DeLay is not a stupid man. Columnist Richard Cohen noted that in early 2001 the Internet was awash with jokes about how dumb President George W. Bush is, but he didn't see them as funny because he doesn't think they're true.[24] This does not mean, of course, that whatever President Bush says about education must be sensible. Like all of the rest of us, he could say something that just doesn't compute.

It is of no help to ignore the irrationality of a statement made by an otherwise competent person. In fact, it seems to me in most circumstances a disservice to the person who says something way off the mark to agree with it or ignore it—but more particularly a disservice to those affected by the statement. In teaching, it is wise to correct errors so that the student does not learn a misrule—doesn't learn a way of thinking about something that is false or will lead to false conclusions or poor performance. Letting children proceed with false information or illogical thinking is no kindness. Neither is letting adults.

And we should be mindful of the fact that making unreasoned statements is part of the human condition, a flaw of human conduct to which all of us are susceptible. We need to be on guard against the tendency to conclude that if a truly intellectually gifted person says something, then it must make sense. People with any level of intellectual capacity can say something irrational or mindless, and most of us do at one time or another.

MINDLESS STATEMENTS OF MANY VARIETIES DEFORM EDUCATION

Mindless statements about education are sometimes made out of ignorance. That is, some of the people making comments or recommendations about education simply don't know what they're talking about. They lack basic information. But in my judgment this is not usually true. In most cases, those who make mindless statements have the basic facts to work with. They simply do a very shoddy job of thinking about them. Their comments fall into the category I have labeled "stupid"—unthinking, irrational, foolish. Their comments demonstrate a lack of willingness to think critically about issues, to use the facts necessary to solve problems. Some use the wrong facts or use them in the wrong way, arriving at a bungled answer just as does the child who tries to solve a word problem in math but chooses the wrong numbers or wrong operation. Strange, but true, as we shall see, is the fact that some of those who make such statements about education do so in the name of something called "critical theory" or argue, rightfully, that we need to teach children to think critically. But they fail to see that we can't do that without specific content to think about, and that an individual's critical thinking about one subject doesn't ensure his or her critical thinking about another.

What are these mindless statements that deform education? I shall take some of them up in considerable detail, but I can't repeat all of them, much less consider them all in detail. The point of this book is not merely to point out the silliness or unintelligibility of particular statements but to encourage readers to ask of *any* statement about education: What does this mean? Can I make sense of it? What would be the likely consequence of making this statement the basis for policy or for teaching? Still, at this point some examples may be useful. I consider the following statements and others like them in more detail in later chapters. For now, consider the gambits of those who say things like the following, each of which is an example of the type of statements I discuss in chapters 3–6.

- *A slogan*: "All children can learn." This has been written and said so often that I attribute it here to no particular person.
- *A self-contradiction*: "The challenge is to provide *an elite education for everyone*."[25]
- *A nonsequitur* (an inference that doesn't logically follow from a premise): "As was decided in the *Brown v. Board of Education* decision, SEPARATE IS NOT EQUAL. All children should be a part of the educational and community mainstream."[26]
- *A misleading statement*: "Separate special education does not work. It does not do so by any measure of assessment—learning, development of self-esteem and social skills, or preparation as student, worker, or citizen."[27]
- *An unintelligible statement*: "I believe that our responsibility is to keep educational research in play, increasingly unintelligible to itself, in order to produce different knowledge and produce knowledge differently as we work for social justice in the human sciences."[28]

Little reflection or critical thinking is required to see the silliness of statements such as these. The people who made them, though smart folks, must have at some point lost their wits (as we are all prone to do from time to time, and most of us have on occasion) or believed that their audiences are comprised mostly, if not wholly, of the witless (as we are all tempted to do in many circumstances, most of us yielding at some time to the urge).

Lack of common sense is often accepted as the norm, left unchallenged even in venues in which more should be expected. Richard Cohen observed that in presidential debates "any stupidity, just as long as it is uttered within the time limits, goes unchallenged."[29] Columnist E. J. Dionne, Jr. noted how in his presidential campaign George W. Bush could "happily ignore the contradictions when his themes collide" and observed that Bush's "calling for an end to finger-pointing and pointing fingers at the same time is a neat trick if you can make it work."[30] Such contradictions appear in academe, too. I recall a letter from a university professor to the Council for Children with Behavioral Disorders, whose journal I co-edited, calling for an end to name-calling while in a not-so-subtle way calling me and my co-editor unconscious racists and sexists (perhaps *unconscious* racists and sexists, but racists and sexists nonetheless).

A question I have asked others and myself is why inane propositions about education—"school reform disorder," I called it—are not greeted with laughter but, instead, are taken seriously.[31] After all, some of these statements are genuinely funny in their emptiness, though the consequences of taking them literally or seriously are anything but funny. So, why not treat them as funny and then take action to avoid the nasty consequences? I think the answer is that at best we're complacent. Actually, I think most people in our society don't really care enough about kids to do what we should. In the end, our careless attitude toward children and their education is revealed by the fact that we embrace or fail to reject notions about teaching and learning and schools that just don't make sense.

Laughing means that we see the humor in silly propositions, even if it's black humor; not laughing at such statements reveals our willingness to take nonsense seriously or let it do its damage without interference. Just because we laugh at something doesn't mean that we shouldn't make a serious response to it. Sometimes laughable propositions are also dangerous. Sometimes our laughter at inanity should be followed by serious countermeasures.

Deformed Education: Joanne, the teacher of our third-grade daughter, Emma, doesn't give children much information directly. She uses what she calls "child-centered" teaching in which she expects children to learn through exploration and discovery. Joanne tells us that she gives children very little feedback on their performance and is careful not to tell any child an answer is wrong. "Kids need to figure out for themselves what's right and what's wrong," she says. Besides, there are no really wrong answers, she feels, although some might be better than others.

Joanne tells us that she does not believe in rewarding children for good behavior or achievement with approval or in any other way because, she believes, rewards undermine internal motivation. She says learning is its own reward, and she can only set up circumstances under which children learn naturally and teach each other. "Learning, has to be authentic," she tells us, "and I'm much more concerned about the *process* kids are learning than about the content. They can always get the content when they need it."

Joanne seems more interested in pupils learning to work together in groups than about their learning mere facts. She believes that standardized tests are bad, and she thinks that higher test scores mean nothing. "In fact, higher test scores might actually mean that children are learning less!" Joanne says. This we do not understand. But, then, she's the teacher.

Joanne says she's committed to reforming education through implementing her ideas about teaching and learning. But Emma has been in this school since kindergarten, and after nearly four years in this school she is still reading on a first-grade level. Still, she's considered "about average" in her class. Joanne tries to reassure us. She reminds us that children develop at different rates and there's always a wide range of levels in a class. Emma will read fine in time, she believes, when she's ready. And then she'll learn to read at her pace, not ours. "We don't want to hurry her," she tells us. And Joanne says we shouldn't worry about what's considered "normal," because, actually, there isn't any "normal." "It'll all come together for her soon," she says. For Emma's sake, we hope she's right.

But we're still worried and more than a little upset. Is it really ok that most of the kids in this class are reading two years lower than their grade level—which is true if Emma is average for her class? Nobody has ever suggested to us that Emma needs special help. She seems bright and eager to learn. What's going on?

STUDENTS ARE USUALLY THE PRIMARY VICTIMS OF VAPID STATEMENTS

As I indicated in my preface to this book, and as the previous vignette illustrates, students experience the real tragedy of statements about education that reflect ignorance or stupidity. Mostly, these are the children in our K–12 schools, but inaccurate information and bad thinking also influence the lives of college and university students, who are shortchanged by poor education. They are the people who suffer from others' foolishness, who are mistreated because people whom we expect to know better say or give assent to ideas that will not withstand reasoned inquiry.

In teaching a course on classroom behavior management, I frequently use a case study describing an exceptionally intellectually talented, athletically gifted, economically successful, self-motivated, self-confident, and seemingly self-aware young teacher who, nevertheless, does some really ridiculous things with one of his seventh grade classes. The kids in his class are not much like him in many respects, it appears from the case. They are mainly poor, ethnic minority kids in a school with a bad reputation for violence. Many or most of them have experienced academic failure, expect more failure to come their way, and seem very uninterested in learning. The big problem with him, my students usually come to understand, is that he doesn't see his students as human beings with feelings much like his own. Had he experienced what they have, he'd probably act much the same as they do, we suppose. He has no point of human connection with them.

In case after case, students in my course are confronted by teachers' stories (the cases we study) in which it becomes obvious that the teacher cannot—or at least does not—understand the student's world, fails to make contact, does not reach out to the student in any meaningful way, does not even inquire about the child's life. How, then, are these teachers to be good behavior managers? We come to see that the artful and successful application of behavior management principles demands understanding how the world looks to the child or youth whose behavior is problematic. This doesn't mean that we see the behavior as ok, not problematic, not to be changed, or simply a function of a bad environment or class struggle. But it does mean that empathy, love, guidance, clear expectations, consistent follow through in statements about contingent consequences, and a focus on attention and other forms of positive reinforcement for desired conduct are essential.

Too often, statements about education or its reform reduce students to abstractions. They become subjects, youngsters about whom we spin theories, write scripts or narratives, but never confront as flesh and blood, as individuals like ourselves. People forget that these are kids who need skills, knowledge, encouragement, and success. It is much easier to pretend that kids don't really need to be taught particular things, that whatever "knowledge" they construct for themselves is fine, that their lives will be improved by our mantras or whatever mumbo-jumbo we may spew. The abrogation of our responsibility is easy, especially when we provide cover for it by talking and writing nonsense. The nonsense doesn't help the kids. It does help those who promote it or acquiesce to it to gain status, security, and power in certain quarters, particularly in higher education and in political contests.

A lot of the nonsense about education, though certainly not all of it, comes from those who are enchanted by "postmodernism," a term that I use frequently throughout the remainder of this book. At this point, I think it is sufficient to say that postmodernism is a rejection of all of the following: The Enlightenment view of science, of reliable ways of finding things out, of knowing how to do anything with predictable good or evil effect, of the notion that one way of knowing is better than another. I caution that some postmodernists contend that they do not reject the Enlightenment, just interpret it in a new light.[32] But obfuscation, self-contradiction, denial of what one just said, and unintelligibility are characteristic of postmodern writing, as I discuss further in chapter 6. This makes postmodernism impossible to define clearly. However, you may note that part of postmodernism is a rejection of belief in the existence of an external world and of any truth that exists independent of one's "construction" of it. The language of postmodernism is often dense, if not impenetrable, but a quotation from a relatively clear exposition might help:

> In postmodernity, the breakdown of the faith in science and rationality has . . . ramifications and associations. We witness a questioning of the scientific attitude, a denial of modernist scientificity [sic] with its emphasis on the universal efficacy of scientific method and the stance of objectivity and value-neutrality in the making of knowledge-claims. . . .
>
> In effect, in the condition of postmodernity, there is a questioning of the modernist belief in a legitimate and hence legitimating center upon which beliefs and actions can be grounded. . . . But the significant thing is that in postmodernity uncertainty, the lack of a center and the floating of meaning are understood as phenomena to be celebrated

rather than regretted. In postmodernity, it is complexity, a myriad of meanings, rather than profundity, the one deep meaning, which is the norm.[33]

This and many other examples of postmodern writing that I provide in this book remind me of "the prime rule of pseudo-intellectual writing: the harder it is to be pinned down on any idea, the easier it is to conceal that one has no ideas at all."[34] Postmodernism has become, as I shall discuss further, a very popular form of know-nothingism that does considerable mischief, particularly in higher education. And if it is popular in colleges and universities today, it is just a matter of time until it pervades teaching in K–12 schools. In a brilliant critique of postmodernism in special education, Gary Sasso wrote:

> In many ways, postmodern critics of special education appear to have given up on children with disabilities. Their recommendations suggest they no longer believe (if they ever did) that children can learn the skills necessary for increasing levels of competence and independence. They act as if it is too hard a task. And, if a person feels that it is too hard to deal with real problems, there are lots of ways to avoid doing so. One of them is to go off on wild-goose chases that don't matter. Another is to get involved in academic cults that are very divorced from any reality and that provide a ready defense against dealing with the world of people with disabilities as it actually is.[35]

Postmodernist theory is only one way of avoiding the reality of disability. Other ways include simply denying that children with disabilities are actually different from those who don't have disabilities. This denial is not peculiar to postmodern nonsense, but it fits the postmodern proclivity for denying that there is a real world external to human beings.[36] So, if postmodern know-nothingism is popular and capturing the imaginations of many and too many reformers are making stupid statements, what should we do? Call it a day and give up the struggle? I don't think so. I think Seymour Sarason has offered a sage response to the question, "Should we just give up?"

> Of course not. Unless you enjoy wallowing in despair, railing against a world inhospitable to your ends, unwilling or unable to commit yourself to what you believe in, retreating as if you have learned nothing and

there are no truths, allergic to approximations that fall short of perfection, there is no alternative to taking a stand. From a purely personal as well as a societal perspective, there is too much at stake. To live in perilous times is no warrant for imperiling your integrity.[37]

PEOPLE MAY DENY REALITY AND
ASSERT THAT SCRIPTS CREATE KNOWLEDGE

Nearly total ignorance of some things and partial ignorance of many things is unavoidable. After all, no one can know everything. Moreover, no one knows everything about anything. In fact, ignorance of the limits of one's knowledge is perhaps the ultimate failure to know. So, fine: We must accept the reality of our own ignorance, though that is often hard. But, then, whose knowledge should we trust? Is all knowledge of equal value? How is knowledge created, recognized, and accepted as fact, or at least the best guess we have about reality?

For starters, I realize that my own statements can easily be discounted. In institutions of higher learning, it has become fashionable to deny that ignorance and stupidity exist. The favored view of many who claim to be "enlightened" by the philosophies I discuss further in chapter 6 is that the words "ignorant" and "stupid" are verboten—except, it seems, with reference to those who reject postmodern doctrine. Among postmodernists, these words are derogatory and should not be applied to any statements or beliefs, regardless what they are. After all, there are many different "knowledges," and because these are constructed differently but have equal validity we cannot describe any as ignorant or wrong (except, as I have said, perhaps disagreement with this premise). As Elizabeth St. Pierre put this point of view, we need to "produce different knowledge and produce knowledge differently."[38] Ideas or statements may be different from those we hold, but they are never legitimately said to be mere superstitions or misleading, so the "reasoning" goes. The "knowledge" we claim to have is merely a meta-narrative, and "ignorant" and "stupid" are derogations applied to "scripts" we don't want to read or don't understand. But to speak of knowledge in this way is nonsensical. Conjecture is a better description than knowledge. And "conjectural knowledge" is an oxymoron, even if Thomas Kuhn, the historian of science who popularized the phrase "paradigm shift," used it.[39]

In special education, James M. Patton has called for "new script writers" to address the problem of disproportional placement of African American students in special education. His contention is that disproportionately few African Americans have "written the script" by which disabilities are described and that "new script writers" will change the way knowledge is constructed and, therefore, the way justice is achieved.

> The underrepresentation of African Americans and conscious [sic] others in the special education knowledge production process has had a strong impact on the character and nature of the knowledge that has been produced. Their relative absence from this story has limited some insightful knowledge production and, accordingly, our deep structure understanding of the disproportionality narrative. The knowledge, meanings, understandings, and principles that have guided the disproportionality discourse have largely been derived from the field's positivistic tradition in the western social sciences. This explanatory framework, largely ahistorical and lacking social, political, and economic considerations, has been inadequate in its explanations and solutions relative to the overrepresentation of African Americans in special education programs. New ways of knowing and valuing and new types of knowledge producers are called for.[40]

This way of "thinking" about the world—or, if you will, of writing a script that reveals or defines truth—is not peculiar to either gender or to any ethnic group. However, some have said that this view is feminist and multicultural, and challenging or rejecting it is sexist, racist, and reflects primitive scientism. Postmodern writings and critiques of them are the basis for my comments here. But I also have personal experiences to draw on, as do others who have challenged the "scripting" view of truth. Letters sent to professional organizations have called my views of science and knowledge sexist and racist—perhaps unconsciously sexist and racist, but no less offensive because I don't recognize the racism and sexism in my own "epistemology."

If you believe that ignorance and stupidity don't exist, then you should just stop reading this book. Do something else. Same if you believe that the only wrong thing to say is that ignorance and stupidity exist independent of a "meta-narrative" about truth. If that is true, then I have nothing of value to say. If Roger Shattuck and others of like mind are wrong—if there is no real external world to be defined—then I am hopelessly intellectually lost, bankrupt, racist, sexist, not to mention ignorant of the nonexistence of reality and wrong-headed in my insistence that it, like this book, and you are really independent of my text, narrative, or construction.

What does this have to do with education? Well, in some respects postmodernism has nothing at all to do with education, as it is only a hopelessly uninterpretable "map" of "knowledges" and a sure road to untenable conclusions. In some respects, though, it has a lot to do with education. For some, it has, become the focus of writing about developmental disabilities.[41] To me, it is a point of view that denies the importance of teaching, and this denial has very serious negative consequences for education. I can't see much point to teaching if ignorance and stupidity don't exist. It seems to me that if one buys into this idea of different "knowledges" and their construction, then about the only thing one can teach is that some people believe this, some that; you should write your own script defining knowledge and truth and understand that it is as good as any other (except, of course, it is better than any script claiming that a world independent of our construction of it exists). Here's what I think it really does to education: It keeps education in an intellectual hole, preventing the education of those who need it most, and it arrogates power to those who claim title to the intellectual rubble they create.

The postmodern retreat from knowledge, about which Gary Sasso has written, has a lot to do with children and education. It is part of the postmodern argument that we can treat facts with contempt, that the way reality is constructed doesn't matter, really. It was part of the tactic of warping perceptions and denying the realities of those who need government assistance, a loathsome practice that became popular during the Reagan revolution and was continued and refined under the Clinton administrations.[42] It led inexorably to the denial of Marcus Stephens' disability: Marcus was born with a seriously deformed heart and died at the age of 13, not qualifying as "disabled" under new government rules designed to reduce waste, fraud and abuse of SSI (supplementary social security benefits designed to help families with disabled children). Marcus, Pierce notes, became an abstraction to government officials, to whom "welfare queens" and other abusers were real (but which, in fact, no government study ever identified). Marcus and those like him, not just the alleged wasters, frauds, and abusers, were the phantoms for those who made the rules.

The retreat from knowledge, the denial of reality, the construction of postmodern phantasmagoria have fathered attempts to alter realities through language. These evil deconstructions and reconstructions of realities—denying rapes, massacres, concentration camps, and other atrocities and calling the shelling of civilians a typical ethnic celebration—have been described by Bosnian writer Aleksandar Hemon.[43] However, the retreat from knowledge does more than encourage the denial of the reality of children's suffering and promote restructuring of social programs to deny benefits to those who need them. It paralyzes any effort to work for the liberal ideas of truth, fairness, justice, and equity.[44] It opens the door and invites into the house such wicked doctrines as the superiority of ethnic or racial groups, the glorification of violence, and the subjugation of women. At the same time, it insures that these malevolent doctrines cannot be refuted effectively because there is assumed to be no actual reality independent of one's beliefs or construction. As Sasso put it, "To violate a person's ability to distinguish fact from fantasy is a demeaning and narcissistic exercise in epistemological hocus-pocus."[45]

SAYING THAT SCIENTIFIC KNOWLEDGE IS JUST ANOTHER SCRIPT IS WILLFUL IGNORANCE

Can someone be ignorant at one time but not at another? Does stupidity depend on the way one deals with what is known or assumed to be true? That is, does ignorance depend on ignoring what we know, stupidity on thinking very poorly about what is known?

I think so. I think we know quite a few things about the real world that were unknown years, decades, centuries, or millennia ago (perhaps unknown even months or days ago in some fields where reliable information about the working of the world is accumulating very rapidly). No one can be rightfully accused of ignorance when knowledge of the matter simply doesn't exist—except, of course, in the case in which someone does not know that something is unknown (is ignorant of the absence of knowledge). Nor can people be accused of stupidity when they don't have knowledge to work with. In that circumstance, they are merely ignorant, not stupid.

Ah, but there is the problem of knowing what and, especially, *how* one knows—*epistemology*, if you want the high-toned, terribly in vogue word for the idea. Since the Enlightenment, when scientific investigation was systematized, the search for truth about the external, observable world has had some reliable, remarkably effective guidelines to follow. These rules have allowed us to build a base of common knowledge about how things work and to answer in many instances the basic scientific question, What will happen if . . . ?[46] Enlightenment science has been remarkably successful in solving many human problems and is an absolute necessity for the discoveries and applications of truths that make the technologies of the developed world possible. Nevertheless, some people maintain that it is outmoded, that alternative ways of knowing—to which they refer as different knowledges or knowledge created differently—are equally valid or useful.

Of course, some information is unreliable or incorrect. The deliberate misinformation of others is, in fact, a time-honored power move. Robert Conquest makes that abundantly clear in *Reflections on a Ravaged Century*.[47] And sometimes new information overturns old ideas. This has been illustrated in essays on science and its history.[48] Still, what is the surest route to truth? Well, many of us would say science— the scientific way of looking at things and asking questions that originated in the era of the Enlightenment, which is usually said to have begun in the eighteenth century.[49]

But if the postmodernist view is correct, then science is just another form of literature, no better for finding things out than telling a story using any alternative "rubric" or "epistemological perspective." I guess that from this postmodern perspective, ignorance simply does not exist, for there is nothing outside one's own construction to be known (except that other people might "know" things you do not because they constructed their own knowledge—but, remember, no construction is superior to another, all knowledges are equally valid, so it does not matter). Neither does stupidity exist, because there is no way of thinking about things that is better or superior to another (except, of course, the way of thinking that rejects the superiority of any way of thinking), a cognitive cul de sac or self-contradiction that does not seem to bother postmodernists.

Gary Sasso reminds us that ignorance can be willful. At least until recently, most people have considered willful ignorance to be a bad choice. Knowing things and being able to figure things out in the traditional scientific sense seem not to be very highly valued in the postmodern world. When bad choices become a definite pattern, then we usually conclude that we are dealing with a stupid person—someone who typically thinks very poorly about what is known.

SOME STATEMENTS ARE JUST GROSS EXAGGERATIONS, BUT NOT ACCEPTABLE OR HELPFUL

Highly questionable statements about education are remarkable for the relief they bring their makers. In most cases, I suppose the person who makes the statement feels that he or she has made a useful observation, if not an important one. To the extent that people feel they have done something useful or important, they ordinarily feel relieved of a burden. Of course, some people do actually make insightful statements, and they, too, typically feel relieved, as well they should.

Far more important is the fact that mindless statements also relieve those who make them of responsibility for guiding or improving educational practices. Moreover, when education goes off-track, gets mired in "reforms" based on unsound ideas, then those whose statements were the basis for silly decisions are very seldom held accountable. We give them a pass, perhaps because so many people fell for the line, bought the junk-reform, and hate to admit it. The rule is this: If you state a goal that is not grounded in reality, something irrational or not testable, then you will be relieved of the responsibility for explaining why you did not achieve it. For example, if you say, "We will leave no child behind," a logical impossibility, then you don't have to explain why, several years later, someone is still behind. Or, to take another example, if you launch a "war on poverty," then I guess you can be "mopping up" forever. The "vision" or fantasy statement gives you an automatic pass. By setting a goal that is actually a real-world possibility, you set up an expectation that it should be reached and that you *might* be held accountable. The same rule applies in other areas of our lives as well. E. J. Dionne, Jr. has noted how President George W.

Bush is not expected to be taken seriously in his talk about tax cuts, as he seems to recommend them for any and all problems. Dionne notes, "The administration is willing to be cynical because it will rarely be called on what it says."[50] I suppose that we should not be surprised that people who say nonsensical things about education will seldom be called on what they say.

Much of the talk about education is confusing. In fact, it appears that many of those who make policy are confused about what they're after. Do they really want to allow localities to choose their "benchmarks" and tests, or do they want a national test that's the same for all students? How much improvement should they expect and from whom and by what measures? These issues are not debated clearly and systematically, and the outcomes are about what you'd expect from haphazard thinking. As Nicholas Lemann wrote in *The New Yorker* about President George W. Bush's education policy initiatives, "The whole world will not be watching. The whole world will be too confused to follow the action."[51] If no one understands, no one will get too upset about the consequences.

Stupid statements are scatter shots, usually missing the mark by a wide margin and ineffectual even if on target. They are based on assumptions or assertions so discrepant from reality that only unthinking persons can take seriously any attempts to implement them in actual classrooms, schools, or student-teacher interactions.

For example, a popular statement of recent vintage is that our education must "leave no child behind," usually expressed by the slogan "no child left behind." Another is that we should hold "the same high expectations (or standards) for all children." But, predictably, few people ask what "behind" means, and few ask whether the same standards are really appropriate for or achievable by all students. But it is a reasonable guess that those who say "no child left behind" and so on feel greatly relieved after having said something they believe will play well with the general public. Bob Chase, president of the National Education Association, has questioned the meaning of these statements, but more questions about them need to be posed.[52] For example:

- What does "behind" mean? Does it mean that no child will be last in achievement in his or her class or instructional group or school? Does it mean that no child will be judged to fail an examination— or that every child will eventually pass the same test that everyone else passes? Does it mean that if a child does not pass a test he or she is, nonetheless, allowed to proceed in grade or to graduate or in some other way to advance so that he or she is not actually "left behind?"

- Does "behind" mean below average? Does it mean scoring below the 25th percentile (i.e., 25% of takers of the test obtain that score or a lower one) or some other percentile (perhaps the 20th or the 30th or the 33rd or the 50th)? Does it mean that no child achieves the lowest score possible—or, does it mean that no child achieves the lowest score of those taking the test?
- Does "behind" mean simply that the child achieves less than we expect? How do we decide what we should expect of a particular child? If we expect less of child A than of child B and both children meet the expectations we hold for them, is A then not "behind" B?

Clearly, if one wants to find the substance, not merely the sugar-coated rhetoric of "no child left behind," then there are severe problems in trying to formulate rational answers to questions like these. Perhaps that is one of the reasons some people reject rationality as a standard for judging the merit of ideas—although quite a few of these same individuals would, apparently, like students in American schools to be able to use logic and evidence to solve problems.

The problem with statements like "no child left behind" is not just that they are meaningless and uninterpretable but that they are seen as serious foundations for policy—laws and rules. Any attempt to build a policy on such nonsense will collapse. Shari Pfleeger stated the problem succinctly:

The Children's Defense Fund urges us to "leave no child behind," but the D.C. Public Schools have misread this important goal. They promote kids who should stay behind because they have not yet mastered the material. How else would a teenager arrive in high school with primary school skills? . . . [The schools must] find out whether [students] can do simple math or read simple text. And then teach them what they need, based on their real level of understanding, not on the grade level they happen to be in.[53]

Pfleeger gets to the crux of the problem: Leaving no child behind academically means that some must be left behind socially; leaving no child behind socially means that some must be left behind academically; and any distribution of either social or academic skills always has a "behind" segment that will not go away. Furthermore, if "no child" is interpreted to mean zero children, then those with disabilities have to be ignored, written off, made to disappear for the slogan "no child left behind" to have any tinge of meaning.

Most politicians understand that you could not build a workable economic policy on the promise that every new business will succeed, that no business will be "left behind." And they do not suggest such nonsense to voters. When it comes to education, however, it seems entirely acceptable to talk nonsense, to propose building a sound education policy on such statements. For example, Rod Paige, at the time president-elect George W. Bush's choice for Secretary of Education, said, "If I'm honored to be confirmed by the Senate, I will dedicate myself every day to the task of assuring that no child in America will be left behind."[54] I have read the "no child left behind" slogan on bumper stickers and other places, and I heard Secretary Paige repeat the rhetoric in a luncheon address in Eugene, Oregon, on March 2, 2001. In late 2001 the U.S. Congress passed and in early 2002 President Bush signed into law the absurdly titled and substantively questionable *No Child Left Behind Act*. If one of the outcomes of this law is that educational practice is typically based on reliable scientific evidence, then we will have reason to celebrate. Unfortunately, I see little reason to believe that if educational practice comes to be based on scientific evidence we can attribute that outcome to this bill.

Secretary Paige is not a stupid man, but I retain my evaluation of the "no child left behind" rhetoric: It is mindless, for reasons I hope I have already explained clearly. Some people have had the good sense to see the exaggeration of the possible in such talk. Robert J. Samuelson noted that although the George W. Bush administration may have moved in the right direction on some education proposals, the "no child left behind" rhetoric is, as he put it using a very kind word, "extravagant." "'No child left behind,' [President Bush] says. With luck, perhaps, fewer children left behind."[55]

The problem of silly rhetoric is not exclusive to the political left or the political right. *Boston Globe* columnist Thomas Oliphant suggested that President George W. Bush's political organization appears to have taken the "leave no child behind" slogan from Marian Wright Edelman's Children's Defense Fund.[56] The fact that the slogan originated with Edelman's or Bush's organization is not related to its silliness. It is meaningless rhetoric regardless of its origin. Oliphant suggests that Marian Wright Edelman and the Children's Defense Fund would like to achieve higher incomes, improved health care, and better housing for poor children. I'm for all of those, including increased expenditures to achieve them, but none of those objectives is flatly impossible, as is "leaving no child behind." Raising incomes, improving health care, and improving housing are all real-world, achievable goals. The following are possible only in fantasyland: no one having the lowest income, no one having the poorest health care, or no one having the most humble abode—even nobody having lower income, poorer health care, or more humble housing than anyone else.

We try to teach children to take on tasks that can be accomplished, to challenge themselves with solvable puzzles, to separate the possible from the impossible. We want them to recognize exaggeration. I do not understand why public officials make statements that, coming from children, we would correct. High aspirations, yes; sophistry or quixotry, no. "Every child well taught." Difficult, but possible.

MEANINGLESS STATEMENTS CAN BE USED WITH DAZZLING EFFECTS ON THE UNSUSPECTING

That contemporary Americans have a strong anti-intellectual bias is an observation made frequently by critics of our culture. This anti-intellectualism may have long historical roots, but it is, in any case, a bent frequently displayed today in American politics and education policy. In the 2000 presidential campaign, candidate Al Gore was frequently criticized not only for being too intellectual but for challenging questionable statements and, especially, for showing impatience with what he perceived to be nonsense. His impatience with nonsense, even though he spouted it himself, may have cost him the election.

Hendrik Hertzberg noted how personality—defined as likeability, and specifically excluding intelligence, knowledge, analysis of issues, or actual prior performance—seemed to become the dominant factor for many voters in the Bush–Gore contest.[57] Craig Timberg and Claudia Deane noted the same dominance of personality over issues in the George Allen–Charles Robb senatorial contest in Virginia.[58] Many voters in the 2000 elections seemed to base their decisions more on whom they would rather have a barbeque or a beer with than on a candidate's analyses of issues or past performance. As National Public Radio's Daniel Shorr put it on election eve, 2000, the presidential campaign was remarkably like mass marketing—not a thoughtful analysis of issues, but a carefully calculated strategy to appeal to voter preferences with the right images and words. The shallow, sound-bite approach to politics didn't spring into being at the turn of the century. It has a long history in American politics, which dates at least to the earliest memories of anyone reading this book.

The intellectual shallowness of the majority of the electorate may account, at least in part, for the vapid statements about education that candidates for public office get away with and promote successfully. Intellectual shallowness may also be a factor in many educators' proclivity for nonsense, as unworkable, even off-the-wall ideas can be counted on to prompt many head nods and imitations but few challenges, if any.

In fact, contemporary Americans seem to consider it rancorous—bad form, mean spirited, ill-tempered, and offensive—to question the meaning of a statement directly. This is not only true in political contests but also in higher education. In higher education, "we find professional unwillingness to be seen to criticize colleagues in the guild."[59] In politics, the public is fed statements by candidates that go unchallenged.[60] Candidates for public office do not actually exchange and challenge each other's statements in any depth in debates. Debate moderators and interviewers of candidates seldom follow any systematic line of questioning to get at the meaning of a proposal. If they do, they are said to be arrogant or rancorous. Not challenging a stupid statement is taken as a sign of respect. The assumption seems to be that most people will see an empty statement for what it is. That assumption doesn't improve public discourse.

Both George W. Bush and Al Gore, as well as many others who propose reforms, speak of "failing schools." As Nicholas Lemann notes and as I discuss further in later chapters, "failing" is not carefully defined for either students or schools, nor is "improvement."[61] Nor are important questions asked to follow up candidates' statements. For example, G. W. Bush stated, "Finally, we will ensure that no child is left behind as we enter a new age of technology. . . . Technology must be harnessed to boost student achievement and close the achievement gap."[62] Notwithstanding the hollowness I have already described in the "left behind" rhetoric, I wonder what technology Bush refers to and just how he thinks it will boost student achievement. Bob Dixon commented:

> I guess technology is hot in education. I attended a meeting in Washington D.C. some time back, during which some fellow from the White House talked about putting a computer on the desk of every child in America, with Internet access. I commented that I thought that achieving such a goal would amount to a cruel hoax on somewhere between one-third and one-half of the school children in the country, if not more. And an *expensive* cruel hoax at that. I must have made quite an impression: The Gore campaign is advocating an internet-connected computer on the desk of every child in the country.[63]

Technology defined as computers or Internet access may well have a role in education, but supposing that access to or use of computers will somehow boost achievement seems to me an empty proposition. What many proponents of reform seem to forget or even reject is that there is a technology of instruction and behavior management that must be harnessed if achievement is to be boosted. And this technology, like that underlying computers themselves as well as many other devices and applications, is ignored at considerable peril. Each individual (mechanic, teacher, aircraft designer, physician) cannot be expected to discover or construct the technology for himself or herself; it is passed on to succeeding practitioners in the process we call education. Resistance to the notion that there is, actually, a science and technology of instruction has ensured that "Our so-called system of education is far less well planned and executed than our system of highways and of mail delivery."[64]

But among educators and education reformers, there is strong resistance to the idea of a technology of instruction and an insistence that instruction, like politics and religion, is best left to personal belief. Bobby Ann Starnes put it this way:

> In other words, from my perspective, we are separated in our vision for and beliefs about what makes good education by the personal values and belief systems that are at the core of our being. No person will be convinced by any amount of research, argument, or evidence that is constructed upon fundamental beliefs that they do not personally hold. That is why we have political parties and so many religious denominations.[65]

With such rhetoric many are persuaded that the evidence supporting any given approach to instruction is trivial at best. Just suppose that highways or mail delivery (to borrow from Roger Shattuck) or medicine (to borrow from Doug Carnine)—or any other area of contemporary life in which technology has been developed and applied—were based on a premise parallel to Starnes's. We would then remain undeveloped in communication, transportation, and medical treatment. We would look like today's third-world countries or, probably, worse.

Given the mindless statements people make about education, particularly about technology, it is not surprising that education is so poorly developed and prompts chronic complaints. Education has been deformed by mindless rhetoric, and until we bring some critical thinking to the task it will go nowhere but through another cycle of forgetting, rediscovery, and religious conversion to the newest fashion. Technology is merely the newest fashion, which, without careful tailoring to students' actual *instructional* needs, leaves those most at risk of failure even more vulnerable. Peter Edelman noted, "As things stand, technology threatens to be yet another wedge dividing our society."[66]

NONSENSE OFTEN DEBASES JUSTICE

Movie critic Bob Mondelo suggested that the 2000 presidential election was stranger than any movie plot a person could possibly make up. Sometimes, truth—or, if you prefer, real life—*is* stranger than fiction. To me, this seems clearly to be the case in some of the contemporary rhetoric about education. What fiction writer would dare to create the "story line" of "postmodern" education? Postmodernism is something

I mention in other chapters and give considerable attention in chapter 6, but for now consider how it deforms education into caricature.[67]

For starters, postmodernism has become immensely popular among educators, having swept through the humanities and much of the social sciences. It is pernicious nonsense, creating a world of trouble in other disciplines before seeping—flooding is probably more apropos—into education. Postmodern mumbo-jumbo and intellectual fraud were not dreamed up by crack-brain educators. Educators have followed the lead of people in other fields who defend crack-brain ideas in the name of "democratic epistemology," including the fool's proposition that all ideas should be treated equally. James Wiseman described its influence in archeology this way:

> Refutation of baseless speculation and repeated resurrections of previously exposed frauds and forgeries is a seemingly unending task. So it seems to the teachers who must explain year after year to new groups of students that reports of Celtic inscriptions in the Precolumbian Midwest or Phoenicians in Brazil are false. The problem is aggravated by a spreading notion in Western society that all opinions should be given equal weight and are valid until proven wrong. In this Post-Modern democratization of ideas, utter speculation by the uninformed ranks alongside the reasoned hypotheses of scholars and other experts in the field.[68]

Yet "postmodern" is said by postmodernists themselves to defy definition. So, the spectacle begins with educators embracing something that they say they can't define but believe in with great fervor and assert is the only ideology that educators can hold without being embarrassed and, eventually, discredited.

Although proponents of postmodernism say it is a "pastiche" or jumble of new and old ideas, they seem not at all embarrassed by the fact that it has no unifying theme, unless that theme is the discredit of all of the "old" ideas of science. In fact, they seem to revel in the disorganized, self-contradictory "thought" of postmodernism, which they assume to be "cutting edge," although, at the same time, they deny the possibility of "progress."

Postmodernists want others to take their basic premise seriously, although their basic premise is that nothing actually makes sense or has a plain meaning. Postmodernism, they argue, is about destroying the rules by which we make sense of things; it is intended to be uninterpretable, unknowable, and impossible. Postmodern research in education should be, as one advocate put it, "increasingly unintelligible to itself."[69]

Postmodernists insist that they make discriminations among ideas, that they don't accept just anything as legitimate. Yet they not only put forward the ideas I have just summarized, but they also fail to state clearly how they would discriminate one idea from another. All ideas are assumed to be valid—except, of course, those that postmodernists find invalid. Invalidity is based, presumably, on criteria to which only postmodernists are privy. As Alvin Kernan put it, those who dare to question postmodernism are confronted by "deconstruction's calm assumption that any view put forward in good faith in an argument by its opponents [is] per se uninformed and ill founded."[70] B. R. Myers captured the postmodern attitude succinctly. "This is what the cultural elite wants us to believe: if our writers don't make sense, or bore us to tears, that can only mean that we aren't worthy of them."[71]

Postmodernists say that they want to redistribute power and work for social justice. However, they fail to state how they would know when social justice has been achieved, except that power would be given to those who are assumed not to have it now (just what these individuals would do with "power" when they got it is not explained). Just how would they work for social justice? By obliterating the justice system now in place? With what would they replace it, and how would they be certain that justice is served? Would they merely eliminate those with whom they disagree or make sure that disagreement with them would not be aired? Would they merely reverse the racism and sexism that was at one time blatant and still exists is some forms, considering payback the achievement of justice? Then what? Moreover, postmodernists seem unfazed by the observation that postmodern ideas ensure the powerlessness of those who hold them, except the power of those in the academy to disenfranchise others with whom they disagree. I am reminded of Richard Feynman's observation about members of the Communist Party and the (ultra rightist) Birch Society: "It's all very well if they have no power. But if they have power, it's a completely different situation."[72] And the situation becomes very ugly when ideologists of the right or the left actually have power, as Robert Conquest has shown.

Consider the visual metaphor of justice — a blindfolded human figure holding a scale. The idea symbolized by this figure, as I understand it, is that the evidence is to be weighed without regard for the accused individual's personal identity — ethnicity, gender, religion, sexual orientation, for example. Now it seems obvious to me that this ideal of justice has often been corrupted by personal identity in courts of law in America and elsewhere in the world, even though it is a great ideal that is worth pursuing and that is the foundation for true justice. That is, there has too often been a double standard (or multiple standards) in which one's race or sex or other identifying feature has tipped the scale in spite of the evidence; justice has looked at the identity of the accused and let it weigh in. I think, frankly, that the scale has often been tipped in favor of white heterosexual males from privileged families, an evil that should be righted. To a significant degree, I think it has been.

However, as I understand "race biased" or "race-based" epistemologies and other postmodern contrivances, the idea they put forward is that personal identity — race, sex, sexual orientation, nation of origin, etc. — not only has been but also always will and *should* tip the balance of justice. This is a complete reversal of the idea of justice in which personal identity should not matter. Who you are gives legitimacy to what you say, so the postmodern, race-based argument goes. This is, I think, a supposed democratization of ideas and truth, allowing "voices" or "script writers" who have been silenced to be taken seriously, to have power. But one can achieve only a false justice by pretending that all ideas are equal, for then the argument that justice is whatever the court decides becomes just as defensible as any other idea.[73] The idea that personal identity should count in decisions involving justice seems to me as misguided and counterproductive as the notion that people will achieve "closure" by witnessing, or at least having confirmed for them, the death of someone who murdered or maimed their loved one. Absolute justice may well be virtually impossible to achieve, but some ideas bring us much closer to it than others. And some ideas so corrupt justice as to make it impossible even to approach.

True, universities need to be careful not to foster so much likemindedness that disagreements simply don't occur or are squelched, as Doug and Lynn Fuchs point out.[74] Diversity of ideas is desirable in universities not just because universities are *supposed* to be about diversity of ideas but also because people in universities have little or no power to influence policies that affect the general population. Remember Richard Feynman's comment—it's all well and good to have people say and believe whatever they wish, as long as they don't have power to create disasters. There is no shortage of truly silly or weird ideas in universities or among the general public—"science's mything links," as one newspaper writer put it so cleverly.[75] If universities, including schools and colleges of education, deliberately nurture off-the-wall ideas, a major risk is that silly ideas sometimes grow profusely and then escape the university's boundaries. Then they can do extraordinary damage, much like the escaped species of flora or fauna (including bacteria) that destroy a hospitable host or ecology. When bad ideas become all the rage, watch out!

Little wonder that scientists Alan Sokal and Jean Bricmont entitled their critique of postmodernism *Fashionable Nonsense* and that philosopher of science Noretta Koertge entitled hers *A House Built on Sand*. And what could be stranger than what is actually occurring among faculty in colleges and universities, including professors of education— retreating from knowledge and disciplined inquiry, presenting jumbled ideas as critical analysis, promoting unintelligibility as desirable, denying that sense can be made, reveling in self-contradiction? It beats any novelist's ability to dream up stupidity among the intelligentsia. But it does give me chills to see how closely postmodernism in American education today parallels Robert Conquest's depiction of the use of the Russian word *intelligentsia* in the Soviet system:

> The condition of being an *intelligent* was defined not by intelligence but by the acceptance of the Idea—so given with the capital letter, and defined as the total destruction of the existing order and its replacement by a perfect society run by none other than the intelligentsia.[76]

Americans may be in many ways anti-intellectual. Nevertheless, the American mind and temperament are at least able and stable enough to see the stupidity of the self-debasing and justice-corrupting rhetoric of postmodernism. Perhaps this, too—postmodernism—shall pass, but not quickly enough for me. It is a form of stupidity that I wish were mere fiction or intended as a joke. Atavism is never pretty, but if the retrogressive ideology of postmodernism becomes the standard in higher education and the rest of public life, then we will be faced with the prospect of ugliness that may be unmatched in American history—or, for that matter, the history of humankind since the Dark Ages.

STUPID STATEMENTS CAN DISTRACT AND CONFUSE PEOPLE AND MANUFACTURE CRISES

Humorist Ogden Nash wrote, "Progress might have been all right once, but it went on too long."[77] Some apologists of postmodernism suggest that the very idea of progress is suspect—but they are not trying to be funny. Psychologist David Elkind, surely one of the most intelligent writers to try to explain postmodernism, suggests that postmodernists reject the assumptions of progress, universality, and regularity.[78] I share his critics' views, that if he describes postmodernism accurately, then it is nonsense.[79]

Elkind suggests that "modernists" (as opposed to "postmodernists") hold the assumption "that societies inevitably move forward in a positive direction."[80] But I think this as well as his depictions of the "modern" (as opposed to "postmodern") ideas of universality and regularity are at odds with most credible scientists' views. Scientists Jared Diamond and E. O. Wilson, for example, certainly do not depict societal change as always forward, positive, upward, or better.[81] One scientist—Stephen Jay Gould, in *Full House*—argues that progress, when it comes to evolution, "does not pervade or even meaningfully mark the history of life."[82] So, to me it seems that Elkind has built a straw person of materials offered by postmodern philosophers without bothering to ask what scientists of our era actually say. Of course, there are arguments about the meaning of the word "progress." But for the present, let us assume that progress means improved or better, a more satisfactory outcome.

Straw arguments aside, what if we assume that no progress can be made, that there are no universals, and that there are no regularities—in teaching, if not in other areas of human effort? Where would that lead us? How would it help us? To me, it is an intellectual poison of considerable consequence. But what if we assume that progress is possible but not inevitable, that things assumed to be universal may apply to the great majority but not to all cases, and that apparent regularities actually may have a margin of error showing that there is variation within assumed regularity? I fail to see what is *post*modern about any of these assumptions. They are the stuff of modern science.

On the one hand, then, postmodernism appears to me to be nonsensical and dangerous, in that it offers only denial of any knowledge, especially denial of the possibility of common knowledge (i.e., it denies that progress, universality, and regularity exist). On the other hand, postmodernism appears to be exquisitely banal (i.e., given that belief in progress, universality, and regularity is tempered by modern scientific understanding). On neither hand does postmodernism offer educators anything other than distraction, confusion, and eventual demise. But, having been involved in the field of the emotional and behavioral disorders of children and youth for several decades, I am aware that sometimes people choose a self-destructive course.[83] That many people may do so at once and in the same manner is of no comfort to me. I see the human ravages and social tragedies created by ideologies of various stripes, and I am not amused. The postmodern "crisis of knowledge" is manufactured.

POORLY REASONED STATEMENTS CAN BE USED TO DEFEND RADICAL DOUBT

Regardless of the complaints of postmodernists or anyone else, there are ambiguities, dilemmas, and paradoxes in this world that must be dealt with. They are problems in the real world that Roger Shattuck posits. Moreover, it is important not to let cynicism lock out fair-mindedness in approaching problems, as columnist William Raspberry has suggested. However, ambiguities, dilemmas, and paradoxes can be manufactured as surely as can problems or supposed crises.[84] Usually, a problem or crisis is manufactured so that someone can sell a particular solution.[85]

A major problem in education—likely in other endeavors, too, but certainly in education—is separating the real crisis, dilemma, or ambiguity from the false or manufactured ones. For example, some of the people urging reforms have referred to a "crisis of knowledge" as if postmodern musings have revealed a true crisis in knowing how knowledge is constructed.[86] Actually, as I see it there is no real crisis of knowledge. The "crisis" is simply a ruse used to persuade people that the "old" rules of evidence are no longer valid and that we must now accept the postmodern view that everything (except, of course, the postmodern view) has been thrown into radical doubt. Those selling a view of education as business would like us to believe that education will be successful to the extent that schools are run along the lines of competitive businesses. Those recommending (selling?) a postmodern view would like us to believe that we have no idea, really, what to believe, except that belief in scientific methodology is misguided and that the propositions of postmodernists must be taken seriously. Gary Sasso has shown how postmodernists argue that any doubt means doubting everything, how absence of the absolute is used to argue that we can make no discriminations.[87] Therefore, as their argument goes, any doubt leads directly to radical doubt. How can they be sure?

SILLY RHETORIC CAN LEAD PEOPLE TO EXPECT EITHER NO PROGRESS OR PERFECTION

One of the myths about many aspects of our lives, including education and schooling, is that they can be perfected. Perhaps this myth is the American way—or some other nation's way, or perhaps just a false hope without national identity. Whatever its origin and whomever its enthusiasts, it is a myth that plays hob with education as well as with many other endeavors. In *Jefferson's Pillow*, Roger Wilkins exposes many myths of our nation's founding, but he expresses deep and abiding affection for America in spite of its imperfections.[88]

The myth of perfection finds particular welcome among those who espouse the "full inclusion" of all children with disabilities in general education schools and classes. For example, Pam Hunt and her colleagues quoted one of their teachers working in a full-inclusion program: "We're here for all kids; we're going to keep working until it is the perfect place for all kids."[89] "Perfect" is often an exaggeration, and when we are not careful in its use we foster disappointment.

The myth of perfectibility causes people to become unhappy with whatever plan or structure is in place and then to argue for radical change. It bloats expectations and is followed inevitably by inane calls for reform. Thus basically sound plans or structures are thrown away or deformed into something unrecognizable.

In some sense, our contemporary "throw-away" culture seems to be extending into the realm of ideas. Good but flawed things that could be repaired or renovated with slight effort are torn down or trashed. The replacements are often poorly tested, if at all, poorly planned, or planned with their obsolescence in mind. Or they may be planned without the long term in mind at all. The users or consumers, unfortunately, often fail to ask or demand answers to the most basic questions about replacing the old with the new. How will it work? Will it work for long? How is it better? Will the same problems or complaints be heard again? So much of the disappointment with educational reforms is highly predictable that many astute observers have wondered why more common sense is not found among the bright people, including captains of business and institutions of higher education, who say ridiculous things about education.[90]

Belief in the myth of perfectibility is sometimes ascribed to scientists (and to those who embrace a scientific understanding of things) by critics of modern science. These critics are for the most part people who espouse postmodernism. Sometimes, in a contortion of reason, people with a postmodern bent may argue that if perfection is impossible then progress or improvement is impossible as well. As I have noted in other discussions of postmodernism, the idea of progress takes heavy hits from postmodernists, who seem to give up the idea that things can be made better.[91]

Regardless of attribution, the tendency of too many reformers is to argue for throwing away something because of its imperfections, never mind the even worse imperfections of the replacement. Thus government deregulation and privatization became the rage of the 1990s, with little, if any, regard being given to the limitations and untoward consequences of unbridled competition and mega-mergers. Some people are now seeing the downside of these enthusiasms for the deregulation of business and turning over public functions to the private sector. The electrical power fiascos in California, for example, are among the outcomes of government deregulation and turning over public utilities to market forces that some have noted. Government rather than private control of certain security operations has become a matter to ponder.

Who among us has not experienced frustration and outrage at the incompetence of banking institutions, privately held utility companies, and other business institutions? Richard Cohen vented his frustrations with AT&T, AOL, and Chase bank, including the bank's slogan, "The Right Relationship Is Everything," which makes a mockery of his banking experience with Chase. He ended one of his columns with this wry observation:

> One more thing. This column is the opposite of what they say in Mafia movies. It ain't business. It's personal.[92]

Columnist Michael Kinsley also wrote a list of familiar complaints about his cable company—not being able to find information about whom to contact, going through a maddening phone tree, being put on hold, being required to give vast amounts of personal information, and finally being shielded from anyone who could help. In his words, "At the cable company, there's an office called 'Consumer Complaints' where skilled experts can take any complaint and explain with genuine remorse that they're not authorized to do anything about it."[93] My own experiences with banks, phone companies, and airlines, to name a few, have led me to compare government agencies' and public utilities' performances very favorably to the performance of private businesses. In fact, a standing joke with one of my colleagues when I get upset about something is his observation, "Jimmy, *this isn't the phone company!*" (I explain the phone company reference further in chapter 4.)

Privatizing education—allowing it to be market-driven—promises the same kind of disappointments and outrage. Keeping education public and not-for-profit does mean learning to live with a system that is less than perfect and not perfectible, although it certainly can and must be improved. But making it competitive in a free market—giving it over to a business enterprise—can be predicted to result in abuses of "customers," whose scathing commentaries will make Richard Cohen's comments on the businesses of banks and phone companies and airlines and dot-coms look kind by comparison. Business can't be made perfect either. Daniel Tanner summarized it well:

> The engines that drive market forces are inappropriate for the schools. Aside from our history, which demonstrates the necessity for public reg-

ulation of these forces so as to protect the democratic public interest, there is the need to recognize that the mission of business, first and foremost, is maximizing profits. The mission of public education is serving the social good.[94]

Education is not close to uniqueness in its tendency to suggest radical and unwise changes in response to observed flaws. A. O. Hirschman and Peter Edelman are among those who have noted how people embrace ridiculous suggestions for trashing economic or social policies because what is in place is not perfect.[95] Anytime we hear someone suggest something like the sentiment that no child will be left behind or that all children will meet high standards of learning or performance or that all schools will be excellent, we should be more than a little skeptical.

Make no mistake in understanding my position here. *I think that we can and must do better for all children.* I am *not* suggesting that we can do no better than we are doing now or no better than we have done at any particular time in our history in any area of business, politics, or the social welfare. But to suggest that we can devise a system in which there are no failures at all is to appeal to the failing side of the human intellect, and this inevitably brings sorrow to happy reformers. In fact, I think it is a mistake not to strive to do better, even to *strive* for perfection. But to pretend in public statements that we can achieve perfection is the kind of mistake that ultimately fuels a backlash of the kind Peter Edelman describes so poignantly in the case of "welfare reform." Besides, our history clearly shows that reforms have never—at least almost never, if not in absolutely zero cases—worked out as planned.[96]

Idiotic suggestions that all failure can be averted are not based on actuarial data or even on commonsensical observation of life's vicissitudes. Perfection may be a human fantasy, but those who talk as if it can be achieved through the reform of social or economic institutions either have severe cognitive weaknesses or knowingly exploit the fantasies of others. Politicians may believe that being honest about our inability to achieve perfection—or rejecting such nonsensical blather as universal excellence—is the kiss of death. But all their dishonesty accomplishes is the long-term death of their reform by strangulation when people finally perceive it to be an ugly brainchild slathered with makeup.

Then there is, as well, the fogged memory of past loves to overcome. Listening to some recall the past, it is tempting to buy the notion that there was a golden era—of the family or the workplace or government, for example—with nonexistent or truly insignificant problems. Death may confer a grace not extended to the living, but we get too misty-eyed about the beauty of times and policies past. This is not to say that nothing from the past is better than what we have at present, merely that if we were to resurrect a policy of the past we would have to confront its flaws. But it is tempting to see earlier times or past policies in an unnaturally romantic light, just as it is to see a proposed policy as—well, just perhaps—perfect. Stephanie Coontz reminds us of this in her wonderful, clear-eyed look at families past, *The Way We Never Were: American Families and the Nostalgia Trap*.[97] She debunks the idea that the "traditional" American family consisted of a working father and stay-at-home mom and helps us understand that throughout history many families have been fatherless and had working mothers. Diverse family forms and family economic and interpersonal struggles are not recent phenomena.

A realistic view of education, as of nearly everything else, is that no solution to any problem is perfect, although some solutions are demonstrably better than others. We can make progress, in the sense of getting better, but we also know that absolute perfection—zero errors, zero problems—has never been achieved and is not achievable. But we can also make things worse. We can be wrong, and we can bring regression. I recall a tribute to former Senator Daniel Patrick Moynihan by E. J. Dionne, Jr., who quoted a 1993 statement of the departing senior senator from New York:

> It is quite possible to live with uncertainty, with the possibility, even the likelihood, that one is wrong. . . . But beware of certainty where none exists. Ideological certainty easily degenerates into insistence upon ignorance.[98]

It is ideological certainty and willful ignorance with deference to the Idea that Moynihan and others have warned us about.[99] Moynihan understood that ideology, liberal or conservative, could demand allegiance to ignorance and to unintelligent ideas. Ideology is, after all, the easiest thing to perfect, as there is nothing outside it against which to judge it. Postmodern ideology justifies itself, including its disagreement with the "facts" of an external world and its denial that such facts exist. Perfect!

We can, actually, be relatively certain of some things. Some of this life's realities are pretty "hard," very unlikely to be overturned. For example, we are unlikely to discover that the world is flat or that we can measure things without producing variance (i.e., a distribution of variation from an average). But other things that we assume are realities may change. In these cases, our best bet is our best guess, based on careful thinking about the most reliable data that we can bring to the task. For example, we may find that blood fats have little effect on heart disease or that mandatory schooling is counterproductive. I doubt that we will find either of these ideas to be true, but it is possible.

Here, I think, is a "hard" reality: Poorly thought out statements deform education, whether their nonsense is postmodern or political or both and even if they're based on poorly done science. Our most helpful strategy is to keep a good head on our shoulders—to think at least as logically and systematically as we expect our students to think. Probably we will be modeling for our students what we expect of them if we refuse to give up the quest for improvement—just as we seek simplicity, if we're smart—but distrust it. Columnist Ellen Goodman wrote of her intelligent distrust of what we call progress, all the while approving of the aspiration for perfection of the improvements we make. She describes the dire warning of the chair of President George W. Bush's Council on Bioethics that the aspiration for human perfection is dangerous and that striving to create perfect human beings is the motivation of scientists for cloning. The chair of the Council invoked a cautionary tale written by Nathaniel Hawthorne in 1843, a story in which a young scientist seeking to perfect his wife kills her. Concludes Goodman, "In my own required reading, I keep a jaundiced eye on progress, but somehow I'm glad medicine didn't stop 'aspiring' in 1843."[100] Hers may not be a perfect essay, but I couldn't have said it better. As she notes, scientists who do stem cell research are not aspiring to make perfect human beings but to improve the treatment of human ailments. Big difference.

NOTES

1. Kaplan (2000).
2. Hirsch (1987, 1996).
3. See Overholser (2000).

4. Cohen (2001b).
5. See Hirsch (1996), Ravitch (2000), Sarason (1990).
6. Gillon (2000).
7. See Northcutt (2000, 2001).
8. Shattuck (1999, p. 106).
9. Shattuck (1999, p. 114, italics in original).
10. Gould (2000).
11. See Becker & Gersten (2001), Carnine (2000), Hirsch (1996).
12. Hirsch (1996).
13. Kohn (1993, 1999, 2000; see also 2001).
14. Hirsch (1996).
15. Hirsch (1996), Kauffman (1993).
16. E.g., Carnine (2000), Shattuck (1999).
17. Edelman (2001).
18. Edelman (2001, p. 126).
19. See Cottle (2001) for an example of anti–special education rhetoric, or Fisher (2001c), who wrote "Special-ed is the gold-plated garbage can of American schooling." See Kauffman (1999–2000) for descriptions of possible effects of such rhetoric.
20. Hirsch (1987, 1996).
21. Northcutt (2000, p. 17); see also Northcutt (2001, pp. 2–3). Michael Shermer observed, "It is one thing to wonder why people believe weird things, it is quite another, and on one level far more important, to understand why *smart* people believe weird things" (2001, p. 319).
22. Northcutt (2000, p. 1, capitalization in original).
23. Northcutt (2000, p. 10).
24. Cohen (2001a).
25. National Center on Education and the Economy (1989, p. 9, italics in original).
26. Stainback & Stainback (1991, p. 228, capitalization in original).
27. Gartner & Lipsky (1989, p. 26).
28. St. Pierre (2000, p. 27).
29. Cohen (2000b, p. A31).
30. Dionne (2000, p. A33).
31. See Kauffman (1992).
32. E.g., Peters (1995b).
33. Usher & Edwards (1994, p. 10).
34. Myers (2001, p. 116).
35. Sasso (2001, p. 188).
36. See Kauffman (1997, 1999a, 1999d).

37. Sarason (1990, p. 133).
38. St. Pierre (2000, p. 27); see also Danforth (2001).
39. See Kuhn (1996).
40. Patton (1998, p. 29).
41. E.g., Danforth (2001), Smith (2001).
42. Pierce (2000); see also Edelman (2001).
43. National Public Radio (2000).
44. See Koertge (1998), Sokal & Bricmont (1998) for elaboration.
45. Sasso (2001, p. 188).
46. See Feynman (1998, 1999). I do not define science or discuss the scientific method in detail in this book because definitions and discussions can be found elsewhere (e.g., Shermer, 1997, 2001). Shermer defines science as "a set of cognitive and behavioral methods to describe and interpret [an] observed or inferred phenomenon, past or present, aimed at building a testable body of knowledge open to rejection or confirmation" (2001, p. 98).
47. Conquest (2000).
48. E.g., Diamond (1997, 1999), Feynman (1998, 1999), Gould (1997a), Gross (1998), Kuhn (1996), Wilson (1998).
49. E.g., Gross (1998), Gross & Levitt (1998), Wilson (1998).
50. Dionne (2001b, p. A17).
51. Lemann (2001, p. 34).
52. Chase (2000).
53. Pfleeger (2001, p. B8).
54. Slevin (2000, p. A6).
55. Samuelson (2001, p. A21).
56. Oliphant (2001).
57. Hertzberg (2000).
58. Timberg & Deane (2000).
59. Conquest (2000, p. 223).
60. E.g., Bush (2000), Gore (2000).
61. Lemann (2001).
62. Bush (2000, p. 126).
63. Dixon (2000, pp. 1–2, italics in original).
64. Shattuck (1999, p. 34).
65. Starnes (2000, p. 108).
66. Edelman (2001, p. 18).
67. For further critiques of postmodernism in science, see especially Gross & Levitt (1998), Gross, Levitt, & Lewis (1996), and Sokal & Bricmont (1998); in the philosophy of science, see Koertge (1998); in education, see Sasso (2001).

68. Wiseman (2001, p. 13).
69. St. Pierre (2000, p. 27).
70. Kernan (1999, p. 192).
71. Myers (2001, p. 121).
72. Feynman (1998, p. 100).
73. See Kernan (1999).
74. Fuchs & Fuchs (2001).
75. Garbeau (2001); see also Shermer (1997).
76. Conquest (2000, p. 86, italics in original).
77. Nash (1957, p. 12).
78. Elkind (1998a); see also Elkind (1995).
79. Brigham & Polsgrove (1998), Sugai (1998); see also Kauffman (1998).
80. Elkind (1998a, p. 153).
81. See Diamond (1997) and Wilson (1998).
82. Gould (1996a, p. 3).
83. See Kauffman (2001).
84. Raspberry (2000b).
85. See Tanner (2000).
86. E.g., Skrtic & Sailor (1996); see also Danforth & Rhodes (1997), Skrtic, Sailor, & Gee (1996), Smith (2001).
87. Sasso (2001).
88. Wilkins (2001).
89. Hunt, Hirose-Hatae, Doering, Karasoff, & Goetz (2000, p. 312).
90. E.g., Sarason (1990), Sasso (2001), Tanner (2000).
91. See Elkind (1998a) for postmodern opposition to the idea of progress and Sasso (2001) for discussion.
92. Cohen (2000a, p. A23).
93. Kinsley (2001, p. A33).
94. Tanner (2000, p. 202).
95. Hirschman (1986), Edelman (2001).
96. Gillon (2000).
97. Coontz (1992).
98. Dionne (2001a, p. A15).
99. See also Conquest (2000), Sasso (2001).
100. Goodman (2002, p. A6).

CHAPTER 2

The Art of the Stupid

"So I stopped—at random—and read the next sentence very carefully. I can't remember it precisely, but it was very close to this: 'The individual member of the social community often receives his information via visual, symbolic channels.' I went back and forth over it, and translated. You know what it means? 'People read.'"

—Richard Feynman, physicist

STUPIDITY PAYS—SOMETIMES

Some people make a living thinking up stupid things to say or do. There is an art to this, even though some people do or say such things quite by accident. When someone says or does something stupid without humorous intent, without apology, and without an obvious profit motive, we typically still wonder what they are trying to sell, even if it is something intangible, like an idea—or, as Robert Conquest puts it, an Idea (an ideology, signified by the capital letter). Some of our greatest comedians have been very intelligent people, but intelligent people can get hooked on an Idea and run aground with it. As Conquest stated, "The true Idea addict is usually something roughly describable as an 'intellectual.' . . . Intelligence alone is thus far from being a defense against the plague."[1] Conquest refers here to the plague of ideology, the Idea run mad, an abandonment of knowledge and judgment in favor of the intrigue of the Idea, which inevitably brings catastrophe.

Sometimes people say stupid things for effect—to poke fun at someone or something, to make a joke, to make people laugh. Such statements have their legitimate place in comedy. Writers and stand-up comics have understood this for a long time and used it with great effect. It's worth noting that stupid statements are funnier if they contain a kernel of truth. Dave Barry uses stupid statements about as well as any humorist. He's a master of the art.

Still, sometimes a comment or behavior might be inane for other reasons—not because we are ignorant people, but because we either don't think carefully or have a reason other than comedy to make an inane statement, usually in favor of an Idea. More frequently than I'd like to admit or believe is fully justified, my wife, Patty, says to me, "That's just plain stupid!" Occasionally, when she tells me this, I meant my comment or behavior to be seen as such, and we laugh about it. And, occasionally, I think she makes a false accusation because she hasn't really thought through something I've said. But too often for me to feel comforted by the realization, what I said or did was just plain stupid, and I had no comedic intention, nor any worthy motive.

Sometimes stupid statements are made for commercial or political reasons in which comedy is not intended. How else do we account for Abraham Lincoln's observation that one can fool all of the people some of the time and some of the people all of the time, but not all of the people all of the time? Fooling people seems to be part of the art of politics. If politics is the art of the possible, then fooling people is understandable, but political horizons are always shortened by the foolery. Eventually, at least some of the people are not fooled. Some people profess to seeing an advantage to a "vision" statement that is detached from reality. I do not. I prefer that my visions be of the possible—very difficult to accomplish, perhaps, even improbable, but still *possible*.

I do understand that people may be told by pollsters or political advisors that they must say such-and-such to get elected, or that saying such-and-so will improve their electoral chances. I understand also that people may see economic or status advantages in making certain statements or taking certain positions on controversial issues. I know that saying certain things may allow one to avoid hazing or other unpleasant social consequences. I admire the person who refuses to say something that he or she does not believe when saying it would obtain for them money or prestige or would avoid criticism. We are all, perhaps, too quick to sell out, to tolerate if not perpetuate nonsense out of self-interest. The art of the stupid is then truly a perversion. Fakery, as part of the art of the stupid, is usually seen as minor and forgivable, a harmless prank. But Stephen Jay Gould noted that "fakery can also become a serious and truly tragic business, warping (or even destroying) the lives of thousands, and misdirecting an entire profession into sterility for generations."[2]

Fooling people is part of the art of advertising. The huckster knows this art well and practices it to near perfection. I'd hope education would include teaching about hucksterism without engaging in it, except as a foil. Dave Barry captured the huckster's art of changing the label perfectly with his usual humor:

> So changing names is a sound idea, an idea based on the scientific principle that underlies the field of marketing, which is: People are stupid.
>
> Marketing experts know that if you call something by a different name, people will believe it's a different thing.
>
> That's how "undertakers" became "funeral directors."
>
> That's how "trailers" became "manufactured housing."
>
> That's how "We're putting you on hold for the next decade" became "Your call is important to us."[3]

And, he could have added, that's how "disability" became "challenge" and how other changes in labels related to disabilities came about.

So, silly things are sometimes said purposely, knowingly for fun, or to sell something. Sometimes, they are said accidentally. Usually, when they are said accidentally, they are regretted. Sometimes, people apologize for them. But regardless of intent, there is an art to the stupid. True, it is part of the arts of comedy, merchandising, politics, and persuasion in academic settings, but sometimes it is an art practiced for purely personal reasons that we may not understand. And here are a few of the ways to practice the art and, often, get away with it:

- Assume that your audience will not think—at least not much.
- Use outliers (atypical cases) as examples of the typical or the universally possible.
- Use the average as representative of all.
- Portray personal experience or preference as more convincing than research.

- Use any ambiguity as an excuse for radical doubt.
- Drive a reasonable proposition into the ground by taking it to its greatest possible extreme.
- Overcomplicate simple things or oversimplify complex things.
- Use or misinterpret a questionable quotation from a person recognized as intelligent or misinterpret an idea.
- When all else fails, spout a hodgepodge of ideas using words and sentences no one will understand.

All of these strategies are found not only in advertising, political campaigns, the radical fringes of multicultural and feminist arguments, and postmodern philosophical writing, but also—the great woe for purposes of this book—in dumb statements about education and its reform. I am very supportive of efforts to achieve fair treatment of all cultural groups and greater equality for women. These are important goals. But the radical fringes of any movement or group, extreme left or extreme right, are prone to artful stupidity of the kind I discuss in this chapter.

ASSUME THAT THE AUDIENCE WON'T THINK MUCH

The assumption that your audience will not think—at least not very much—about what you say is a tried and true strategy. It is, actually, the foundation for all the other strategies I discuss. It seems to be the assumption behind a lot of successful slogans—the educational slogan "All children can learn," as well as the advertising slogan "Wouldn't you really rather have a Buick?" Both are what Owen Meany, the central character of John Irving's 1989 novel *A Prayer for Owen Meany*, whose voice was always represented by capital letters, would say are MADE FOR TELEVISION![4] That is, they are made for unthinking responses, demanding that any powers of intellect be put on hold. I recall something I wrote in 1990 as president of the Council for Children with Behavioral Disorders.

> Special education is in a precarious position today, partly because we have not developed and expressed Owen Meany's scorn for claptrap, half-truths peddled without shame, overgeneralizations presented as

sureties. For too long, we have allowed outrageous propositions and pronouncements to be taken seriously. It's time for us to model for each other and for the kids we serve the kind of reality testing that is an antidote for made-for-television statements on the reform of regular and special education. We need to give Owen Meany's response to reform rhetoric that doesn't match what we know about the real world, to wit:

"The challenge is to provide an elite education for everyone." MADE FOR TELEVISION!

"What is known about the education of students labeled as handicapped? First, separate special education does not work." MADE FOR TELEVISION!

"What is possible in one place is possible in every place." MADE FOR TELEVISION!

"There was no evidence in the past and there is no evidence now showing that removing disabled children from the mainstream and putting them into special classes or schools is an advantage for them." MADE FOR TELEVISION!

"One promising approach to serving the vast majority of special education students without using labels has been to restructure general classroom instruction." MADE FOR TELEVISION![5]

It might be worth noting that all of the quotations I called MADE FOR TELEVISION! were taken from the literature of education reform. None was made up by me.

People who make witless statements often seem to be betting that no one will ask substantive questions about what they say or write. About such slogans as "All children can learn," they do not see a need to formulate an answer to simple questions, such as "What can they learn? In what period of time can they learn it? They can learn it with what investment of resources?" Purveyors of such nonsense may even add such seemingly redundant qualifiers as, "And all means *all*" without so much as a thought that someone might ask, "By all, do you mean *each and every* child, *no* exceptions?"

The assumption that consumers of education rhetoric will not think much seems pretty safe, given education's history. Were the assumption true only for teachers, who are mistakenly assumed by many to be typically slow-witted, reforming education would not be so problematic. The unfortunate reality is that people in every walk of life, including school board members, legislators, and executives in business and politics, too frequently disconnect their powers of reason when confronted by problems of public education.

USE EXCEPTIONS TO PROVE THE RULE

Using outliers—exceptions to the rule—as examples of what is typical or universally possible assumes that people won't think much about variations in human beings, won't understand statistical distributions, or will simply deny that statistical distributions exist. We see this strategy in the use by tobacco companies of outliers to illustrate the noneffects of smoking on health. A Marlboro-Man-like character who has smoked for years, yet is in robust health, is used to refute the conclusion that smoking is an unhealthful practice with severe consequences on respiratory and circulatory well-being. Are there actually people who smoke heavily for years, yet live long and healthful lives? Well, yes, but they are outliers in a statistical distribution, not typical of smokers.

Alternatively, tobacco companies may use the lung cancer of someone who has never smoked as evidence that smoking does not cause lung cancer. Again, the statistical outlier is used to discount or disprove the general conclusion—smoking greatly increases the risk that someone will get lung cancer. Some people in positions of authority, like United States Senator Jesse Helms (not to mention tobacco company employees), have argued that scientists have no clinical proof that smoking causes cancer. Scientists have, as Senator Helms has said, "only statistics." The Senator's misunderstanding or misrepresentation of science and statistics notwithstanding, science is about statistics—probabilities. And the statistics are clear on this: smoking substantially increases a person's risk of having vascular disease (heart or blood vessel problems), lung disease (e.g., lung cancer or emphysema), or both.

I suppose one could argue that it is the consumers who buy misrepresentations of cigarette smoking who are not smart. Yet, the argument that outliers disprove the causal relationship between smoking and ill health is, surely, false whether consumers are tricked by it or not. The fact that a sucker is born every minute does not mean that the presentations for which they fall are not stupid—except in an economic sense for the tricksters who con them. My previous point should be recalled: Sometimes stupidity pays, and handsomely.

In education, too, deceptive claims are sometimes based on statistical outliers. The child who learns to read with no instruction at all or some children's learning to read with instruction that results in the failure of *most* children to learn to read satisfactorily by third grade, for example, may be used to defend instructional practices that are worthless, or next to it.

Alternatively, the failure of a few children to learn to read satisfactorily with instruction resulting in a very high percentage of children learning to read is used to discount the worth of generally effective reading instruction. Thus ineffective instructional methods are adopted and promoted while effective instructional methods are bypassed or rejected on the basis of unrepresentative cases.

But instruction is not the only topic in education for which outliers are employed to make absurd arguments. Extraordinary teachers who overcome outrageous odds—including, for example, lack of instructional materials, crumbling buildings, very high class size, extremely low pay—to produce unusually high achievement outcomes are used as examples of what every teacher should be able or expected to do. How many people would buy into such nonsense in other areas, say in athletics? Would most people consider it reasonable to expect that the Olympic gold medalist in swimming shows us what any swimmer can or should be able to achieve? The fact that highly successful people spend a lot of time practicing and don't attribute their achievement to luck or to natural talent but to hard and persistent practice is quite beside the point. First of all, not everyone can or wants to show such ardent commitment to a particular task. Second, not everyone who invests a given amount of time and effort in a given task will come out at the same level of functioning.

Alternatively, of course, outliers in the other direction—for example, the teacher who fails to produce reasonable achievement outcomes in spite of having a small class, a high salary, access to a fantastic array of instructional equipment and materials, a beautiful new building—are used to indicate that these resources do not make any substantial difference. In short, the outliers don't prove the point. I suppose that we could remind ourselves that one swallow doesn't mean spring has come.

USE THE AVERAGE TO REPRESENT ALL CASES

Using the average as representative of all is just the inverse of using
outliers as examples of the typical or representative, and it is no less an
artful presentation of the stupid. It is the kind of thing that drives outliers crazy because they are assumed not to exist or not to matter much,
if at all. The extra tall, the extra short, the extra large or small often experience the unfittingness of the average for their needs. That is why
we have boutiques that serve the outliers for whom the average, the
typical, the range of sizes that fits the vast majority, is too restricted.

But it is in education that I think the average is used most inanely to
represent all students or all cases. Whenever someone suggests that all
students should learn this or that, I cringe at the presumption that all
should be taken literally—to mean each and every. To me, it seems too
obvious, so undeniable, so important to consider that there are exceptional children, students who do not fit the average mold by a long shot.
Some reformers' rhetoric seems to discount a certain percentage of the
student population, to ignore or deny or discount the needs of kids whose
cognitive capacity or behavioral control is way, way below that of their
typical age mates or of those whose intellectual power or virtuosity in
some area of performance is way, way above that of their age peers.

Similarly, some very bright people have been tempted to discount all
educational research because the typical or average study in education
is not very good. The conclusion that some would have us make is that
no educational research at all is really worth paying attention to, that it
is all trivial or worse. This generalization ignores the fact that there is
a considerable body of educational research that does have real meaning for how students should be taught, if only people would pay attention to it.[6]

The same sort of mindless rhetoric of the average applies to schools
and teachers as well. Is American public education failing, or is it a remarkable success? Depending on how one defines success or failure,
we could make the case that the public schools are not doing a very
good job or, alternatively, that they are doing a superb job. But in either
case, the general conclusion avoids the outliers—in the case of the conclusion that the schools are failing, those that are successful; in the case
of the conclusion that the schools are great, the ones that are failing.

Marketing is usually based on the average performance of a product, not the full range of performance, which, of course, usually includes breakdowns, failures, or other unsatisfactory outcomes. Medications, cars, foods, beverages, and nearly all other products are sold as if the typical is true for all cases, never mind the allergies, breakdowns, dietary restrictions, and so on that consumers must understand.

Truthful and helpful talk about education recognizes the fact that nothing applies to literally all—to each and every case. David Elkind's distorted portrayal of "modern" assumptions notwithstanding, most of us do understand that many "universals" are not literally so.[7] The fact that there are exceptions, as I noted earlier, is sometimes used to reject a generally effective practice. The idea of a "universal" is sometimes rejected because it refers to the vast majority of cases, though not to each and every instance (although some universals in physics and mathematics may actually apply to each and every case). Nevertheless, the education rhetoric that does not allow for exceptions to the general rule is stupid and destructive. It is, for example, the basis for such misbegotten policies as zero tolerance, in which the same rule is assumed to apply to all cases regardless of any extenuating circumstances.[8]

So, what can or should be expected or demanded of literally *all* students (i.e., each and every one)? Not much, in my opinion, simply because the variation among students is so dramatic and important. Maybe "doing your best" or "learning all you can" would be appropriate for all, but "your best" is rather difficult to define, and "best" is a concept beyond the apprehension of some learners of extremely limited cognitive ability. And "learning all you can" will drive some children with high capacity and high motivation to unhealthful and unwelcome extremes of effort. However, if we accept that "all children" or "every American" really means the great majority, but not literally every living child or citizen, then a core curriculum, a standard set of expectations, may make very good sense.[9]

MAKE PERSONAL EXPERIENCE MORE IMPORTANT THAN EXPERIMENTAL RESEARCH

Portraying personal experience or preference as more convincing than experimental research is a favored tactic in marketing and postmodern argument. The pain reliever television commercial featuring a man saying that he doesn't care what studies show, he knows what works for him, is the model for this artful ploy. But it is a popular tactic of education rhetoric and is the basis for commentaries such as Timothy J. Landrum's "Why Data Don't Matter."[10] Landrum points out how, when it comes to education, people accept personal preferences rather than data as the basis for decision making.

Saying that all educational research is meaningless or untrustworthy or simply unconvincing because personal experience is a better guide to truth and success is a senseless gambit with a long history in education. You may recall a quotation of Starnes in chapter 1: "No person will be convinced by any amount of research, argument, or evidence that is constructed upon fundamental beliefs that they do not personally hold."[11] Now, this may be true, in that a person may consider teaching to be in a province where data do not matter (Tim Landrum's point). But this is precisely where stupidity reigns: Personal belief cannot be swayed by data, is disconnected from evidence, and is assumed to be true regardless what reliable, objective assessment of the outcomes of instruction might be.

Well, yes, a person might believe that preparation A provides superior headache relief regardless of any objective evidence to the contrary or that prayer is superior to antibiotic X for fighting a given infection regardless of what research may say. But the important question for those of us who embrace the ideas of the Enlightenment is whether belief is aligned with evidence where evidence is available. To hold out for personal belief in the face of clear evidence to the contrary is, as I have suggested elsewhere, a mulishness that might well be considered stupid.[12]

Several caveats are necessary here. First, it is possible that a person giving testimony against evidence is an outlier in the distribution of effects of a particular treatment. For example, the person saying, "I don't care what research shows about _____, I know what works for me" may have found that _____ doesn't work well for him or her but an alternative does. This is possible. But then to urge others to ignore the evidence that the alternative is *generally* better—works better for *most* people—is to make the mistake of arguing that outliers are typical. In education, some people make the argument that because they personally do not like or do not believe in a given instructional procedure, it is not superior, regardless what the best research evidence shows.

Second, some so-called research is very poorly executed and is, therefore, unreliable. Educational research is often made fun of or pooh-poohed, and sometimes rightfully, as some of it is nothing short of ridiculous. So is the so-called research in nearly every—if not literally in every—field of inquiry. Sometimes research is faked or biased or nonsensical. Think of the claims of researchers a few years ago that they had produced cold fusion, claims that were eventually proven false.

Third, some people are really inept in applying research to the solution of problems. They may not understand the basic concepts on which the method is based. They may understand but be unable to implement the method properly. If a method of teaching (like a method of doing surgery or repairing a car or anything else) is not implemented with fidelity to that of the researcher, then we might expect that it would work poorly, if at all.

Fourth, for some things, scientific research does not provide or cannot provide an answer. As Richard Feynman has suggested, science can only tell us what will happen *if we do X*; it cannot tell us whether *we should do X*.[13] And, of course, science doesn't *always* tell us what will happen *if we do X* for two basic reasons. First, not knowing what will happen is the reason for doing science—to find out. Many things remain unknown. Second, science gives us a probability that X will happen if we do Y. For the vast majority of scientific investigations, if not literally for all, there is a margin of error. Scientists try to come close or closer to being able to predict with absolute certainty what will happen if we do X, but in very few cases is the prediction 1.0 or 0.0, particularly if the decimal places are extended to many digits.

It is precisely on this point that much of the criticism of "modern" science rests. And it is also the point on which "postmodern" suppositions rest, with their peculiar irony of suggesting that we know only one thing for certain—that no one knows anything for certain.

Finally, it is important to remember that personal preferences are legitimate and to be respected, if not protected, in many areas of our lives. The clothes we wear, the makes of cars we choose, the music we listen to, the particular foods we eat, and many other things may be marketed by scientific principles, but our freedom of personal choice is defensible. But in other areas of our lives, we are considered derelict as professionals if we do not make choices based on evidence other than our personal predilection. We do not allow a car manufacturer, for example, to take a postmodern view of the high, centered brake light that has become mandatory.

The postmodern view might be that my own experience and that of people I know does not confirm the so-called objective scientific data indicating that the brake light centered high on a vehicle reduces accidents. Furthermore, a postmodernist might say, "I don't like brake lights in that position." A postmodernist might argue that the requirement of the brake light is hegemonic and oppressive. Some radical feminists might say that it is masculinist, and some radical multiculturalists could argue that some cultures have few rear-end collisions without the brake light, so it is actually just a culturally embedded idea that has no true advantage. Thank goodness that as a society we have agreed that such a (personal preference) view of brake light location is silly and irresponsible if it becomes the basis for a policy governing the sale of vehicles! Why, I and many of my colleagues ask ourselves, do we not demand that in teaching children we base as many of our decisions as possible on the most reliable evidence we have?[14] Why do we allow personal preference to determine the instructional programs that teachers use?

Why, indeed? But we do. Cathy Watkins reviewed what happened in Project Follow Through. Follow Through was a Congressionally mandated experimental comparison of nine instructional approaches used in Head Start. (It was mandated in the 1960s under the Johnson administration by Public Law 90-92.) It was a well-designed comparison involving 51 sites around the country. The long and short of the comparisons is this: Direct Instruction beat all other programs hands down in improving children's performance in basic skills (math and reading), cognition (thinking), and affect (feeling good). Did that mean that the federal government got behind Direct Instruction as a preferred model? No! What happened is a sad story that is much like what happens today.

> The purpose of the Follow Through planned variation experiment was to identify effective educational methods. However, there is little utility in

identifying effective methods if they are not then made accessible to school districts. The Joint Dissemination Review Panel and the National Diffusion Network were created to validate and disseminate effective educational programs. In 1977, Follow Through sponsors submitted programs to the JDRP. "Effectiveness" was, however, broadly interpreted. For example, according to the JDRP, the positive impact of a program need not be directly related to academic achievement. In addition, a program could be judged effective if it had a positive impact on individuals other than students. As a result, programs that had failed to improve academic achievement in Follow Through were rated as "exemplary and effective." And, once a program was validated, it was packaged and disseminated to schools through the National Diffusion Network.[15]

Ernest Boyer, then the Commissioner of Education, objected. "Since only one of the sponsors (Direct Instruction) was found to produce positive results more consistently than any of the others, it would be inappropriate and irresponsible to disseminate information on all the models."[16] But Boyer's objection wasn't heeded, and I doubt any similar objection would be heeded today, and for the same reasons.

The JDRP apparently felt that to be "fair" it had to represent the multiplicity of methods in education. Not only did this practice make it virtually impossible for school districts to distinguish between effective and ineffective programs, it defeated the very purpose for which the JDRP and NDN were established.[17]

In an article reprinted from the November 15, 1994, *Newsday*, Billy Tashman summed it up this way with reference to Follow Through: "The good news is that after 26 years, nearly a billion dollars, and mountains of data, we now know which are the most effective instructional tools. The bad news is that the education world couldn't care less."[18]

Whom do we blame for the idiocy Cathy Watkins and Billy Tashman describe? Tashman lays the blame on "the education world," but Watkins discusses how this world includes policymakers, colleges of education, teachers, school districts, publishers, and the public. All of us who do not make good decisions when we can—and all of us who fail to point out the lunacy of being "fair" rather than discriminating good from bad and best from better—bear a measure of blame.

Besides the fairness and equity notions regarding teaching methods, the line of argument defending a "pastiche" of instructional methods is well known, though based on falsehoods: data are conflicting, with equally valid claims being made for many different approaches, or the data are meaningless, actually showing nothing much. The assumption, sometimes implicit in arguments, sometimes explicit, is that teaching is not and cannot be made scientific in any meaningful way. As I discuss in other chapters, there are certainly important aspects of teaching that can and have been subjected to scientific investigation. Others and I have urged decisions based on such scientific information.[19]

It is not stupid to suggest that some things should be left to personal preference. In my judgment it is both mindless and hurtful to students to suggest that science cannot or should not enlighten instructional procedures. True, the science of education is not the same as the science of chemistry or physics (or any of the other "hard" or natural sciences), but this is not to say that education cannot practice the same sort of skepticism that underlies the natural sciences and depend for much of its practice on evidence obtained from experiments in which disconfirmable hypotheses are tested. The science of education is much like (and closely related to) the science of psychology. Much education— and much psychology—is not science, and in both fields of study some practitioners reject the methods of science and scientific knowledge. Still, the basics of scientific inquiry apply as surely to many problems in education as they do to any other field of knowledge.

Deformed Education: I wear several hats in my school system. I'm a teacher of children with special needs in an elementary school, a mother of a son who is learning disabled and receives instruction in reading from a resource teacher, and I'm the building representative for the local teachers association. As a building representative, I'm expected to go to the school board meetings and report to the teachers in my building what the board proposes. Last month, one of the board members suggested that the school system adopt a whole-language reading program and that we also hire professionals to present workshops on this method. After the board member's suggestion, I spoke about the fact that over 30 percent of our students are considered at risk and that we also have a lot of special education students whom special education teachers are having trouble integrating into the regular classrooms.

Because of the large number of at-risk and special education pupils, the special education teachers hoped for a more structured program for these students. I offered to bring copies of research studies about the ineffectiveness of the whole-language approach with low achieving students and special education students, and I also gave the school board the name of a leading researcher in the field who teaches in the education department at the local university.

After I spoke, the board member who suggested the whole-language curriculum frowned, thanked me for my opinion, and immediately spoke to another board member, Harriet Lane, or "Dr." Lane, as she prefers to be called. She asked Dr. Lane, "What about this whole-language, Dr. Lane? Tell us about it."

Dr. Lane has been in the education department of the local university for over 25 years, teaches science education, hasn't published since obtaining tenure, and is a joke among students because she never seems to read a journal article. However, Dr. Lane said, "Well, reading is not my area of expertise, but I know credible people in this area, and I'll be happy to discuss this with them and get back to you."

To my dismay, whole-language reading was a done deal with the school board on the strength of Dr. Lane's recommendation. She reported to the board that she had contacted "the top people" in the field at several universities in the country (without naming them), and that they felt that this was an excellent program (based on what information, she did not say). She said she knew that her niece had learned to read using a whole-language approach and that she'd asked her niece's teacher about it and that teacher had strongly recommended it and that was good enough for her. When I asked Dr. Lane if she would tell us whom she contacted or if she could give us the published sources of her information, she frowned at me and asked, "Are you doubting my integrity?" The whole board laughed as if she'd said something very funny.

I just sat down, then. I wanted to tell Dr. Lane that I didn't doubt her integrity, but that I did doubt her credibility. I wanted to know if the "experts" she contacted really know anything about reading instruction, if they are acquainted with the latest research on other methods of instruction, how whole-language stacks up against other programs used for at-risk children, and where parents could learn more about the efficacy of this method. But I didn't ask any of those questions. I sat down. I know who butters my bread, and I'm a single parent with a child with special needs. I need my job.

MAKE ANY AMBIGUITY A
REASON TO DOUBT EVERYTHING

Postmodernists show an affinity for using ambiguity as an excuse for radical doubt. In my opinion, no one has described how postmodernists do this more clearly than Gary Sasso. As he notes, postmodernists use the defensible observation that *absolute* objectivity is theoretically or philosophically if not practically impossible to achieve, then conclude that objectivity does not exist at all because it can never be absolute. The very idea of objectivity is untenable, they argue. Sasso uses analogue arguments to show how postmodernists could likewise conclude that neither black nor white exists because absolute purity of blackness and whiteness cannot be demonstrated to exist, only shades that may appear to be very close to black or white. And since everything is merely a shade, the density of the shade is trivial. In the case of objectivity, postmodernists argue, subjectivity of any degree is permissible because absolute objectivity is not provable as a philosophical proposition and is, therefore, unbelievable.[20]

Postmodernists use such theoretical or philosophical gimmicks to argue against common sense and for radical skepticism.[21] In a column on failure to count all of the ballots in the 2000 presidential election, William Raspberry first noted how a theory may show that it is impossible to walk across a room (i.e., the distance between the starting point and the other side of the room is always one half of the remaining distance, so you can never actually get there, so the philosophical argument goes).[22] Although Raspberry does not mention postmodernism in this column, his crossing-the-room illustration is clearly the type of philosophical ambiguity used by postmodernists to justify their radical doubt. But it is doubtful that most of us who cross rooms, describe room-crossing, and ask others to cross rooms can take the can't-cross-the-room theory seriously in everyday life. Even the most earnest postmodernist would likely have to snicker, not bicker, if asked in a public forum to cross a room to demonstrate the impossibility of doing it.

But in the warped world of postmodern posturing, theory and practice are often confused. No practice is acceptable that is based on what postmodernists view as flawed theory, no matter the real-world consequences. In the postmodern world, theory is a matter of deduction from acceptable propositions, and practice must conform to philosophy. In the world of everyday life and of science, however, theory is constructed, assembled, induced from observations of what actually happens under given circumstances. Scientific theory must be based on the observed results of practice. A real world is assumed to exist outside our theories, and theory has to be consistent with our observations of that real world. Putting theory in the driver's seat, making a philosophical proposition the test of acceptable practice, is the modus operandi of communism, as Robert Conquest has described so clearly.[23] That it (Marxist communism) didn't work well in practice, primarily because of its detachment from the real world, probably tells us something about where postmodernism is going. But the probability of ending up at an address in Nullville, Nowhereland, has so far not been a deterrent to postmodernist enthusiasts.

Gary Sasso best portrays the twisted thinking of postmodernists about making discriminations when he discusses their rejection of objectivity in research and their descent into propaganda:

> This [objectivity is unbelievable] is a desirable conclusion for postmodern cultural relativists, because they think it protects them from being faulted for research that is blatantly subjective or politicized (see Danforth & Navarro, 1998), since both truth and knowledge for its own sake are delusions. However, the same logic starting at the other pole will prove the opposite conclusion: There is no such thing as subjectivity. Single-factor logic can be made to work backward, too. It is the failure to continue the process of finer distinctions that render all-or-nothing arguments false and misleading. Once this corruption by belief becomes a habit of thought, the power to see what is really there is severely diminished. That is why advocacy research is not research at all: It is propaganda.[24]

In short, the postmodern proclivity for confusing the roles of theory and practice and for using any ambiguity as an excuse for radical doubt gives stupidity a green light—well, that is, given that any light can be judged green or any statement can be judged senseless! This fondness for using ambiguity as cover for stupidity turns common sense on its head. For example, it allows or even fosters the nonsensical propositions that objectivity is unbelievable as a characteristic of scientific research and that it is possible to have an education system in which no child is left behind or in which all education is special education. And it does so with such panache, such verve, such undisguised chutzpah and obscurantist language as to fool many who should know better.

In real life, ambiguity has a distinct and important role, but it is not used as an excuse for radical doubt. Ambiguity may be purposeful in law, for example, as the alternative ensures injustice.[25]

TAKE A PROPOSITION TO THE GREATEST EXTREME POSSIBLE

Using ambiguity as an excuse for radical doubt is just one instance — but currently a very important one for postmodernism — of a more general strategy of driving a reasonable proposition into the ground by taking it to its ultimate extreme. As Michael Shermer pointed out in *Why People Believe Weird Things*, it is the tactic known as *reductio ad absurdum* — "carrying the argument to its logical end and so reducing it to an absurd conclusion."[26] Closely related is the "slippery slope" argument, that if you take the first step in one direction, then you start an inevitable slide to the end. For example, Shermer uses this example to illustrate the fallacy of reducing an argument to the absurd to avoid a slippery slope: If you eat one scoop of high-fat ice cream, then you are putting yourself at risk of becoming morbidly obese and dying prematurely of heart disease. Sometimes people who take that first step off the straight and narrow road slide all the way down the slope; usually, they do not.

Sometimes, as Shermer notes, it is useful to take an argument to its logical end to see whether the argument is valid, given that the logical end is something possible and it can be tested by experimentation. However, the frequent result of taking something to its most extreme is an unyielding stupidity that becomes rabidness, madness, preoccupation, and an excuse for the most extreme of "solutions," such as suicide bombing and other forms of self-destruction or murder. It becomes, as Robert Conquest puts it, not just another idea to be evaluated but an

Idea to be served at any cost, even the cost of rationality.[27] It becomes ideology, a certainty that Senator Daniel Patrick Moynihan warned about.[28] It becomes the excuse for demanding that the world—at least that part of the world in which the Idea is the issue—be seen in high-contrast black and white terms.

By driving a reasonable proposition into the ground, we arrive at all manner of extreme, rationally untenable, destructive positions on a variety of issues. The Idea becomes a matter of faith, a position held with religious fervor if not with the justification of a religion. Some such Ideas have to do directly with education; others do not. This art of the stupid is in practice when the infamous "one drop" rule is the standard defining someone with one drop of ancestral blood from a given ethnic or "racial" group as belonging to that "race." It is seen in the conclusion that a special class or a special school for students with disabilities is an evil form of segregation, usually a conclusion arrived at with reference to the statement that "separate is inherently unequal." It is behind the insistence that reading instruction must involve "whole language" or "phonics" alone, uncontaminated by the other instructional method.

Among the most interesting—to me, anyway—of life's questions is this: How do people become radicalized, such that judgment and reason go out the window? How do people become terrorists and murderers in defense of an ideology? Ellen Goodman, writing of Oklahoma City bomber Timothy McVeigh, who murdered hundreds to make some twisted point about the evils of American government, made the following trenchant observation: "I wonder how many other Americans have forgotten that acts of war or martyrdom or terrorism throughout history were—still are—often motivated by deep beliefs, not dysfunction."[29] We tend to forget that ideologies (Ideas) have created the greatest horrors of the last century, as Robert Conquest has reminded us.[30]

Perhaps people seek simplicity when it is inappropriate, which I discuss in the next essay. Perhaps it is starting with a reasonable proposition and being reinforced, by adulation and other forms of social encouragement, for taking increasingly extreme views on a particular issue. Perhaps it is a form of madness we will never fully understand. Whatever its cause, however it comes about, it is the abandonment of judgment in favor of an absolute. Perhaps people are looking for absolution, for something that will save them or set them aright in spite of their other "sins." Who knows?

But human judgment is less than perfect. This is why people object to "slippery slopes," believing that if any judgment is allowed then all is lost. The "slippery slope" argument is an all-too-familiar but silly defense against reasonable limits of nearly every kind. The arguments go like this: Require that guns be registered or ban assault rifles, and there goes the whole of the right to bear arms. Put any limits on the definition of disability, and there go all disability rights. Let teachers use time-out as a form of punishment, and before you know it teachers will be locking children in isolation and forgetting them, and perhaps beating them, too. Allow screening of school children for emotional or behavioral disorders, and all family privacy is lost. We could think of many other examples. In the case of the extremes I have used as examples, each starts with a reasonable proposition, to whit: The United States Constitution grants the right to bear arms. The rights of people with disabilities must be recognized and assured. Teachers may be abusive in their use of punishment. The right of families to privacy is important.

The slippery slope was at the bottom of many people's objections (including the objection of two United States Supreme Court justices) to allowing Casey Martin to use a golf cart in PGA (Professional Golf Association) tournaments. You may recall that Martin is a golfer with a serious degenerative condition of his right leg (Klippel-Trenaunay-Weber Syndrome), such that he simply cannot play a round of golf if he has to walk the course. In a 7–2 decision, the Supreme Court held that the ADA (Americans with Disabilities Act of 1990) applies in this case and that Martin must be allowed to use a golf cart, although other competitors walk in a tournament. Many people, including newspaper columnists and sports writers, weighed in on this controversial decision. The primary objection of the two dissenting Supreme Court justices and many commentators was that if Martin is allowed to use a cart because he has a disability, then we'll not know where to stop in giving people breaks in sports because they have an ostensible disability. Objections to the decision about Martin went like this: Allow Martin to use a cart, and next thing you know little leaguers with ADHD (attention deficit-hyperactivity disorder) will be demanding and be granted four strikes instead of three; or, let Martin use a cart, and first thing you know some 50-year-old fat man with a bad back and sore ankles will be claiming he has a disability and will sue for the right to use a cart for his tournament game. One could go on and on in a similar vein. As S. Scott Rohrer wrote, the *PGA Tour Inc. v. Martin* was about basic human decency, which requires judgment about what a disability is and what should be done in the individual case to accommodate it reasonably.[31]

The truth is that any slope and every slope is slippery. There are no nonslippery slopes. This is important to understand so that we are on our guard against sliding into decisions or policies that are evil. But another truth of at least equal importance is that staying off a slope guarantees a grotesquely mindless, absolutist policy that fails to address circumstances or come to grips with dilemmas. Zero tolerance in school discipline, for example, is a wrong-headed policy that fails to take extenuating circumstances into account.[32] Uniform or mandatory sentencing rules tie the hands of judges, substituting certain stupidity in many cases for the possibility that indefensible sentences will be handed down in some cases.

You may be tempted to conclude that one judgment is as good as another if we do not embrace an absolute. Relativism is decried by some, and "moral relativism" comes in for more than its share of denunciation. But just because a commandment may be broken under extenuating circumstances—that is, that judgment is allowed, one evil is judged against another—does not mean that someone's judgment must be accepted willy-nilly. Judgment is required to distinguish good judgment from bad, and I think it is usually bad judgment—perhaps not always, but very nearly so—to exclude human judgment in the individual case. Relying on judgment does allow the possibility of evil, but disallowing judgment ensures evil.

There is the myth that scientists are certain of many things, if not most, a myth on which I have commented elsewhere.[33] Scientists often reply to questions, "That depends." And in education we try to teach children to think things through, which means, if we are successful, that they will often reply the same and understand the folly of absolutism. But, as I explain further in the next chapter, education itself is not *the* answer to life's persistent questions, including this one: Why is this person unwilling to allow someone else to make a judgment?

OVERCOMPLICATE SIMPLE THINGS OR,
CONVERSELY, OVERSIMPLIFY COMPLEX THINGS

A time-honored art of the stupid is to overcomplicate simple things or to oversimplify complex things. This art is not peculiar to education. People in all of the social sciences and humanities seem to be particularly good at it, too.

Overcomplication of simple things is funny in its pomposity, as long as it is not taken seriously, in which case it is truly maddening to those who look for readily understandable language about simple things. Richard Feynman has given us a funny description of the overcomplication of language by a sociologist in a paper written for an interdisciplinary conference. Feynman says that he couldn't make any sense at all of the sociologist's paper until he started reading one sentence at a time and translating from pompous language into plain English.

> So I stopped—at random—and read the next sentence very carefully. I can't remember it precisely, but it was very close to this: "The individual member of the social community often receives his information via visual, symbolic channels." I went back and forth over it, and translated. You know what it means? "People read."
>
> Then I went over the next sentence, and I realized that I could translate that one also. Then it became a kind of empty business: "Sometimes people read; sometimes people listen to the radio," and so on, but written in such a fancy way that I couldn't understand it at first, and when I finally deciphered it, there was nothing to it.[34]

The banality of the paper to which Feynman refers is similar to that of many writings of "deconstructivists" or "postmodernists," which others have pointed out. When people write in jargon and we try to figure out just what they are saying, it often turns out that they are saying something so obvious, so vacuous that it is no wonder they tried to hide it in a blizzard of unnecessary words and obtuse phrases. Educators may be prone to blow-hard banality, but they are neither the inventors nor the masters of it. B. R. Myers has noted the problem with reference to contemporary literary style:

> The "literary" writer need not be an intellectual one. Jeering at status-conscious consumers, bandying about words like "ontological" and

"nominalism," chanting *Red River* hokum as if it were from a lost book of the Old Testament: this is what passes for profundity in novels these days. Even the most obvious triteness is acceptable, provided it comes with a postmodern wink.[35]

Now it is true that many seemingly simple things are complex and that seemingly simple things are often things we never fully understand (e.g., the way of a man with a maid, if you want an old Biblical reference). There is an element of truth in the observation that everything is too complicated to understand completely, but this partial truth can be used to mask the larger truth that we can often sift out the active ingredient, the fundamental process, or the big idea that's important.

The other side of this art is to hide the complexity of an issue by suggesting that it is really simple. School choice and "accountability" are probably among the most obvious cases in point. Another case that may be less obvious, although it is a popular oversimplification in rhetoric about education, is *individualization*. Even the federal special education law called the *Individuals with Disabilities Education Act* (IDEA) has since its inception in 1975 called for Individualized Education Plans (IEPs). An IEP is supposed to be designed to meet the "unique" needs of each student with a disability. The ideas of uniqueness and individualization bear closer scrutiny.

Maybe my tendency to want words to have their agreed upon (i.e., dictionary) meaning is misguided. Some of my critics have told me so. Nevertheless, I think "unique" *usually* means "not like any other; one-of-a-kind." True, a dictionary may list "unusual" as a meaning of "unique," and if "unique" is taken to mean "unusual, but not actually like no other," then I can make sense of the call for meeting these unusual needs. There are at least two reasons that "unique" taken in its first "like no other" meaning is nonsensical. First, the sheer number of students with disabilities (several millions in the United States) and the nature of education (e.g., learning to read) preclude actual uniqueness in the educational needs of these students. There are not millions of different ways to teach anything, at least not if "different way" has any actual meaning. Second, the only way effective educational methods are devised is to look for samenesses, likenesses, similarities among children—to find out how students are alike for purposes of instruction.[36] So I wonder why the law did not refer to "unusual" or "atypical" needs rather than "unique" needs. Maybe lawyers and advocates for students with disabilities thought "unusual" was accurate but wouldn't have the punch of "unique," even though "unique" is not quite accurate.

But if uniqueness is an oversimplified concept in education, the idea of individualization is more so. Bob Dixon, discussing how the assumption that technology, specifically computer-based instruction, will be better *because* it is individualized wrote the following:

> I contend that this assumption is a bit oversimplified and isn't necessarily true all the time. As a simple example, given the choice between teaching [reading] to one child or to five well-placed children, I'd rather teach five. . . . The . . . reservation I have with the general notion of *individualized* instruction is that the whole idea is just too broad: we don't know the *basis* upon which instruction is individualized.
>
> For instance, some schools of thought suggest that computer-based instruction could be individualized upon the basis of *student interest*. In that approach, one child works on multiplication facts with basketballs in the background (because that child is interested in sports), while another child sees leaves in the background (because that child is interested in Mother Nature). First no one has even begun to demonstrate that accommodating student interest thusly improves a child's achievement. Second, we could hypothesize that those differing backgrounds could constitute a distraction from the task at hand, thereby having a detrimental effect on achievement. Either hypothesis could be tested, but to my knowledge, neither has been.[37]

Catch phrases of school reform rhetoric are often oversimplifications of rather complex issues. Having "the same high expectations for all students" sounds simple, but upon close examination it becomes an obviously silly phrase because it ignores the complexity of deciding just what is reasonable to expect from a student and what is not. It's as unthinking as saying that we should pay the same high salaries to all employees or have the same high expectations of musical or athletic performance for all individuals. For some students of any given age or grade, a given expectation (e.g., in reading) will be unreasonably high; for others, it will be way too low.

Of course, some who support such statements will say that they are not to be taken literally to mean that the same expectation should apply to all students. But, they may say, we should expect all students to strive to do better. But the question is how much striving and how much improvement, and should there be the same formula for all students? Besides being a grotesque oversimplification of the matter of expectations, the phrase runs head-on into the idea of individualization—differentiating, having different expectations for different children depending on their characteristics.

So, what does "the same high expectations for all students" mean? Maybe the intended meaning is merely "expect all students to make progress." If so, I wonder why people don't say that instead of saying something manifestly empty of thought. I also wonder how expecting all students to make progress is different from what the vast majority of teachers now expect. Besides, expectations without instruction have a very marginal effect, if any at all, on what a student can attain. It's time we give up magical thinking about expectations—thinking that if we just expect students to do something then they will.

USE A QUOTATION FROM A SMART PERSON TO SUPPORT AN UNTENABLE POINT

Another strategy for presenting the stupid as sensible is to use a quotation of questionable sense from a person recognized as bright or, alternatively, take a bright person's quotation or concept and misinterpret it. A prime example of the quotation gambit is the use of F. Scott Fitzgerald's well-known statement that "The test of a first-rate intelligence is the ability to hold two opposed ideas in mind at the same time, and still retain the ability to function."[38] One possibility is that Fitzgerald was thinking of competing but not opposite or contradictory ideas. Perhaps by "ability to function" he meant resolving the competition of ideas or weighing the evidence that one is more defensible than the other.

We do not know precisely what constraints Fitzgerald might have intended to put on interpretations of his statement. And, of course, he could have said something wrong, even though he was a very bright person. It appears to me that he meant competing, not contradictory, for he continued, "One should, for example, be able to see that things are hopeless and yet be determined to make things otherwise." I suspect that he meant "be able to see that things *appear* hopeless." Otherwise, there really is no reason for hope. But I could be wrong in my assumption about his intended meaning.

I have sat through meetings in which truly silly ideas were presented. Sometimes the leaders of these sessions asked us to remember the famous statement of nineteenth-century philosopher Arthur Schopenhauer that all truth passes through three states: (1) ridicule, (2) violent opposition, and (3) acceptance as self-evident. The leaders of such meetings seemed to be suggesting that if an idea is revolutionary but true, it must first be ridiculed. And, of course, opposition to a silly idea merely confirms its truth, which will eventually be recognized. But, as Michael Shermer discusses, Schopenhauer's statement is inaccurate. Many revolutionary ideas are neither first ridiculed nor violently opposed before being accepted, and many ideas that are ridiculed or violently opposed are completely discredited and forgotten. "For every Galileo shown the instruments of torture for advocating a scientific truth, there are a thousand (or ten thousand) unknowns whose 'truths' never pass muster with other scientists."[39]

The fact that a person has won a prize—even a Nobel Prize, for example—does not necessarily mean that his or her comments on every topic are defensible. In fact, some Nobel laureates have made statements about matters other than their prize-winning work—or, in a few cases, even their award-winning work—that are indefensible.[40] I am not suggesting that those who are awarded prizes for their work are usually or even often "wacky." I merely note that sometimes people thought by their contemporaries to be creative geniuses are indeed crazy. Sometimes their mental aberrations are chronic and pervasive or they have an idea that seems to be a breakthrough but in actuality is silly or perverse. More often, they are just uninformed (ignorant) about topics other than those in their field of work and their comments outside the field of their genius are off-target. The point is simply this: genius in one line of work does not preclude idiocy in another.

One of the great temptations in today's social environment is to attribute knowledge of education to people who have succeeded in other fields of study. We suppose that if someone is capable enough to win a

Nobel Prize, for example, then they must be able to figure out problems of all kinds—especially educational problems, which people assume are relatively easily solved because they are not "rocket science." But this assumption is not borne out by experience.

I, too, must be careful not to let my admiration of the intellect and ability of someone to explain how science works color my evaluation of their comments on education. I must admit to being a great admirer of the late physicist and Nobel Prize winner Richard Feynman, whose descriptions of science and pseudoscience I find both highly readable and dazzling.[41] And his descriptions of educational and psychological "experiments," which he classifies as "cargo cult science," and of judging books by their covers (literally) are nothing short of hilarious.

In my judgment, Feynman is rightfully scornful of much or most of what passes for scientific method in education and psychology. Nevertheless, I do not agree with his apparent conclusion that education (especially K–12 education) is beyond the reach of science. "The science of education, for example, is no science at all," he states in *The Pleasure of Finding Things Out*.[42] True, much of what passes for science in education is not. But we can test instructional methods in the objective and skeptical way that scientists approach any other problem of finding the answer to the question, "What happens if we _____?" The answer is a probability statement, to be sure, but so is the answer to all other scientific questions. And as Siegfried Engelmann, Doug Carnine, and others have shown, the probabilities arrived at through careful and skeptical inquiry can be highly meaningful in guiding educational practices, just as they can be in medicine, engineering, or any other field of applied science.[43]

This is not to suggest that education can or should be free of the value judgments that science cannot answer. Not all of education can be addressed as a science. But what kind of intellectual derelict would suggest that that part of education open to scientific investigation should not be investigated scientifically? Surely Richard Feynman, were he alive, would not suggest such abrogation of responsibility to acquire reliable knowledge about how things like instruction work. Still, sometimes scientists not familiar with education as a science can, out of ignorance of a field other than their own, dismiss rigorous inquiry as unknown or infeasible.

Perhaps the greater danger is the misunderstanding, misinterpretation, and misapplication of ideas coming from the "hard sciences" (e.g., physics, chemistry, biology) by educators and others who work in the social sciences. Alan Sokal and Jean Bricmont have described in considerable detail how philosophers and social scientists have often misunderstood basic principles—botched the meanings of ideas in physics, for example, such that their attempt to apply these ideas to social or interpersonal problems begins with a basic intellectual error.[44] Then the attempts to relate these ideas of physics or mathematics to social phenomena are further botched by the misapplication of the ideas to problems they do not fit. The consequence is bizarre, sometimes magical thinking about social problems that serves no one well (except, perhaps, the person whose irrationality obtains recognition through publication or requests for public speaking or university promotion). In chapter 4, I mention this kind of misapplication of the Heisenberg principle of uncertainty. But postmodern writing is shot through with such warped and off-target ideas. "Ecology and the New Physics"—an article published in 1987 that attempted to draw implications for working with emotionally disturbed children from a variety of notions said to represent the "new physics"—is perhaps now the classic example of such nonsense in special education.[45]

The thesis of this book is that sometimes intellectually gifted or influential people say vapid things about education and get away with it, are rewarded for it, and are imitated. So, if a highly visible, otherwise successful person endorses something known to produce poor or unpredictable results, there is the danger that it will be taken seriously. This is the problem with presidential candidates, presidents, governors, and other high government officials or high-profile athletes, people in show business, or people in corporations making statements that do not compute or that are not backed up by sound data. Their assertions may support corporal punishment or any other hare-brained idea; no matter, it will not be easily discounted.

THROW WORDS TOGETHER IN A HODGEPODGE NOBODY WILL REALLY UNDERSTAND

When all else fails, spout a hodgepodge of ideas using words or sentences that no one will understand. This is pretty much the gambit of the postmodernists, whose unintelligibility I discuss in chapter 6. The postmodernists are not the only ones to use this strategy, which can be practiced at the level of art. However, in recent years it has become difficult to find examples of unintelligibility not attributable to postmodern influences in education. This is simply because postmodern views seem now to dominate in publications of the American Educational Research Association and some other organizations catering to educators. To be sure, the American Educational Research Association does sometimes publish articles defending scientific evidence and reason, although postmodernism seems now to take inordinate space in the association's journals.[46] But do not be fooled into thinking it is just educators who spout nonsense. The problem infects all of the humanities and social sciences, not to mention politics. I give examples from education because that is my field of study.

I think that the use of jargon fools mostly those in the professional group in which it is spoken or written. Those outside the professional enclave where it (the jargon) is familiar see it for what it is: pure poppycock or extremely mundane statements dressed as erudition.

Please do not misunderstand. For some things in education and psychology, as well as in physics or chemistry or any other field, a technical language is required. For example, terms like "discrimination" (being able to notice a difference), "reinforcement" (increasing the probability of an act by altering its consequence), "conduct disorder" (serious misbehavior including disobedience and aggression), and other terms are necessary for efficient and accurate communication. Nevertheless, sometimes people needlessly complicate communication with their own professional colleagues and stymie communication with a more general audience by using language that is dense or worse.

After reading things like the following excerpts, I always say to myself, "I hope I write more clearly than that." It is not difficult to find examples like the following in the publications of educators — and, I warrant, in the publications of other professionals, too. First, consider the last paragraph of an article titled "The Culture of Redemption and the Administration of Freedom as Research" from *Review of Educational Research*, a publication of the American Educational Research Association. The writer is apparently summarizing the contribution of his article to the understanding of something.

I hope to contribute to a rethinking of the politics of knowledge by his-
toricizing the overlapping of the culture of redemption with the social administration of freedom. The very research interests in the emancipatory
effects of "practice" are an effect of power through the inscription of an
overlap of discourses about progress, science as a redemptive culture,
and populism. As the effect of power, these discourses are constructed
historically through the relation of the state, social science, and pedagogy in the governing of the soul. I pointed to the dangers of the redemptive culture in inserting the actor who should be saved by academic
research. This conflates different forms of political action into a unidi-
mensional practice classified by intellectual work. As is obvious in the
discussion of power and inclusion/exclusion, my concern is to address
the historical amnesia in which researchers and policymakers forget the
social relations inscribed in the culture of redemption.[47]

Next, excerpts from the middle of "Inquiry Cantos: Poetics of Developmental Disability," an article published in the journal *Mental Retardation*. Apparently, the author is attempting to explain why no type
of knowledge is better than any other—the postmodern argument that
all ways of knowing are equal (except objective scientific knowledge,
which is troubling because it is associated with power and should be
abandoned in favor of multiple subjectivities).

An important tool used by those (often unintentionally) guarding knowledge borders is the creation of idea taxonomies and hierarchies of knowledge. Some knowledge—or more precisely, some knowledge expression—
is deemed of greater value than other knowledge expressions: "other
knowledge is considered 'lower' if expressed in different idioms, for example, the writing of journalists but also writing in unconventional academic styles."[48] Knowledge presented in the conventional written forms
and codes of positivist research, forms typically used in representing developmental disability research, is given greater cultural value than knowledge
presented in other forms, such as poetry, drama, fiction, and the like. . . .
    Qualitative researchers have begun to move across the ideological di-
vide from objectivity to subjectivity. Some disability studies and postmodern researchers, seeking a way out of what is seen as a simplifying
binary of objectivity/subjectivity, look to avoid this dualism by assuming
multiple subjectivities. One anonymous reviewer, responding to an earlier version of this text (and so this text itself becomes multiple, nesting
within responses of reviewers and the counter-texts of myself as author),

noted poetically that "the call of subjectivities (plural, positioned, multi-voiced, contingent, inconstant) is the hope of pluralistic community and idiosyncratic individuality, of a particularity, of experience, of hope, of suffering" . . . This described, for me, a vision of an inclusive community of researchers, self-advocates, support providers, family members, and others—a community that finds troubling the power ensconced in developmental disability research journals and texts that deny access to the writing and reading of self-advocates. . . .

So, with others, I began to look around at what has been called the crisis of representation, to find new ways of understanding the lives of labeled Others through alternative textual practices. . . . I realized that I needed to move beyond typical analytic and writing practice in developmental disability research. I would need to develop and create text acts outside of typical academic prose.[49]

Or, read a paragraph from "School-Linked Services Integration: Crisis and Opportunity in the Transition to Postmodern Society." This article appeared in *Remedial and Special Education* and is an attempt to explain, well, I'm not sure, actually. The following passage, though, seems to be an explanation of the implications for special education (and other human services) of the philosophy of Michel Foucault. Foucault's "antifoundationalism" is a rejection of professional and scientific knowledge in favor of a "perspectivist" or relativist view. In essence, antifoundationalism defines human and institutional practices as "texts" or "discourses" that can be read or interpreted in a variety of ways, none of which can be demonstrated to be correct in a scientific sense.

The principal figure behind this line of criticism [antifoundationalism] is Michel Foucault, the moral philosopher whose work emphasizes the political implications of the knowledge, practices, and discourses of the "human sciences," an inclusive term for the social sciences and social professions. . . . His work focuses on the various modes by which modern societies turn human beings into subjects for investigation, surveillance, and treatment, practices that regularly involve various forms of medicalization, objectification, confinement, and exclusion.

The notion of disciplinary power raises serious moral and political questions for the social professions—questions concerning the nature and effects of the practices and discourses of investigation, surveillance, medicalization, objectification, treatment, confinement, and exclusion that these professions have developed and refined over the course of this century. . . . What makes these questions even more troubling, of course, is the epistemological implications of antifoundationalism. Not only must the social professions respond to these questions, but they also must do so knowing that there is no way to justify their practices and discourses by an appeal to scientific authority. This, then, is the epistemological and moral crisis that antifoundationalism poses for the social professions at the close of the modern era.[50]

Perhaps I just do not understand the depth of passages such as these. Maybe I have not attained the intellectual level required to comprehend their significance. Or, just perhaps, they indicate the depth of the muck into which we educators have fallen.

A few words about Michel Foucault may be in order, as he has become an icon in the postmodern world. Many postmodern education writers cite his work and attempt to pattern their philosophies after his.[51] But, as Roger Shattuck describes Foucault and his philosophy in *Candor and Perversion*, both the man and his teaching are loathsome to most people who are not antisocial. Shattuck describes Foucault's admiration of the Marquis de Sade and his defense of sadomasochism, sexual promiscuity of people infected with the AIDS virus, pedophilia, the elevation of power to the highest good, and other disgusting positions on moral and social issues.

Here are a few sentences from *Candor and Perversion* in which Shattuck describes Foucault's philosophy and behavior in a chapter titled "Second Thoughts on A Wooden Horse: Michel Foucault."

Foucault convinced himself and his admirers that his own crapulous behavior merited some kind of perverse moral justification. But what he referred to as "the limit-experience" of sadomasochistic experimentation led—so far as we can tell—to no illumination beyond itself.

Readers familiar with [the Marquis de] Sade's work may perceive the true direction of Foucault's project: to seduce and to pervert, following the doctrine that elevates power above truth. But you would not grasp this project from an uncritical reading of Foucault's abstract, obscurantist prose.[52]

There is more than enough obscurantism in writings about education and its reform. And I get the impression that much of the reading of those who cite Foucault has been casual, at best. But what Shattuck calls Foucault's "cantata style" and "evasive language" are now widely imitated. I hope those who revere his philosophy and cite it in support of their own views do not really understand its depravity. If they do, then the yogurt into which we have fallen is deeper than is apparent from the postmodern style of writing.

Crapulous (sickening) is an apt word for Foucault's behavior and philosophy. *Execrable* (detestable, horrifying) is fitting too, I think. Both words also appropriately describe the postmodern cant parodied by Frederick Crews in *Postmodern Pooh* and the imitations of that language in the literature of postmodern education.[53] In my view, such lingo is best flushed promptly—rejected as scholarship and as serious adult discourse, at least in education.

NOTES

1. Conquest (2000, p. 8).
2. Gould (2000, p. 9).
3. Barry (2001, p. E10).
4. Irving (1989).
5. Kauffman (1990a).
6. E.g., Forness, Kavale, Blum, & Lloyd (1997), Lloyd, Forness, & Kavale (1998), Watkins (1996).
7. Elkind (1998a).
8. See Kauffman & Brigham (2000a).
9. E.g., E. D. Hirsch's notion of what every American needs to know; see Hirsch (1987).
10. Landrum (1997).
11. Starnes (2000, p. 108).
12. Kauffman (1999c); see also Conquest (2000).
13. Feynman (1998, 1999).
14. See Carnine (2000).
15. Watkins (1996, p. 61).
16. Watkins (1996, p. 61).
17. Watkins (1996).
18. Tashman (1996, p. 67).
19. E.g., Carnine (2000), Engelmann (1997), Engelmann & Carnine (1982), Kauffman (1993, 1999a).
20. Sasso (2001).
21. Shattuck (1999).

22. Raspberry (2000c).

23. Conquest (2000).

24. Sasso (2001, p. 183).

25. Kauffman (1990b).

26. Shermer (1997, p. 58).

27. Conquest (2000).

27. See Dionne (2001a).

29. Goodman (2001a, p. A6).

30. Conquest (2000).

31. Rohrer (2001).

32. See Kauffman & Brigham (2000a, and references cited therein); see also www.indiana.edu/~safeschl/publication.html.

33. Kauffman (1999c).

34. Feynman (1985, pp. 281–282).

35. Myers (2001, p. 104).

36. E.g., Engelmann (1997), Engelmann & Carnine (1982).

37. Dixon (2000, p. 2).

38. Fitzgerald (1945). See www.quotationspage.com; see also *Columbia Quotations*.

39. Shermer (1997, p. 50).

40. See Golden (2000) for examples of silly, crazy, or deviant ideas and behavior of Nobel Prize winners.

41. Feynman (1985, 1998, 1999).

42. Feynman (1999, p. 242).

43. See Engelmann & Carnine (1982), Carnine (2000), Crockett (2001).

44. Sokal & Bricmont (1998).

45. Rhodes (1987).

46. See Richard Mayer (2000, 2001) as exceptions to postmodernism.

47. Popkewitz (1998, p. 27).

48. Sibley (1995, p. 122).

49. Smith (2001, pp. 382, 384–385, 386); see also Smith (1999).

50. Skrtic & Sailor (1996, p. 275).

51. Besides Skrtic & Sailor (1996), see Peters (1995a), Scheurich (1997), Usher & Edwards (1994).

52. Shattuck (1999, pp. 78–79).

53. Crews (2001); see also Bain (1995), Peters (1995a), Scheurich (1997) and other works proposing or supporting postmodernism in education cited in other chapters, especially chapter 6.

CHAPTER 3

Slogans and Other Trivialities

"Let us begin by acknowledging that there are as many ways of teaching as there are teachers."

—Alfie Kohn, freelance writer

SLOGANS AND OTHER TRIVIAL, MEANINGLESS STATEMENTS DON'T IMPROVE EDUCATION

Slogans are useful for selling objects and ideas and for rallying the masses. Commercialization and hoi-polloi aside, slogans have no value in analysis of problems. In fact, slogans often work against the acquisition of understanding. As Seymour Sarason noted, "Sloganeering as a defense against the acquisition of knowledge is all too frequent."[1]

Slogans give an impression, but below the level of image they are hollow. That is why we refer to them as slogans, catchwords, or catch phrases and to using them to change an image as sloganeering. They are, as Gary Clabaugh and Edward Rozycki have pointed out, designed to give the impression of consensus without conveying any substance.[2] They are familiar to anyone who reads about education, but they are not the peculiar province of educators. For example, Marc Fisher, writing about Virginia's legislative support for posting "In God we trust" in schools and requiring students to say the pledge of allegiance, commented, "I thought government-mandated wall slogans and mass recitations were supposed to go out with the Berlin Wall and the Evil Empire."[3]

An argument can be made that a slogan may help to rally public opinion and force political action for a good cause. This is no doubt true. But if the slogan then becomes the basis for policy—laws and rules—it is bound to give a policymaker free rein to promote injustice in the defense of thoughtless rhetoric. Given that social progress is actually possible (I believe it is), I'm not sure that sloganeering is the best way to achieve it. Sloganeering assumes that people can be distracted from thinking through propositions in a logical way, of dealing with reasonable complexity. When people defend sloganeering as necessary to achieve social progress, I feel they are appealing to base human characteristics and revealing that they have low, not high, expectations of the public, not to mention low expectations of the typical students in our schools. I think we can and must do better than that.

In chapter 1, I mentioned the exquisite banality of postmodern rhetoric. But banality is not the exclusive tool of postmodernists. The hackneyed and the trite are commonly found among other comments about education and its reform that are intended as serious discourse. In chapter 1, I also discussed one of the new century's most popular slogans, which includes the words "leave no child behind." This has become a mantra of candidates for high public office.[4] That such statements are trite makes no difference to politicians. Legitimate as they may be for rallying public opinion or fostering an image, slogans are not helpful in books, articles, and speeches intended to guide reflection or thoughtful action. "The thinking person's slogan" is, of course, an oxymoron.

All slogans are trivial, except for the purposes served by catchwords and catch phrases, but not all trivial statements become slogans. Sometimes statements intended to be profound, even revolutionary, are essentially meaningless.[5] In this chapter, I focus on slogans and trivial observations about education, although many of these may be traced to ideas put forward in other disciplines. One example will suffice. In *The Schools Our Children Deserve*, Alfie Kohn begins his description of two models of schooling with this statement: "Let us begin by acknowledging that there are as many ways of teaching as there are teachers."[6] There are, in fact, millions of school teachers in America. Are there millions of ways of teaching? I don't think so. In fact, to the extent that we try to make millions of distinctions in teaching I think we are engaging in a trivial pursuit. This is not to deny that teachers are unique human beings. But suggesting that the individuality of human beings is important to successful teaching trivializes the real differences among instructional strategies. There are not as many ways of teaching as there are teachers unless "way of teaching" is reduced to a triviality.

One more point about slogans: Most of them, if not all of them, contain elements of truth. They perpetuate myths or misimpressions precisely because you can find at least a little shard of truth in them. The truth may be small, but a kernel of it is there, nonetheless; the slogan is usually not a pure, unvarnished lie. This is what makes the slogan stick, makes it attractive, and draws people into a larger falsehood. Many are the thinkers who, like E. D. Hirsch, Jr. have noted that half-truths are more dangerous than outright lies. Slogans are a tricky business, and the trick is to find just enough truth to fool people without telling them the whole truth. A big lie is sold one partial-truth at a time.

POPULAR SLOGANS
DOMINATE THE WORLD OF EDUCATION

Too many slogans have been used in education for me to try to mention them all. You will no doubt be able to recall or recognize some that I do not mention—some old, some new. In early 2001, I asked participants in a special education email discussion list to send me their favorite slogans. Here, in no particular order, is most of what I got from respondents, with some of my own favorites added randomly into the list:

If you can read this, thank a teacher.
It takes a village to raise a child.
Treat all the children the same.
Leave no child behind.
All children can learn.
All children are special.
All education should be special education.
Label jars, not people.
Celebrate deviance.
The problem is not in the child.

Every teacher is a reading teacher.

All means ALL.

Special education is not a place.

Celebrate diversity.

All teachers should teach all students.

Children are more alike than they are different.

Those who can do; those who can't teach; those who can't teach teach teachers.

Good teaching is good teaching.

Inclusion: It's the right thing to do.

Kids don't fail, their teachers fail.

Every school an excellent school.

Values, not science.

Every child will be average or above in academic performance.

Brain-based learning (or education or teaching).

A few of these are slogans I had not previously encountered. A few seem to be summaries of ideas captured by other slogans (e.g., "Every child will be average or above in academic performance" may be another way of saying "We will leave no child behind").

In *The Schools We Need and Why We Don't Have Them*, E. D. Hirsch, Jr. provides a guide to educational terms and phrases, many of which are slogans. He describes with particular clarity and insight the way these words are used:

> Prospective teachers and members of the general public are bemused, bullied, and sometimes infected by seductive rhetorical flourishes like "child-centered schooling" or bullying ones like the dismissive words "drill and kill." These terms and phrases pretend to have more soundness, humaneness, substance, and scientific authority than they in fact possess. Promulgating this system of rhetoric has been an ongoing function of American schools of education, whose uniformity of language and doctrine ensures that every captive of the teacher-certification process and every professor trained to continue the tradition is imbued with educationally correct phrases. Consensus-through-rhetoric has been one of the main instruments of the Thoughtworld's intellectual dominance. . . . Repetition and consensus give the phrases a self-evident, not-to-be-questioned quality which induces those who repeat them to believe them earnestly and implicitly.[7]

Hirsch's list of misleading terms and slogans is too long to reproduce in full here, but it includes terms like these: "learning to learn," "life-long learning," "child-centered schooling," "developmentally appropriate," "learning styles," "discovery learning," "constructivism," "co-operative learning," "holistic learning," "mere facts," "teaching for understanding," "critical thinking skills," "multiple intelligences," "authentic assessment," "portfolio assessment," and many kindred neologisms, meaningless combinations of words, and trivial observations. Terms like these are now popular not only in education but among those who sell education to the public. Alfie Kohn, among the most popular of the current freelance writers about education, uses many of these terms and more in his article "Fighting the Tests: A Practical Guide to Rescuing Our Schools."[8] Kohn and others who share his views write in the tradition of what Hirsch calls "romantic developmentalism" and "naturalistic pedagogy." They object to a "tool-conception of education" and express antipathy toward emphasis on subject-matter content in teaching. They call for "real learning" as opposed to learning facts. This tradition fits the anti-intellectualism of Americans, who now often refer to facts as "factoids," as if facts are trivial knowledge and knowing facts makes a person a nerd.

In the remainder of this chapter, I discuss some of the slogans I consider most vapid and destructive of sensible education. I highly recommend Hirsch's glossary, which exposes the hollowness of much of the terminology used in rhetoric about education.[9] Keep in mind that not only educators and teacher educators use these slogans and trivial statements. These statements have become, as Hirsch notes, part of our public discourse about education and are used widely by politicians. Witness the current popularity of the meaningless phrase "no child left behind."

Deformed Education: We questioned our fifth-grade child's teacher, Natalie, about her "progressive" ideas about school reform. She told us that she has had recent training from a "high-powered" faculty member from a university's school of education. She assured us that the schools' top administrators and the school board were instrumental in arranging this training.

Natalie thinks these people—the university professor and her school administrators—must know what they're talking about, and she isn't

about to question them. Furthermore, she says, she's read in recent education journals that her methods are "brain-based" and that she ac-
commodates different "learning styles." Well, we think, better base
learning on the brain than some other organ! And we wonder what
"style" has to do with learning basic math or reading.

Seriously, we don't see the evidence that her methods are effective.
Lots of the students in Natalie's fifth grade class still don't know their
basic number facts—addition and multiplication tables—and can't
solve simple word problems in arithmetic. Natalie says the facts aren't
terribly important, that kids have calculators from which they can get
the facts any time they need them. She just wants her students to learn
to make good guesses and then compare to what their calculator says.
We worry that if the students don't know their addition and times tables
they won't have a good idea whether the answer they see on the calculator is right or wrong. In fact, they won't even be able to tell when
they've obviously made a mistaken entry on the calculator.

Natalie says we shouldn't be so concerned, because her math curriculum has the stamp of approval of major professional organizations
and the school board, as well as the superintendent and principal. Our
son Skip will do just fine without learning the number facts we learned,
she assures us. She tells us that although we learned the facts, he's learning the process of finding the facts, which she says is more important.

But we're looking into a private school for Skip and considering
whether to hire a tutor. Either way, we're angry about paying taxes to
support schools that don't teach students basic things we think they
should know. Is Skip going to be able to use a calculator on the state
test? Even if he is allowed to use one, we think he'll be a lot better off
if he learns how to do basic arithmetic without one. How will he fare
in high school or the world of work or even manage his own money
wisely if he doesn't know the basic math facts? The school's explanations aren't making sense to us.

"ALL CHILDREN CAN LEARN" IS
EMPTY OF ANY SIGNIFICANT MEANING

"All children can learn" is a familiar mantra with about as much meaning as "all children are young" or "all children grow." As my colleague

Dan Hallahan and I suggested a long time ago, "all children can learn" begs many questions.[10] "All children can learn" does not begin to address the actual problems of teaching and learning. It glosses over the obvious—that children differ enormously in what they can learn, how quickly and easily they learn particular things, and what level of performance they can eventually attain.

Some children must struggle to learn basic reading and math skills by the time they are teenagers, even with the best teachers. Others will have mastered reading and/or basic math before they are five years old. "All children can learn" is, I tell my students, a prime example of a throw-away line, a statement of no real meaning to anyone who is even vaguely familiar with educational problems or able and willing to assess the meaning of a slogan. It is like saying "Money can be used to buy things," or "A job is work to do." "It is fill, 'like, you know, but uh, kind of thing,'" I sometimes say.

Now, I have considerable sympathy with the observation that many students who are "written off" as nonlearners can be taught, can learn a lot more than their teachers imagined, and can be educated in meaningful and important ways. So I want to be as careful as I can to make myself understood on this point: *We must be careful to discriminate a teacher's inability to teach a child a particular skill from that child's ability to learn it. But we must also be careful to discriminate those skills a child can learn from those the child cannot.* Not all students are capable of learning all things, and there are a few children (a minuscule percentage of the child population, but probably a growing percentage as medical science saves more severely physically damaged children) who can learn only the simplest of tasks, and then only with extraordinary instructional effort. Some children are permanently unconscious due to severely damaged or missing upper brains, and for them "education" seems to me to be out of the question, although training a simple response to a particular stimulus might be possible.

Do not misunderstand this, either: I think these children, who I consider ineducable, are entitled to and must be given humane, life-supporting care. The acceptable alternative to education for these children is not neglect or maltreatment. Rather, the alternative is to provide other types of care, other services in which the object is not to teach the child a skill. Education, in my judgment, implies teaching, and there exist in this world some children for whom teaching is a fruitless activity. In my opinion, it is wise to recognize this fact, not cover it over.

If the slogan "All children can learn" is intended as a counterweight to the sentiment "This child can't learn a thing!" applied to a child who is sentient but difficult to teach, then it represents responding to silliness with something sillier still. It seems obvious to me that "All children can learn" is vapid on two counts. First, it is a meaningless statement unless qualified in ways I have suggested. Second, if "all" is taken with extreme literalness, to mean each and every living child, no exceptions, even for the unconscious or those with no cerebral cortex, then it is, I think, patently false unless we are talking about learning at the most fundamental behavioral level, which we can induce in fruit flies, worms, and a variety of very simple animal species that can be trained to make simple responses to specific stimuli.[11] The difference between training and education may be, at least in part, an important issue here.

"All children can learn" is usually stated without qualification. If it is intended to state that all living children can be taught something, like a simple motor response to an intense stimulus, then I don't see an argument in the making, simply because the slogan is such obvious fluff. But there are those who take it with extreme literalness and earnestness, such that children who lack a cerebral cortex are said to be educable (never mind whether their brains function properly, they simply don't have a cerebral cortex with which to think or process information, a condition called anencephaly). Furthermore, argument about whether children with brains that function very poorly and children without upper brains at all, whose lives are being sustained merely by the function of their brain stems, must be "educated" has reached the federal courts, including the United States Supreme Court.[12] The issues have become legally moot, as the U.S. Supreme Court admits of no exceptions whatever to the law demanding the education of every single child, no matter how disabled, under what is now the *Individuals with Disabilities Education Act* (IDEA). The issues have also become extremely contentious, and comments about the view that some children are not educable are sometimes vitriolic. The Supreme Court's decision on the matter of educating all children regardless of their educability does not mean that all children are educable. However, for views like mine on education, people are likely to be called Nazis. Unwillingness to accept a slogan can earn you a loathsome moniker.

"ALL CHILDREN ARE SPECIAL" IS AS MEANINGLESS AS "ALL CHILDREN CAN LEARN"

"All children are special" and its variants are popular but patently silly. Well, ok, all children are genetically unique (identical twins excepted, maybe). And children exhibit a tremendous variety of characteristics. And all children could conceivably be and should be special to someone, who values them above all others. But this slogan is not intended to indicate specialness in these ways. It is, rather, intended to mean that all children are special when it comes to teaching them. Every teacher is to see every child as a special child, an exceptional child in some way, and to teach each child like no other. The slogan is used to argue against seeing only some children as exceptional, only some as needing a special education. From "all children are special" we go to "all education should be special education."

For example, Dorothy Lipsky and Alan Gartner concluded an article with this gem of self-contradiction: "It is time to move on to the struggle of changing the educational system to make it both one and special for all students."[13] They blithely ignore the inherent contradiction of the concepts *same* and *special*. They might as well have said something like this: It is time to move on to the struggle for standards of excellence not derived from comparisons. Language like this belies any intention of reformers who use it to bring intellectual integrity to the task of educating children or their teachers. It carries a peculiar irony when the ostensible intention of reformers is to promote critical thinking or, as the National Center on Education and the Economy put it, to prepare students to "render critical judgment" and produce students "whose understanding runs deep."[14]

The ideas of universal specialness and universal excellence are so appealing as bases for slogans that I fear they may be ineradicable. Reformers seem to bask in the image of *special* or *excellent* but, at the same time, make sure that they disassociate themselves from the implications of both words. Specialness and excellence require discrimination (in the sense of discernment, ability to see a significant difference). They require judgment, the recognition that all are not equal in achievement, that some are better than others at doing something, that there is a distribution of valued characteristics. In America and other nations embracing democratic ideals, we do hold the view that one person should not be judged more worthy than another *as a person*, that all people are created *equal before the law*. But that does not mean that we must believe that all people are equal in every which way.

George F. Will has perhaps best captured many Americans' disgusting unwillingness to make any judgment that might reveal an elite in his commentary on art.

> So the word "art" has become a classification that no longer classifies, there being nothing it excludes. How perfect, now that "inclusive" is the day's ultimate accolade because it is an antonym of "judgmental.". . . The question . . . is whether this democracy is capable of a cultural policy unapologetically oriented toward excellence. Neither the studying nor the achieving of that is something to which everyone has equal "access."[15]

The rhetoric of egalitarianism is so enchanting that it pulls those who should know better under the sludge of irrationality. How else can we explain the statement of the National Center on Education and the Economy that "The challenge is to provide *an elite education for everyone*"?[16] *Universal* excellence, giving everyone the VIP treatment, providing the elite for *all*—well, what can we say, except that this is not the kind of thinking we want our children to exhibit? It represents the kind of nondiscrimination among performances that E. D. Hirsch, Jr. attributes to the romantic notions undergirding "progressive" education.[17]

Maintaining belief in the slogan that all children are special when it comes to education simply insures that no child is, actually, seen as special. Why do we laugh when someone says, "Oh, yes, I'm special, just like everyone else?" Why don't we laugh when someone says, "All children are special?" When we don't laugh, I hope it's because we think it's a bad joke, not because we believe it isn't a joke. I hope that someday soon we will laugh people out of positions of public trust for suggesting things like "all children are special" for education.

"ALL CHILDREN WILL COME TO SCHOOL
READY TO LEARN" WAS NEVER A REALISTIC GOAL

"By the year 2000, every child will enter school ready to learn" was a slogan devised by the creators of the "America 2000" education goals in the early 1990s. Obviously, it is a slogan that was not fulfilled, even though it was embraced by members of both Republican and Democrat political parties. More important, it was a slogan that never could be fulfilled in any meaningful way, regardless of the year (changing it to 2005 or 2010 or any other year would make no difference). It could well be characterized as dead on arrival, as rhetoric not matched to the realities of this world. It expresses a nice sentiment, but it means nothing more. It is sentimentality gone political.

First of all, it is not at all clear to me—or to anyone I've asked about it—just what "ready to learn" means. It seems to imply at least that the child will have acquired the skills necessary to receive instruction— skills like sitting still, paying attention to the teacher, being compliant with a teacher's requests, and so on. It might refer to a high degree of motivation to learn whatever a teacher attempts to teach. But perhaps it should be taken to mean that the child has acquired some of the skills of discrimination necessary to learn to read—to hear and be able to imitate differences in speech sounds, for example, or perhaps even to associate some of these sounds with letters of the alphabet. Or, perhaps it refers to certain basic numeracy skills, such as counting or one-to-one correspondence.

Of course, there is the matter of the age at which the child enters school. Not all children start school at the same chronological age. Perhaps we should assume that the reference is to age five or to kindergarten.

Actually, it doesn't much matter what "ready to learn" is taken to mean or the age at which the child enters school. There is no way in our society to ensure that every child will come to school ready to learn by any reasonable definition. We could say that all children are, actually, "ready" to learn when they come to school. It's only a matter of the teacher discovering their readiness. If that is the case, then there is no reason to set the goal of all children coming to school ready to learn, as they're already ready!

The slogan has any vestige of sense only if "ready to learn" means the children were supposed to be somehow different in that readiness in the year 2000. Consider that neither schools nor any other social agency in our American society (or in any other democratic society that I am aware of) has the right or the charge of compelling parents to get their children "ready to learn" by the time they enter school. Thus even if the slogan can be given some sort of meaning, it would be impossible in our society to achieve its ostensible goal.

I do think it is possible and important to encourage families to do a better job of childrearing, to nurture children, to help them learn the basic skills of self-control and paying attention that are required for successful school performance. I think more parents should be helped to teach their children basic phonological awareness (awareness of how the sounds in words are alike and different), one-to-one correspondence, counting, and a variety of other skills that most successful students have when they enter school. But that is not the same as setting a goal that is both meaningless and clearly impossible.

"EDUCATION IS THE ANSWER" IS WRONG

"Education is the answer" and similar slogans remain popular, even though history has demonstrated repeatedly that education does not solve many problems, particularly social and personal problems. After a student shot some classmates in San Diego on March 5, 2001, President George W. Bush suggested that students need to be taught right from wrong, as if that were the answer to school shootings. Other politicians have seen the limits of education more clearly. Writing of the late Robert F. Kennedy's views as a United States Senator, Peter Edelman observed that "He [RFK] had come to see that education was not sufficient by itself."[18] RFK saw that education is a dead end without economic development resulting in people being employed in jobs that pay more than poverty wages. But there are other reasons as well why education alone is not *the* answer to much of anything.

Here I refer to education as sharing or imparting knowledge, informing people so that, presumably, they can and will make better choices. And it's true that sometimes telling people things works wonders, a bit of knowledge that my colleagues and I think every teacher should have.[19] But the larger truth is that telling—informing—though the simplest and most straightforward approach to problems in which knowledge could make a difference in how someone behaves, often fails to change behavior. Problems sometimes persist in the face of clear evidence that bad choices are being made. Of course, good choices do not *necessarily* eliminate problems, leading some, I suppose, to conclude that choices make no difference.

Choose a personal or social problem—smoking, diets high in saturated fats, lack of physical exercise, drunk driving, dropping out of school, glorification of violence in the media, whatever—and someone is likely to suggest that people's behavior will change when they know the negative long-term consequences of their conduct. However, short-term payoff beats long-term negative outcome for lots of people. Behavioral psychology has revealed this reality many times and in many ways.

Both history and experiments tell us that education in this sense of sharing or imparting information has severe limits in solving personal and social problems. In a chapter titled "The Answer Is Education," Robert Conquest describes how high levels of education have often failed to prevent homicidal and even suicidal Ideas from gaining sway in the twentieth century.[20] In fact mental aberrations have often been devised by people of high educational standing, and these poisonous mental seeds have often been grown first in colleges and universities.

Three major points contraindicate education as an easy or sure answer to human problems. The first is described admirably by Richard Feynman: if you can teach good, you can teach bad; if truth, also falsehood; if the helpful, then the unhelpful as well.

> There have, in the past, been great enthusiasms for one or another's method of solving a problem. One was that education should become universal, for then all men would become Voltaires, and then we would have everything straightened out. Universal education is probably a good thing, but you could teach bad as well as good—you [could] teach falsehood as well as truth.[21]

So we must come to grips with the reality that education per se is only a tool that, like science, can be used for good or bad purposes. And it is often the case that the bad or untrustworthy will be sold to students or the general public as good and reliable. The substance as well as the semblance of education can be corrupted.

The second contraindication of education as *the* answer to human problems is that people often do not do what they know they should or do what they know they should not. This understanding is at least as old as the observations of the Apostle Paul, who remarked: "For the good that I would I do not: but the evil which I would not, that I do" (*Holy Bible*, Romans 7:19, King James Version). If only understanding what we should do were followed reliably by our doing it!

Third, education, like every other social policy, may produce unintended consequences. Informing people may induce them to make choices that seem at first good but are later understood to be bad. Changing people's behavior through education may produce consequences that were not merely unintended but that create new and more serious problems. After they are "educated," people may construct social policies with the best of intentions only to find that things have gone awry, in part because of the very policies they constructed.[22]

So, what is the answer? Actually, I don't think there is any, if "the answer" is an ultimate fix. However, although I don't think we know exactly what to do, I think we do know what not to do. I think the answer is decidedly not to choose ignorance over knowledge (i.e., to embrace willful ignorance or deliberately to keep people from finding things out) or to assume that no useful predictions can be made about anything. I discuss the predictable and wretched consequences of the willful ignorance and nihilism of postmodernists elsewhere in this book. But I think a wise person will come to understand that "education is the answer" is a slogan as hollow as they come.

"KIDS DON'T FAIL, TEACHERS FAIL" HURTS BOTH KIDS AND TEACHERS

"Kids don't fail, teachers fail" and similar indictments of adults are often used to blame good teachers and induce guilt on the part of teachers whose students are unsuccessful, regardless of the quality of instruction that has been offered. It is a pity that a slogan should be used to indict teachers who do their best, even teachers who offer excellent instruction. Part of the problem here is the concept of teaching. Part of the problem is also in the recognition that teachers often have failed and do fail kids.

Many people have observed that teaching and learning are closely linked, and some have said that without learning there is no teaching. That is, a teacher cannot use the cop-out, "I taught him, but he just didn't learn!" Anyone who has studied teaching and learning understands how dangerous it is to allow teachers to use this kind of statement. Teaching can be very bad, and even mediocre teaching can account for the student's lack of learning. And some teachers blame students for failures that can be attributed to their inadequate instruction. Teachers should be expected to find and use instructional strategies that result in their students' learning whenever they can.

Nevertheless, every teacher has hit the wall with a kid—done his or her best using the most reliable instructional practices, yet observed little or no progress in the kid's learning. True, we have often been too ready to blame children for teachers' faults, but the world is not set right by being too ready to blame teachers for children's failures to learn. Teachers can fail; so can their students.

So, can one teach something that the student does not learn? If teaching means exposing the student to certain things (like the teacher's reading or lecturing or presenting a problem) in the presence of which some students have learned the skill in question, then the answer is, obviously, yes. Furthermore, any child, living or dead, can be taught if *that* is the definition of teaching. If teaching means presenting the student with tasks that result in the student's acquiring a new skill, then the answer is, obviously, no. Using this definition, no learning means that no teaching has occurred; the teacher failed. If teaching means using instructional practices that are known to result in most students' learning the skill in question, then the answer is, obviously, maybe. I think it is reasonable to assume that it is possible for a teacher to use best instructional practices, yet have a student who learns little or nothing of what has been taught.

Best practices are those instructional strategies that are usually successful for a particular type of student who is being taught a particular skill. It is necessary to qualify this statement with the type of student and particular skill because students differ dramatically in their prior learning, and skills differ dramatically in their instructional requirements. Many excellent teachers find that they must try multiple approaches to teaching a particular skill to a particular student, even though most of their other students learn the skill with a standard strategy. But many excellent teachers also never find a way to teach some children some skills. Does this mean they have failed? A similar question could be asked of physicians. If a patient does not recover from an illness, does that mean the physician has failed? Not necessarily, I think.

I suppose it is human nature to want to have someone to blame, some whipping boy, someone to hold accountable for what goes wrong. It may be an American predilection, but it is a destructive attitude. Anyone *can* fail, but often we don't know who did or why. Saying that students don't fail, only their teachers, is grotesquely unfair to teachers (not to mention their students) and, if it is taken seriously, will drive many good teachers from the profession. True, teachers' organizations sometimes protect bad teachers, just as other professional or labor organizations protect their incompetent members. That must be recognized and condemned, for it contributes to bad practices and to the harm of others. But teachers are particularly easy targets for the poison pen and the bad mouth. It's also tempting to look for a facile "solution" to the problem of children or schools that don't meet with our expectation. For example, William Raspberry has described the problem as one of low expectations. To his credit, he does not simply blame teachers for having low expectations but indicts others as well: "The critical change . . . is in expectation: on the part of teachers, of course, but also on the part of the rest of us, emphatically including the parents of these children."[23] This does not change the fact that if improved performance were simply a matter of increasing expectations—those of teachers or of parents or of both—then improving performance would be a piece of cake. Nearly all teachers, even most of the very good ones who have high expectations for their students, understand this.

"CELEBRATE DEVIANCE" IS A GROTESQUE IDEA

"Celebrate deviance" is a slogan—or, at least, *was* a slogan—of a professional organization of which I have been president and a long-time member, the Council for Children with Behavioral Disorders (CCBD). I must confess that I was never comfortable with this slogan, even though I have accepted buttons and other materials on which it was printed. I don't think CCBD had any evil intentions, but I think the catchy words reflect sloppy thinking about behavioral disorders and deviance.

I suppose that "deviance" may be taken by some to mean mere "difference" or "deviation" (presumably from a mean or from any expectation we may have for another individual). "Deviance" could be confused with "nonconformity," I suppose. But the terms "deviance" and "deviant" are usually taken to mean differences of a particular nature—those that are unacceptable, that cross the line into emotional or behavioral disorder or mental illness or the illegal. People who celebrate deviance may have attached an unusual meaning to the term or may argue that deviance is actually welcome, as it is merely a difference from an oppressive, normative type of behavior and all differences are to be welcomed and celebrated. Norms, whether academic or behavioral, are said by some to be inherently oppressive and should be resisted.

But I have a problem with "celebrating" anyone's illness, sickness, accident, or social behavior that I think is unacceptable. To me, it is sort of creepy to celebrate someone else's misfortune. Some of my colleagues will argue that, actually, an emotional or behavioral disorder (or any category of disability) is not a *mis*fortune, just a different way of being that is equally as good as not having a disorder or disability. Some people with disabilities, whether university faculty members or not, will argue the same. Actually, they will contend, we are all pretty much the same, and disabilities are just differing abilities, not conditions to be lamented. I think I do understand the necessity of valuing people whether they have disabilities or not, the importance of getting on with one's life whether one has a disability or not, the need to get past lamentation. But I cannot bring myself not to care or not to want to help change a disability into an ability—and in my judgment any humane society will care enough about people with disabilities to want to do the same.

Some differences are ok, some are not; some differences are inconsequential, others enormously important. We need balance, judgment, discernment about difference and sameness, characteristics often lacking in stupid statements.[24] In a classic, moving editorial about mental retardation, Richard Hungerford commented about sameness and difference:

> Some of this talk of sameness is the talk of charlatans. An easy way to solve a problem is to say that it does not exist; ignorance and ignoring have a moral as well as a semantic affinity. By charlatans, the complex, the boring, the disturbing are made simple by fiat. To charlatans all men want the same, all men are the same.[25]

Note that Hungerford says *some* of the talk of sameness, not all of the talk, is the talk of charlatans. His topic is the difference we call mental retardation and how people tend to deny or ignore it, or to remain ignorant of it, preferring to say that all of us are the same. People seem to have a tendency to deny that deviant behavior is, in fact, deviant until it becomes intolerable. Teachers and school psychologists and school administrators experience considerable pressure from each other to deny deviance until it is protracted and extreme. Of course, this kills any hope of preventive action.[26]

I see deviance as a difference that is a reason for concern and action to correct matters, not as a reason for celebration. Deviance is an unpleasant difference. I know that some of my colleagues will argue that an emotional or behavioral disorder is a difference or deviance that is "not in the child." In fact, there is a point of view in my field that just as kids never fail (only their teachers fail), so problems are never in kids (only their environments have problems). If the environment were the way it should be, they believe, then the kid wouldn't have a problem.

Oh, yes, we can be too quick to pull the trigger of blame on kids and fail to see that the environment needs changing. However, regardless *why* the child behaves in ways judged by most people to be deviant or unacceptable, the fact is that he or she *does* behave in this way and his or her behavior must be changed.

Recognizing difference and deviance is critically important. So is understanding the charlatanry that shows us only sameness where there are important differences. But do not mistake my line of argument here. Recognizing samenesses, commonalities, shared characteristics is also important. Whether difference or sameness should be our focus and how particular sameness and differences should be responded to—

these are critical issues for education (and I discuss them further in the following text and in chapter 5 under the topics of special education and multicultural education).

"LABEL JARS, NOT PEOPLE" SHOWS A MISUNDERSTANDING OF LABELS, JARS, AND PEOPLE

"Label jars, not people" is a slogan that I find not only preposterous but also particularly destructive. It not only offends common sense, it leads people to believe things that are counterproductive. It is used often in special education, though not exclusively in that field, to counter the notion that children and adults can be categorized in meaningful ways. But it reflects a kind of thoughtlessness that makes the problem of labeling worse. The labels to which people object most vehemently (for themselves or other people) indicate that something is wrong—that the person has a disability, deficit, disorder, or problem that needs correction.

Any student who is treated differently from others is inevitably labeled. The issue is, really, whether all students should be treated the same (no labels) or some should be treated differently (which requires labeling). Some people have suggested that special treatment can be provided without labels, but that is clearly only a fantasy, not a possibility. We cannot speak of difference or special needs without words (labels). We cannot call children nothing (i.e., we call them something). Moreover, either our labels for disabilities or special problems signify concern (something unsettling, not positive) or they are worthless for describing what needs to be changed.

The social reality of disabilities cannot be hidden with anti-labeling rhetoric. Today's euphemisms are tomorrow's epithets. For example, "challenged," a euphemism of the 1990s, is already in our lexicon of derogations. Calling someone "intellectually challenged" is at least equally as transparent as calling someone "mentally retarded," and it has the additional sting of the wink and nod that goes with the obvious lie. True, we need to use the least offensive labels that clearly describe a problem. However, we don't need to believe the fantasy that the label is the problem or that a new label will fool people for very long. People's objections to particular labels may be judged legitimate or frivolous, but these objections are not the same as suggesting that labeling or categorizing per se can be avoided.

Besides, categorizing—and every category has a label, because otherwise we don't recognize that we have a category—is fundamental to all intelligent activity. Jars need labels that tell us their contents. People need labels describing their characteristics if we are to understand who they are and what they need. The fact that some people may misunderstand or abuse a particular label does not mean that the label is at fault. The point is that if we lose labels, then we have no way of making sense of the world, whether the labels are for people or objects.

Very little research evidence supports people's concern for the negative effects of formal labeling. If a disability label carries social stigma, for example, that stigma typically precedes a formal label for disability. That is, we observe a difference and label it; we do not label a person and only then notice a difference. Social stigma typically goes along with being different, whether a person is officially labeled or not. Disability labels themselves do not add appreciably to stigma. In fact, formal labels may actually assist in the explanation of a disability and the formation of a more positive identity.[27]

Nevertheless, some people retain powerful anti-labeling sentiment. In fact, the sentiment against identifying any student as different in any negative sense is so strong that some people argue against the label "at risk" applied to individual students. They wish to speak only of high-risk *environments*, as if some how the risk can be decoupled from the person. As I have noted before,

> When we decline to use labels responsibly, the individuals whose problems they designate become rogues or unmentionables—those with unspeakable characteristics. Some may argue that "person first" language (i.e., "_____ with _____" such as "child with behavioral disorder" or "person with mental retardation") is a partial solution, others that individuals do not actually *have* disabilities but are merely assigned them in some socially acceptable conspiratorial fashion or have merely developed a *reputation* for behaving in certain ways, or that we should label only programs or services, not the people who receive them. These are tortuous and self-serving philosophical games that delay and deny help to the suffering, whether they are the individuals who exhibit the problem behavior, those who must live, learn, play, or work with them, or

those who simply care about them. When we are unwilling for whatever reason to say that a person has a problem, we are helpless to prevent it. In some instances, we call those who demonstrate such unwillingness to label a problem "enablers" because they support maladaptive behavior such as substance abuse or spouse abuse through their refusal to call it what it is.[28]

The insistence on "person-first" language is particularly troubling to me for what it reveals about the objections to the ordinary use of language. As others have pointed out, when we label people by what they do, we don't insist on person-first language. We speak of bankers and bakers, not people who bank (or people with employment in banking) or people who bake. We speak of mechanics, not people with experience in car-repair. Most people do not object to labels like man, red-head, short, or tall. In my estimation, the insistence of disability advocates on person-first language has the opposite of its intended effect. Person-first language does not attenuate people's attention to disability, does not help people think of the disabled as just another person who happens to have ____. Rather, it sets disability apart, calls attention to it, gives it special and wide linguistic berth, and creates a backlash of mockery in which person-first language becomes the stock of laughter. "Person with male genes" for male prompts snickers. Combined with euphemisms like "challenges," the language is even more demeaning. "Person with height-challenge" for short man, "man with folic challenges" for bald or balding man, and other person-first euphemisms make the point—we are using silly language to pretend to hide what everyone knows we are talking about.

A lot of students with disabilities get the label du jour among their age peers for those who are misfits. These informal labels can be extremely cruel. A formal label used in psychology or special education may actually prevent some of their peers' misunderstanding and rejection of kids who are slow, who don't get it, who don't fit in. And these formal labels are better than the attempts to hide meanings by tortured linguistics.

Unfortunately and ironically, peoples' horror of labels of any kind merely heightens the stigma associated with the labels we use. When people object to labels that indicate a human characteristic or problem, they inadvertently reveal their negative attitudes toward the difference they ostensibly believe is not or should not be stigmatizing. We don't object to labels for things we value or for things we think are different, maybe not particularly desirable for ourselves, but at least ok. We don't do linguistic stunts for things we find commonplace or nonthreatening, only for things that disturb us deeply. It is the things we really abhor or want to hide for which we don't want to use common names. We have left the era in which homosexuality was referred to as "the love that dare not speak its name," but we have entered an era in which we dare not speak the name of a disability—mental retardation, for example—without fear of reprisals. Thank goodness for the acceptability of words like "homosexual," "gay," and "lesbian," that we no longer feel shame in saying these words and understanding their meaning, that we aren't expected to use such linguistic contortions as "person with sexual orientation toward the same gender" in place of gay. Mental retardation and other forms of disability will not lose their shame in our society until we can name them without being shamed.

Richard Hungerford had some pertinent comments about recognizing differences and the use of words for them:

> We must not let an awareness of difference keep us from trying with everything that we have to eliminate it or ameliorate its unpleasantness. But in our desire to rid ourselves of the frustration of such a staggering responsibility, we must not forget that some of the different differ—differ so much that they need protection. We are our brother's keeper. We are our son's keeper. The word "keeper" has fallen upon evil days; but it comes of proud lineage.[29]

Like "keeper," a lot of very ordinary words describing human differences have fallen upon evil days. The politically "correct" and, perhaps, expedient attitude is expressed today in unwillingness to call something what it is unless it can be construed as a positive characteristic.

"THOSE WHO CAN DO; THOSE WHO CAN'T TEACH; THOSE WHO CAN'T TEACH TEACH TEACHERS" SHOWS MISUNDERSTANDING OF TEACHERS AND TEACHING

"Those who can do; those who can't teach; those who can't teach teach teachers" is surely one of the most distasteful slogans to teachers and

teacher-educators. It's not silly simply because it is distasteful to teachers and those who teach them. The logic of the proposition makes it
silly, and the evidence doesn't support it.

Ah, but there is an element of truth—just a shard—to the slogan,
enough to make it a popular way of demeaning teachers and, particularly, educators of teachers. Some teachers are slow of wit, and some
educators of teachers I regard as near witless. But I think mental slow-
ness characterizes neither most teachers nor most of their educators.
Moreover, I think the larger truth is that many people do other things
because they can't teach. Teaching well is really quite difficult, and
many gifted people give it up, as do many whose intellect is dull. I
am quite sure that many critics of teachers have never been teachers
themselves—at least not in the sense of being responsible daily for
teaching children in public schools for a semester or more. They may
have dabbled in teaching, perhaps having visited a classroom briefly or
read a story to a group of children, but they have not walked in the
shoes of the classroom teacher. Many critics of teacher education have
never taught anything for a semester in a college or university, let alone
thought about what is important to convey to teachers in training and
how best to convey it or how acts of teaching are improved.

Generally, we do not presume to criticize from outside a profession
the work we do not know and do in our daily rounds. Physicians generally do not presume to teach others medicine when they do not practice medicine themselves. And they do not presume to teach a particular specialization when they are not specialists themselves in that area
(e.g., a cardiac specialist does not presume to teach psychiatry). Shame
on those of us who teach teachers but are not teaching in schools of the
type where our students are likely to take jobs. True, we are teaching,
we are in classrooms, but they are not often the classrooms in which we
are teaching teachers to practice. When someone practices an art or
profession sporadically or frivolously, we call him or her a dilettante.
Dilettante might describe some teacher educators, but it is even more
apt for those who have never been teachers in any institution.

Critics' lack of experience can be forgiven or overlooked, I suppose,
at least in part. Our criticisms of presidents, senators, judges, truck
drivers, waiters, physicians, and so on should not be entirely discounted because we have not done their jobs. True, some of our criticisms may be blunted because we simply do not understand how other

people do their work or how their resources constrain their performance. But making the fact that a critic has not done our job the central
point of our response to criticism—well, it misses the mark a bit.

One of the great misconceptions about education is that if you just
have content knowledge you will be—or at least *can* be—a good
teacher. If you really know math or engineering or English literature or
whatever, you can teach it to others, so some believe. Having been a
university faculty member for more than three decades and having
served in various administrative capacities in addition to being a member of promotion and tenure review committees at all levels (Department, School of Education, University), I recognize this for the distor-
tion of fact that it is. Content knowledge is necessary, but it is far from
sufficient to make a good teacher. Every good university recognizes
this fact, and many universities have programs that help faculty learn
how to teach in their discipline—in effect, they have teacher education
programs, usually outside of schools of education, that train faculty to
teach. There is no reason to believe that just because a person has content knowledge he or she can teach that content well at the elementary
or secondary school level either. Furthermore, research reviewed by
David Berliner and Linda Darling-Hammond and others has reviewed
the insufficiency of content knowledge to make a good teacher.[30] The
truth is that many of those who "can do" (other things) can't teach unless they are taught how to teach.

Teaching is not something that comes intuitively to most people,
whether they are highly intelligent or not. The same is true of writing,
singing, playing music instruments, and most skills. True, a few people
seem to possess intuition at a high level. Probably, intuition in any area
of learning is highly variable and distributed across the population
much like general intelligence or height or weight. Having a high level
of intuition about one thing doesn't mean that a person will have it
about another. Most people don't have enough intuition about most
things to rely on it as their primary mode of learning. They require instruction, guided practice, feedback, and many trials to learn particular
skills (piloting an airplane, playing the drums or the bass, singing, an-
nouncing the play-by-play for a sport, or writing an essay, to give just
a few examples). Teaching well, like other skills, requires more than
just being smart; it requires specific training in how to do it well.[31]

But, of course, many things can be muddled through. Many people get away with a low level of skill at what they're doing. Teaching seems to be one of the tasks at which we are too willing to allow people to muddle and then justify low-level skill with stupid rhetoric. Furthermore, we allow people to demean teaching without knowing anything about it—except that they have experienced it. This is rather like allowing passengers to critique a pilot's performance without any knowledge of flying—except that they have been passengers on airplanes. Taking this kind of criticism seriously is rather like taking seriously the raging of the couch potato at the performance of an athlete or coach that he watches on television.

Anyone who has been around universities with education schools and other professional schools must admit that some teacher educators are failed teachers, just as some law faculty are failed lawyers and some business faculty have but little business sense. But I think that in neither law nor in education nor in any other professional school have the typical faculty members left their practice of the profession because they could not do it or did it very poorly. Proof that "those who can't teach teach teachers" would be found in data showing that teacher educators are, for the most part, those who failed as teachers. I have never seen such data, and I doubt that such data exist.

But a question any reasonable person will ask when contemplating teacher education is this: Who decides what should constitute teacher education? As Paul Sindelar and Michael Rosenberg have noted, teacher educators in colleges and universities actually have rather little to say about how the preparation of teachers is carried out.[32] State legislatures and school boards set requirements for teacher certification that may be contradictory, silly, or impossible to meet. Those who teach teachers often do so under adverse conditions that include public misunderstanding fostered by legislators' and school boards' irrationality and ineptitude. And state legislators and the media have sometimes grotesquely misrepresented the abilities of teachers.

Teacher education needs improvement. I think that's obvious. But I hope teachers' complicity in misrepresenting reality won't continue. Clarke Fowler, though, suggests in the conclusion of his essay on the Massachusetts Teacher Tests that it will. He refers to "Reformed Fritz," an invented institutional character, as "a lad who, thanks almost entirely to his wise elders' high expectations, stern reprimands, and severe sanctions, has turned his life around," and Fowler supposes that very few teacher educators will reject that characterization.[33] He predicts that teacher educators will preserve a new fiction—that they have improved in response to the older fiction that nearly 60 percent of Massachusetts's prospective teachers couldn't pass a test of eighth to tenth grade skills.

SLOGANS REPRESENT PRETENSE, NOT A SOLID FOUNDATION FOR EDUCATION POLICY

Slogans are the language of pretense and humor. We use them in part to shield ourselves from confronting distasteful realities or to have fun. Unfortunately, our cowardice in confronting unwelcome realities only leads us into cognitive dead ends where exceptionality is denied.

We also see how misbegotten slogans inject humor into everyday life. Bob Thaves created a Frank and Ernest cartoon for January 30, 2001, depicting a travel agency with the slogan "Go Away!" "Maybe we should change the slogan," the cartoon character suggests.

In a previous publication, I noted how we use slogans as if they represent realities, deluding ourselves in the process.

"All children can learn"—as if we need not worry about the fact that they cannot all learn the same things or learn with the same speed, allocation of resources, and ultimate level of performance.

"Children are more alike than different"—as if a list of ways in which children are similar might somehow disguise their differences.

"All children belong in regular classrooms where they have access to the rich and varied general education curriculum"—as if being in the presence of a curriculum is sufficient to ensure learning and obviate the need for different instruction.

"We consider people to have mental retardation or to be unintelligent simply because of our own biases and limitations in understanding their intelligences"—as if we ourselves can assume the burden of their difference.

"People with cognitive disabilities or behavioral disorders exhibit different behavior, compared to the normal expectations, but their behavior is not inferior"—as if these differences do not really matter, that one way of behaving is as good as another.[34]

We can do better than this. We must demand better of ourselves and of those we elect or appoint to public office. When we hear slogans about education, we must challenge them—but not with another slogan. Slogans that make us laugh or set us up for mockery shouldn't be the basis for education policy.

NOTES

1. Sarason (1990, p. 87).
2. See www.members.home.net/erozycki/Slogans.html.
3. Fisher (2001a, p. B1).
4. See Slevin (2000).
5. Sokal & Bricmont (1998) and Koertge (1998) as well as Shattuck (1999) have given numerous examples, primarily in areas of study other than education.
6. Kohn (1999, p. 2).
7. Hirsch (1996, pp. 239–240).
8. Kohn (2001).
9. Hirsch (1996).
10. Kauffman & Hallahan (1993); see also Thomas & Bainbridge (2001).
11. See Kauffman & Hallahan (1993), Kauffman & Krouse (1981), Weiner (1999) for further discussion.
12. See *Timothy W. v. Rochester, New Hampshire School District* (1989).
13. Lipsky & Gartner (1987, p. 73).
14. National Center on Education and the Economy (1989, p. 20).
15. Will (2001a, p. A19); see also Will (2001c).
16. National Center on Education and the Economy (1989, p. 9, italics in original).
17. Hirsch (1996).
18. Edelman (2001, p. 40).
19. Kauffman, Mostert, Trent, & Hallahan (2002).
20. Conquest (2000).
21. Feynman (1999, p. 113).
22. Gillon (2000).
23. Raspberry (2001b, p. A19).
24. See Kauffman (1997; 1999d).
25. Hungerford (1950, p. 415).
26. Kauffman (1999b).
27. See Hallahan & Kauffman (1994), Kauffman (1999b).

28. Kauffman (1999b, p. 452).

29. Hungerford (1950, pp. 415–416).

30. Berliner (2000), Darling-Hammond (2000). Nougaret (2002) compared 20 alternatively licensed special education teachers (i.e., they had taken no more than 2 special education courses) and 20 traditionally licensed special education teachers. All were evaluated during their second semester of teaching by trained evaluators unaware of the teachers' licensure status. On all measures, traditionally licensed teachers significantly and substantially outperformed those with alternative licenses. The lowest performing traditionally licensed teachers were in the range of the highest performing alternatively licensed teachers. However, there were no statistically significant differences between groups on self-perception of teaching skill, suggesting that alternatively licensed teachers did not know that they lacked skill in teaching.

31. Berliner (2000), Gawande (2002).

32. Sindelar & Rosenberg (2000).

33. Fowler (2001, p. 780).

34. Kauffman (1997, p. 132).

CHAPTER 4

Self-Contradictions,
Nonsequiturs, and Denials

"The challenge is to provide *an elite education for everyone*."

—National Center on Education and the Economy

SOMETIMES PEOPLE CONTRADICT
THEMSELVES THROUGH THEIR CHOICE OF WORDS

Just suppose that someone were to say something like one of the following:

1. "The challenge is to foster democracy without involving ordinary citizens."
2. "The challenge is to find a standard of excellence not based on comparison."
3. "We must nurture all possible bio-diversity while eliminating those species that threaten such diversity."
4. "To be truly useful, educational research must be unintelligible to those who do it, not to mention those who apply it."
5. "The challenge is to provide *an elite education for everyone*."
6. "Education money comes with too many strings attached. We must eliminate these strings while requiring accountability from our schools."
7. "Actually, there is nothing wrong with kids who have disabilities."
8. "The failure of our schools can be addressed by making them competitive, like businesses."

Why would we not respond with laughter to such silly self-contradictions and denials or, at least say to the person who wrote or uttered them, "Say what? You contradict yourself!" But we don't—at least not in education, as I noted in the early 1990s.[1] Three of the above self-contradictions are actually in the literature on education: the fourth, saying that educational research *should* be unintelligible, from an article published in *Educational Researcher*;[2] the fifth, saying that *all* children should have an elite education;[3] and the seventh, suggesting that there's nothing actually wrong with children who have disabilities, from a book on critical issues in special education.[4]

Self-contradiction seems not to matter to many who comment on education and its reform. In fact, self-contradictions are sometimes said to reflect superior intelligence. Only people with high intelligence, so the argument goes, can understand how and why two statements may be contradictory and, at the same time, both be true. As I noted in chapter 2, sometimes F. Scott Fitzgerald's famous quotation, "The test of a first-rate intelligence is the ability to hold two opposed ideas in mind at the same time, and still retain the ability to function," is used to justify self-contradiction.[5] Never mind questions of Fitzgerald's meanings of "opposing" (contradictory or competing?) or "function" (avoid the opposition or resolve it by finding out which is more defensible?). Never mind the constraints he himself *may* have wanted to put on his statement or the possibility that he *could* have said something inane, even though he was a very gifted writer.

Sometimes a seeming contradiction (e.g., this piece of metal is solid, but it is made up mostly of space) is used to justify an actual contradiction (e.g., education should be under the control of local politicians, but federal regulations should govern education). Actually, all things are mostly space at an atomic level (which means there is, actually, no contradiction in the example about a solid). In our system of governance, federal regulations always supersede state and local regulations (so that in the example about education there is a real contradiction about control of education).

The oxymoron and its closest companions (sentences including self-contradictions) are common in silly talk about education and its reform. (I note here that "oxymoron" is a word to which some of my colleagues react in horror or forbid their students to use because it contains "moron," a demeaning label for mental retardation—make that "intellectual challenges," one of the euphemisms currently in vogue.) In fact, it appears that oxymorons have become downright presidential and bipartisan.

"Educational excellence for all," "elite for all," and so on may make successful sound bites, but they do not reflect the kind of thinking that the creators of these inane combinations of words say they want children to learn. In one essay in chapter 3, "'All Children Are Special' Is as Meaningless as 'All Children Can Learn,'" I noted how "special" and "excellent" are drained of any meaning when applied to all, and I quoted George F. Will's commentary on the world of art. Education, notwithstanding its ostensible purpose to help students learn to make judgments, to be discerning, to know serious talk from flim-flam, gets the same treatment by many who should know better. For example, David Broder wrote, "educational excellence for all is a national issue and at this moment is a presidential priority."[6] Now, it may well be possible for all schools to reach a reasonable standard of performance, and that floor of performance might be said to be good. But *excellent* has a meaning beyond *good*, I think. If it doesn't, then a lot of its traditional meaning is lost. If it's lost, then I suppose it's only a matter of time until we speak of extreme excellence, super-excellence, or ultra-excellence or some other term to indicate those that stand out from the pack.

Sometimes I wonder this: Do we really have to point out the stupidness of ideas like "universal excellence" or "elite for all"? Maybe we do, and we might need to do so more clearly, for such statements are still being made. Are the majority of people so empty-headed that such statements are taken seriously by them? I hope not. Maybe it is time for politicians and others making statements for public consumption to start assuming that the public intelligence is not to be insulted. Otherwise talk of education reform can be only self-contradictory—"I demand excellence on terms that cannot possibly be achieved."

SELF-CONTRADICTION HAS BECOME COMMON IN POLITICAL RHETORIC

Consider some of the political rhetoric we might encounter about education and its reform. Michael Kinsley described the self-contradictions in George W. Bush's campaign statements about reforming education.[7] Bush proposed, for example, to close the gap (which one?) in academic

achievement, set high performance standards, promote character education, and ensure school safety. However, he also suggested that states
would be freed from federal regulations — but, nonetheless, be held accountable for results.

The self-contradictions in rhetoric about holding schools accountable
are transparent, especially when they come from a political conservative
opposed to federal control of education. Kinsley first questions why
something that is said to be a state's prerogative (education) should be the
centerpiece of a campaign for federal office. However, assuming that education is a national issue, why not have a national government policy and
have the federal government enforce it (something G. W. Bush opposes)?
If local control has made shambles of education, why insist that the key to
improvement is local control? If the federal government should stay out
of the business of education, how can one justify spending billions of dollars on it and claiming that federal policy and federal authorities will see
to its improvement? Obviously, the rhetoric just doesn't add up to a rational view of the problems of education or their solution.

Michael Kinsley suggested that George W. Bush may be capable of
thinking through his self-contradictions about education but just
doesn't want to be bothered by them. Maybe he just likes to hold two
opposing ideas at the same time — something he's good at — regardless
of ability to function (in this case, as an education policymaker).
"Maybe two ideas aren't that much harder than one, if you're starting
from scratch."[8] Here are some of the questions that statements like
those of G. W. Bush should raise in a reasonable person's mind:

> When he says that local control of schools is vital, criticizes his opponent
> for wanting to "federalize" education, promises as president to impose
> various requirements on schools, complains that federal money comes
> with too many "strings," calls for after-school funds to be used for "char-
> acter education," endorses a federal law forbidding state lawsuits against
> teachers and so on, does he have a path through this maze of contradic-
> tions? When he promises a federal school voucher program and then de-
> flects criticism by saying "vouchers are up to states," is he being dense
> or diabolically clever?[9]

Would to god that people running for political office were the only
source of self-contradictions. The tragicomic fact is that some self-

contradictions come from people who are not running for office but say they want school reform that puts more emphasis on developing students' critical thinking. To these "reformers," it seems not to matter that a bright school child can catch their self-contradictions. Do they intend to tell school children to think through what they themselves have not? Even worse, the very idea of teaching critical thinking as an abstract skill is not supported by what we know about learning.[10] Critical thinking requires content, and precious seldom has education itself been the content of critical thinking!

Now I do understand that the deregulation fever means that the sheer number of regulations might be reduced, that money might be given in block grants, and that states or localities might be given ostensible freedom to make certain choices of tests to monitor student performance. Nevertheless, "accountability" always, by its very nature, implies "strings," and replacing many small strings with a rope seems to me only cosmetic, not a substantive cutting of strings. Perhaps being killed by a single blow is preferable to being pecked to death by ducks, but one ends up dead all the same.

SOMETIMES AN INFERENCE DOESN'T FOLLOW FROM THE PREMISE

Sometimes the silly talk about education comes in the form of a nonsequitur—an inference that does not follow from the premise or the transposition of a condition and its consequent. For example, we might encounter the argument that because the election results are close, a careful recount of ballots is unnecessary. Or, to take a popular example, because Werner Heisenberg demonstrated that it is not possible simultaneously to measure with absolute accuracy the velocity and position of a subatomic particle there is uncertainty about (here you can just plug in your personal favorite, ranging from the speed and position of aircraft to election results or the behavior of children in classrooms or the facts in a criminal case). Among my favorite nonsequiturs is this proposition, of which some politicians and school boards have become enamored: If we teach children that humans evolved from (here you can plug in apes or any other form of life or, even, primordial mud), then they will act like (here you can use apes, Neanderthals, animals, and so on). The person who uses a nonsequitur in argument seems to have forgotten that the "then" doesn't flow logically from the "if."

A temptation to which too many yield is ascribing fondness for non-sequiturs to teachers or "educationists." However, keen observation isn't required to find nonsequiturs in the writings of people from all walks of life, including many very smart people who should know better. Alan Sokal and Jean Bricmont in *Fashionable Nonsense* and Noretta Koertge in *A House Built on Sand* describe the nonsensical applications of the Heisenberg uncertainty principle and other ideas from quantum mechanics and theoretical physics to human affairs.[11] They demonstrate the fondness of academicians in the arts and humanities for statements in which premise and inference are unrelated.

Columnist Charles Krauthammer—a very intelligent man whose reasoning I usually admire—wrote in the *Washington Post* about the uncertain outcome of the presidential election of 2000.[12] He illustrated the use of nonsequitur by invoking Heisenberg's principle of uncertainty about simultaneous measurements of multiple aspects of subatomic particles in his conclusion that the uncertainty regarding Florida's presidential votes in the year 2000 could not be resolved. Certainly, I agree with Krauthammer's observation in late November 2000 that there was considerable uncertainty regarding the outcome of Florida's votes in the presidential election, and undoubtedly any method of vote counting contains a margin of error. But I fail to see how quantum mechanics or the simultaneous measurement of two properties (e.g., velocity and position) of subatomic particles has anything whatever to do with counting votes. Krauthammer could as easily, and perhaps more advisedly, have said that any measurement contains a margin of error (a mathematical proposition that applies to all measurements, although it does not keep us from measuring some things with extraordinary accuracy, which is to say with extremely small margins of error). Perhaps Krauthammer intended to use the Heisenberg principle only as a metaphor, but if so I think it was an inept use of metaphor. A good metaphor draws on basic similarities (in this case, errors in counting and adding). A good metaphor is a figure of speech that makes a statement more understandable, not one that fosters confusion of ideas.

Selma Wassermann, a retired professor writing in *Phi Delta Kappan*, also illustrated the use of nonsequitur in comparing standardized testing to quantum theory and the uncertainty principle. First, in her argument that we put too much faith in numbers, she seems to ignore completely the fact that Richard Feynman (whom she quotes in support of her anti-testing views) was a scientist who put great stock in precise measurement. In my judgment, her article reflects a complete misunderstanding of Feynman's points (e.g., she quotes from his essay on values in support of her argument against testing). She complains that "a new standardized testing movement reappears, with nauseating regularity, every few years."[13] She fails to mention the regularity with which standardized tests are demonized. And she seems to see quantification of educational performance as both immoral and misleading.

Wassermann's use of a play (*Copenhagen*) by Michael Frayn to explain Heisenberg's uncertainty principle demonstrates the laughable, but too typical, misunderstanding of science and measurement.

> In the play, Heisenberg, the originator of the uncertainty principle, describes its meaning to an audience largely untrained in science: "You can never know everything about the whereabouts of a particle, or anything else . . . because we can't observe it without introducing some new element into the situation—things which have an energy of their own, and which, therefore, have an effect on what they hit." Because of this, he continues, "We have no absolutely determinate situation in the world." Heisenberg's uncertainty principle "shatters the objective universe." The uncertainty principle limits the simultaneous measurement of conjugate variables, such as position and momentum or energy and time. The more precisely you measure one variable, the less precise your measurement of the related variable will be.[14]

I think the vast majority of physicists would not assume that Heisenberg's principle means we can't measure anything without changing it significantly or that it has shattered the objective universe. The principle of which Heisenberg spoke applies to measuring subatomic particles. To my knowledge, and that of the scientists with whom I've discussed the matter, the Heisenberg principle doesn't apply to macroscopic measurement, and its extension to mental measurements is pure nonsense. Lest you think that I exaggerate Wassermann's extension of theory about subatomic particles to testing children's performance, consider this: "If quantum theory has any validity, then it should cause us to pause and consider the kinds of numbers that serve as indicators of student performance on standardized tests." I consider this *nonsequitur ad nauseam*. I hope it is not the kind of "thinking" we teach children.

Physics professor Steve Reynolds of North Carolina State University kindly wrote me about the Heisenberg principle as follows (and I quote with his permission):

The Uncertainty Principle *does*:

1. Tell us that there are particular pairs of measurable quantities whose values cannot be simultaneously known with infinite precision for a particular object or system (example: east-west position and east-west velocity).
2. Tell us that there are far more possible pairs of measurable quantities that can (at least in principle) be measured with arbitrarily high precision (example: north-south position and east-west velocity).
3. Give us a numerical value for those minimum uncertainties, based on Planck's constant h = 0.00000000000000000000000000000000000663 joule seconds (6.63×10^{-34} JS).

The Uncertainty Principle *does not*:

1. Make all measurements uncertain (for example, it doesn't apply to measurements involving discrete counting).
2. Destroy the possibility of objectivity.
3. End experimentation in physics.
4. Have any significant quantitative application whatsoever to objects larger than a single molecule.
5. Cast any doubt at all about the nature of cause and effect.
6. Allow you to ignore other possible practical sources of uncertainty, which are almost always dominant in any real measurement.

Wassermann and others who attempt to apply quantum theory and the uncertainty principle to the macroscopic and social worlds appear to be missing a relatively small but crucial bit of understanding: the scale of measurement has to be appropriate for the phenomenon and purpose. Stephen Jay Gould was commenting on measurement in paleontology and geography in the following excerpt, but I believe his observations apply also to using the Heisenberg principle and quantum mechanics to explain education and other things in macroscopic and social worlds:

> Many commentators (and research scientists as well) ally themselves too strongly with one of the oldest (and often fallacious) traditions of Western thought: reductionism, or the assumption that laws and mechanics of the smallest constituents must explain objects and events at all scales and times. Thus, if we can render the behavior of a large body (an organism or a plant, for example) as a consequence of atoms and molecules in motion, we feel that we have developed a "deeper" or "more basic" understanding than if our explanatory principles engage only large objects themselves, and not their constituent parts. . . . One scale doesn't translate into another. No single scale can be deemed more important than any other; and none operates as a basic model for all the others.[15]

Chaos theory, the observation that some mathematical phenomena are not predictable, has captured the interest and imagination of many. The mathematics of chaos have been "translated" into bizarre and pernicious notions about children and their education, as well as into unworkable ideas about all human interactions. Now, it is true that we cannot predict some phenomena with extreme accuracy and over the very long term. Some phenomena, such as weather, are particularly difficult to predict over the long haul, and the mathematics involved may demonstrate what has come to be known as "chaos" or "chaos theory." But, does it follow that chaos is the principle behind everything we understand very poorly? Probably not. And even more important, if a phenomenon is, in fact, mathematically chaotic, what does that say about our systematic use of the phenomenon to solve problems in which the chaos is irrelevant? Probably nothing.

In his arguments for postmodern perspectives on the behavioral disorders of children, David Elkind uses weather and the dispersion of cream in coffee as examples of essentially chaotic phenomena that have implications for teaching difficult children.[16] His assumption seems to be that kids, like the weather, are unpredictable. But even if we conclude that the weather and coffee cream–dispersion are mathematically chaotic, does that matter for all purposes related to these phenomena?

Obviously not, I think. The practical implications of our inability to predict the pattern of dispersion of cream in coffee are, for the purpose of creaming coffee, precisely zero.

Some chaotic phenomena are trivial for achieving a particular purpose in which they play a part. The fact that the dispersion of cream in coffee is chaotic in no way impairs our ability to predict with a high degree of accuracy, and with good effect, the color, taste, and caloric value of a given amount of coffee to which a given amount of cream is added. Even against a background of mathematical chaos at some level of measurement, some predications are helpful. Climatology and meteorology can still give us highly useful short-term warnings. Improved weather predictions are advantageous, allowing individuals to avert risks and harm, even if accurate long-term weather predictions are impossible due to the mathematical chaos of the long-range effects of climatic events. Physicist Steve Reynolds wrote to me with reference to both Heisenberg and chaos theory:

> Even if we can't predict in detail the pattern of cream being stirred into coffee, we can with high precision predict the average behavior of important quantities like the coffee temperature. This is analogous to how, even though Heisenberg tells us to take care in predicting the behavior of individual subatomic particles, by the time you have an object containing a trillion trillion such particles (like a baseball), you can predict the average behavior extremely reliably.

Some of the silliness about science may come from people's misunderstanding of it. Misunderstanding is probably fostered by front-page headlines like this: "'Laws' of physics may not stand test of time: Team's reported findings cast doubt on one such tenet."[17] Some people undoubtedly do not read beyond a headline like this, using it to suggest that all principles or laws of physics have been called into question by physicists themselves. Others may read an article and still not understand that the findings have not been replicated (i.e., confirmed). Still others may fail to note a statement like this one of an astrophysicist: "'Exceptional results deserve extraordinary proof.'"[18] Or people may not understand that the findings are measurements that may overturn some arcane aspects of theoretical physics but have no implications whatever for the typical laws of Newtonian physics that we encounter in our everyday lives.

Most of us believe in a real world governed by very reliable laws of physics, and these are extremely unlikely ever to be overturned or suspended for anyone. However, postmodernists apparently do not share that belief. They seem to believe that no real world of material things exists, only our constructions of it. As I mentioned in chapter 3, they may use any doubt as an excuse to embrace radical doubt. To me, postmodernism represents a breathtaking jump into an intellectual, moral, and political abyss. It makes as little sense to me as jumping from an airplane flying 2000 feet above the ground without a parachute. The consequence of such a jump is, for most of us, highly predictable and not very pretty.

But the real damage to education comes from the idea that social interactions and social development are unpredictable in any meaningful sense. Taking seriously the idea that regularity and predictability in human behavior have been overturned—particularly as such predictability is related to teaching and managing classroom behavior—leaves teachers unable to develop their craft. Consider some comparisons. Creative and competent musicians find the repeated patterns in chords and scales. Without them, they can produce nothing that we recognize as music. Creative, productive mathematicians analyze the regularities in quantitative relationships. Creative linguists find the patterns we call grammar. Without finding the predictable relationships, the regularity of patterns, no artist can make sense of anything, and neither can any scientist. Understanding the predictable patterns in students' behavior is essential to the art and the science of teaching. A creative and excellent teacher has to see the recurrent patterns in students' behavior. That such regularities exist in behavior and that their recognition is essential to teaching seems, to me, now beyond question.[19]

Argument by analogy has its pitfalls, among them the yawning hole of premises and inferences that are not closely matched. Among the most obvious nonsequiturs in education, as I have suggested, is the use of the Heisenberg uncertainty hypothesis and other ideas from "new physics" (i.e., theoretical physics in which mathematical approximations are proposed to account for the behavior of subatomic particles). Principles of physics are invoked by some misguided souls to suggest various "implications" for working with children. Likewise, chaos theory and other mathematical phenomena have been "applied" to teaching. The predictable results have been chaotic "thinking." Some of these silly analogies have actually found their way into the professional literature.[20] Others have been submitted to me in one of my editorial capacities, and I have not supported their publication for obvious reasons.

THE BROWN DECISION ON SCHOOL DESEGREGATION IS OFTEN MISAPPLIED

Among the most maddening nonsequiturs in arguments about reforming general and special education is the use of the 1954 United States Supreme Court decision, *Brown v. Board of Education of Topeka* to suggest that any grouping of students by any category or ability is unlawful.[21] It is particularly maddening because it uses the correction of a great social injustice to argue, illogically, that another law promoting fairness is unjust. It confuses the issue of fairness by equating disability with skin color. The argument, which has been made repeatedly by proponents of the "full inclusion" of children with disabilities in regular classrooms and neighborhood schools, goes like this:

> The third and by far the most important reason for including all students into the mainstream is that it is the fair, ethical, and equitable thing to do. It deals with the value of EQUALITY. As was decided in the Brown v. Board of Education decision, SEPARATE IS NOT EQUAL. All children should be a part of the educational and community mainstream.[22]

To understand the passion behind this argument and to understand why it is a nonsequitur, we must note the history of racial segregation in American public schools and see the *Brown* decision in its historical context. Racial segregation was one of the most egregious forms of discrimination practiced in American public education. When forced racial segregation was declared unconstitutional (in 1954 by the *Brown* decision), the question before the court was whether such segregation deprives minority students of educational opportunities equal to those provided to white pupils. Chief Justice Earl Warren wrote for the court:

> [Racial segregation] generates a feeling of inferiority as to their [African American] status in the community that may affect their hearts and

minds in a way unlikely ever to be undone. . . . We conclude that in the
field of public education the doctrine of "separate but equal" has no
place. Separate educational facilities are inherently unequal.[23]

In *Brown*, the Supreme Court concluded that the racial segregation
of schools was unconstitutional. However, that decision does not mean
that the court also outlawed placement of students with disabilities in
classes or schools outside the mainstream. The statement that separate
is inherently unequal certainly cannot be applied to any and all grouping of students for instruction. Nevertheless, it is used willy-nilly in objections to the placement of any children with disabilities in special
classes and special schools.

The misuse of the *Brown* decision to defend full inclusion of children
with disabilities is a nonsequitur that in my opinion demeans both the
civil rights of ethnic minorities who were mistreated by racially segregated school systems and the civil rights of students with disabilities
who may require education in a class or school separate from the regular classroom and school. It is demeaning to the civil rights of ethnic
minorities because it makes skin color or ethnic origin seem to be a disability. It is demeaning to the civil rights of students with disabilities
because it makes educational disability seem to be merely a difference
in appearance. The basic premise for achieving fairness in the case of
color is different from that in the case of disability.

The 1954 *Brown* decision and school desegregation were based on
this simple observation: Separating children according to skin color or
ethnic identity is unfair because these demographic characteristics have
nothing to do with ability to learn or profit from instruction. However,
the 1975 federal special education law (now known as the *Individuals
with Disabilities Education Act*, or IDEA) was based on a different observation: Failure to separate some children with disabilities is unfair
because their learning characteristics (e.g., need for structure, direction,
repetition, level of instruction) demand teaching that cannot be provided reasonably and effectively in the context of the regular classroom. One question is whether we want the same or different things for
children. Fairness, as many people have noted, doesn't always mean
giving everyone the same. In the case of children differing only in ethnicity, most people would argue that fairness demands that they be
given the same thing. In the case of children who differ dramatically

from the norm in ability to learn, most people would argue that fairness demands that they be given instruction different from that which is normative. And most people would argue that it is extremely important not to mistake one for the other—ethnic identity and ability to learn.

Furthermore, as Anne Proffitt Dupre has noted, appeal to the *Brown* decision ignores the disappointing outcomes and unintended negative consequences for African American students of the insistence of *Brown* that black students would benefit from being in schools and classrooms with white students.[24] The underlying message of *Brown* was not entirely or unequivocally complimentary to African Americans. Similarly, Barbara D. Bateman noted how inclusion rhetoric that demands placement of students with learning disabilities (or other forms of disability) in regular classes is fundamentally demeaning.

> The parents, advocates, and courts who urge that a child who has a disability must be placed with those who do not have a disability too often send the message that children who have disabilities are not peers and are not fit to be with. Something is terribly and not very subtly insulting about saying a bright learning disabled student ought not attend a special school with other students who have learning disabilities because he needs to be with non-disabled students.[25]

Goals and the means of achieving them are often confused. Separating students from the mainstream of education is often mistaken for making them second-class citizens. Melvyn Semmel and his colleagues observed that "confusing the social goal of equal opportunity with place of opportunity distracted social scientists as well as the lay public from attention to what were appropriate educational means to reach desired ends."[26] Mixing up the reasons for separate schools for children differing in ethnicity with the reasons for separate programs for children with disabilities is surely worse than mixing metaphors, and the consequences are not funny.

But let us examine more closely the patent absurdity of assuming that *Brown* applies to the separation of students (i.e., their segregation in separate schools or classes) on *any* basis for instruction or for any other function of schooling. My colleague John Lloyd and I have explored the obvious questions such an unqualified interpretation of *Brown* raises.[27] How should students be grouped for instruction? Does *Brown* outlaw private schools, public schools of choice, magnet schools, schools designed to teach particular ages, groups of students, or different subjects? To what distinguishing student characteristics does the *Brown* decision apply (e.g., to gender, age, academic interests, performance on academic tasks, disability as well as color)? To what level of placement does *Brown* apply (i.e., does it apply to classrooms and to locations within classrooms as well as to school buildings and school systems)? Does *Brown* prohibit separation or segregation of students when it is voluntary, follows informed consent, or follows due process of law on a case-by-case basis as well as when it is forced and uniform? If *Brown* really has no bounds, then probably all schools and classes are illegal under that Supreme Court ruling, as they set some boundaries around the group of children they teach—they do not randomly assign students to schools or classes, and, besides, classes and schools are all separate and so inherently unequal. *Brown* without bounds is absurd. So is its application to the education of children with disabilities.

Most people understand that it is difficult, if not impossible, to offer all curricula with equal finesse in the same place at the same time. Furthermore, people generally acknowledge that students differ in what they know and in what they need to learn, what they want to learn, and, perhaps, how they are best taught. And it seems to me obvious that these learning differences are far more closely related to disabilities than to colors of skin or to ethnic identities. Granted, the legal racial segregation of public facilities, including public schools, is despicable, the hyperextension of the notion that separating students on any basis for instruction is inequitable brings us recursively to the issue of fairness. James J. Gallagher made this observation: "Fairness does not consist of educating all children in the same place at the same time (and with the same curriculum?) but in ensuring that the student has basic needs met and is traveling a well thought-out road to a career and a satisfying life style."[28]

To be sure, both children of color and children with disabilities are entitled to fair treatment in schooling, and children in both groups have suffered discrimination. But in the case of children of color, the discrimination has been denial of access to the same education as white children. And in the case of children with disabilities, the discrimination has been denial of access to different education from that provided to children who have no disability. Of course, we could say that children from different ethnic groups need education that is different from that which is appropriate for other ethnic groups, and we could also say that children with disabilities need education that is exactly the same as that which is appropriate for those who are not disabled. And if we do either, then I think we are right back where we started—education that is unfair. Maybe that is the stupid kind of mistake we are likely to make. And if we do make it, then maybe it is true that the only thing we learn from history is that we don't learn from it.

DENYING THAT STUDENTS WITH DISABILITIES HAVE DIFFERENT NEEDS ISN'T SMART

Among the outright denials I find most frustrating is the argument that, actually, students with disabilities are just like everyone else. We should not see students with disabilities as needing something special because, well, so the argument goes, they are not *really* exceptional. They're just students, like all the others, who are different from each other. One line of argument is that we should not see students with disabilities as requiring different treatment; we should treat them just like everyone else. Another line of argument suggests that there is nothing wrong with children who have disabilities except our failure to provide educational environments that match their learning needs. The problem is only our insistence that students with disabilities have problems.

The denial of the differences that we call disabilities has become part of the popular rhetoric about inclusion, even among special educators. I admire much of the work of Jim Ysseldyke, Bob Algozzine, and Martha Thurlow. I like them, as I do many of the people whose assertions I criticize. But the following statement puzzles me and, frankly, it strikes me as the kind of thoughtless prose that helps kill educational programs for kids who are not educationally normal.

> The human service practices that cause providers to believe that clients (students) have inadequacies, shortcomings, failures, or faults that must be corrected or controlled by specially trained professionals must be replaced by conceptions that people with disabilities are capable of setting their own goals and achieving or not. Watered-down curricula, alternative grading practices, special competency standards, and other "treat them

differently" practices used with "special" students must be replaced with school experiences exactly like those used with "regular" students.[29]

You've got to be kidding! I say to myself. There's really nothing wrong with students who have disabilities, except perhaps that we treat them differently? They should be treated like everyone else in school, have the same experiences as those who don't have disabilities—same curriculum, standards, grading? They set their own goals as they wish, and they either achieve these goals or they don't—whatever—it's up to them? But, no, Ysseldyke et al. were not writing tongue in cheek (or whatever the expression for writing a spoof should be—finger in palm, perhaps). Jeez, I think, I don't understand this. I just don't get it! What am I missing here? All along, I thought disability meant a person couldn't do some particular thing or could do it only with extreme difficulty, and some of these disabilities have to do with school learning. Special education must have been a horrible mistake to begin with, I guess! If we had only recognized that kids with disabilities don't actually have deficits needing correction! Well, if we treat them just like all the other kids, then they won't be set apart and they'll do ok in school. I don't really believe this, but it seems to be the meaning of the statement of Ysseldyke et al. that I quoted.

If the statement by Ysseldyke and his colleagues were a unique denial of disability or an unusual self-contradiction, then I might write it off as a fluke. Unfortunately, these authors have company in their topsy-turvy, self-contradictory rhetoric of denial. Alan Gartner and Dorothy Lipsky are among those who have urged the reform of education, particularly the merging of general and special education into what they describe as a unitary, supple, responsive system in which all students succeed without being identified as "special" and without being set apart from their peers. I take up some of their misleading statements again in chapter 5. But, here, consider how they embrace the same sort of denial as Ysseldyke and his colleagues—that there's really nothing wrong with kids who have disabilities. Here, however, the implication is not that the school environment should be exactly the same for all students, but that if a student is perceived to have an "impairment" it's not really that something is wrong with the student but with the teacher, who is thwarting the student's progress by failing to match instruction to the student's needs. And, as their argument goes, a teacher must create a single classroom environment that matches *all* students' needs. Therefore, students with disabilities are not really "different" or "exceptional" in ways that other students are not.

> The current practice of special education operates on a deficit model: that is, it identifies something as wrong or missing in the student. When a student has a learning or behavior deficit, the current model leans toward finding cause in terms of an impairment.
>
> The new concept will frame the student's "problem" in a different context, seeing it as the result of a mismatch between learning needs and the instructional or management systems. Therefore, the child will be viewed not as a disabled person but as a learner whose potential is being thwarted by an educational mismatch.[30]

In chapter 3, I noted problems with the slogan that kids don't fail, only teachers fail. We can pretend that there is nothing wrong with students who have disabilities, but I doubt that it is in the best interests of the children involved. Such pretense seems to me likely to result in failure to provide effective programs that help children learn what they should or change their behavior.[31]

Rhetoric like that which I have described in this essay and the previous one led me to write an imaginary news release as follows:

Special Education Dies As New Millennium Is Born:
Those with Disabilities Free at Last

WASHINGTON, DC: Apartheid, the Berlin wall, Jim Crow, and special education. All were once very much a part of our lives and consciousness. But special education today joined the list of structures and policies that once stood for the brutal separation and segregation of others.

Across the nation, celebrants are rejoicing in a new era in which education is no longer divided into special and general, students need not qualify for so-called special treatment, and all students are provided a common education for a common purpose—to be simply citizens and students with equal rights and responsibilities.

"No more special rules, no more special privileges, and no more labels, that's the one rule we have now," said the U.S. Secretary of Education. She continued, "What is good for one student is good for *all* students, and that is to be treated as an individual who is not like anyone else."

A professor of education who formerly was involved in the special education system but is now an advocate for all children said, apparently not aware of her contradiction of the Secretary, "Students are more alike than they are different. We teach *all* children, not just some, and we prepare teachers to teach *all* children—and *all means all*."

Signs in large block letters reading "SEPARATE IS INHERENTLY UNEQUAL" were waved on the mall by educators and parents who hailed the end of special education as the beginning of a new era of freedom from children's being labeled and funneled into a costly, bloated, and segregating system.

One parent who identified himself as a school board member put it this way. "IDEA was a horrible idea that said only *some* kids would get treated in a special way. Now *all* kids are seen as special and they're *all* eligible for anything they need. That's the long and short of it, and that's why we're so happy. Now we can just say and act as if a kid is a kid is a kid."

The process of merging special and general education has been gradual until very recently. People started talking about it in the early 1980s. Now, 20 years later, their dreams have been realized. Special education is no more. Gone are the labels and categories of disabilities. The law and the bureaucracy are gone. So are special appropriations. And most observers feel it's good riddance.[32]

If special education really is an evil system, as some contend, then I'd like to be among those who contribute to its death. In fact, the sooner it goes, the better. But if special education is really a good idea that is often poorly practiced—as I think is the case—then I'm opposed to killing it. We need to improve it, but not stamp it out. But about this we should have no doubt: The rhetoric that denies children's differences or fobs them off as teachers' ineptitude threatens the very existence of special education. Its logical end is captured by the hypothetical news release I've written.

MAKING SCHOOLS INTO BUSINESSES ISN'T A GREAT IDEA

A popular notion today is that schools need competition, that if they were run like competitive business enterprises (or if they actually *became* such enterprises), then the schools would be "fixed" and all the "customers" of education (which is to say, in our society at present, all children) would be better served. This idea represents either extreme naiveté or malice toward children who are not economically privileged—or both. I don't think someone can think carefully about both the business world and education and hold such an empty idea. True, those with sufficient money can buy just about anything, including a marvelous private education. People of average means can't purchase the best of much, particularly not most high-ticket items like education. And poor people, well, any reasonably intelligent person knows they can't afford the best of anything and just manage to scrape by. Cogs are slipping, I think, when it comes to education as business, unless it is to become a commodity like cars and houses. If the goal is to make education "work" or make it good for everyone, regardless of their economic circumstances, then the proposal to run schools like businesses is a self-contradiction—it calls for equity while proposing a system that cannot deliver it.

Daniel Tanner has described how inappropriate the business model is for education. So has E. D. Hirsch, Jr.[33] And Seymour Sarason has made his view clear: "I do not take kindly to assertions that schools will improve to the extent that they adopt the presumably successful managerial style and values of the private sector. . . . To imitate the private sector would be both irrelevant and another faddish disaster."[34] Their points are very well taken. But no genius is required to ask some important questions about the business model of education.

First of all, I suppose a reasonable person would ask this: If business principles are so sure a route to success, why do so many businesses fail or require a government bailout? Would the education business be so very different from most businesses that most or all companies in the education business would succeed? Is there a "magic" associated with the business of education that would protect it from failure and prevent it from abusing its employees or customers?

My guess is that education businesses will fail, too, and probably at a rate at least equal to that at which public schools are said to fail. Taxpayers might remember they are still paying for the bailout of savings and loan companies that went bad and that they had to bail out the Chrysler Corporation. We might remember the abuses of employees and shareholders by the now defunct Enron Corporation.

Second, what happens to employees and customers when a business goes under? Is this what we want to happen to teachers and kids? Can firms doing the business of education be required to provide services through the remainder of a school year at private (business) expense when they founder? It's just a guess, but I imagine lots of kids and families, not to mention schoolteachers, would be left in the lurch when education businesses go down the tubes. A situation involving charter schools with parallels to private enterprise was described in a story appearing in the *Washington Post*. Three charter schools, which parents apparently chose over "failing" public schools, were closed by the District of Columbia Board of Education. "The move puts hundreds of children in academic limbo less than four weeks before the start of a new school year."[35] Why were the schools closed? Board members cited absentee rates ranging from 45 percent to nearly 100 percent, lack of educational curriculum and materials, poor classroom management, and financial irregularities.

Third, can small businesses succeed in education and resist the hostile takeovers or buyouts that would make them part of a large conglomerate? And if education businesses become very large, will they also become, like other gargantuan businesses, impersonal? Will education businesses that are not locally owned be sensitive to local needs or conditions?

Fourth, will businesses put their customers' (students') interests first, or their stockholders'? How will schools be run like today's businesses if the bottom line for shareholders (or very high compensation for the executives) is not the primary concern? For example, the rail passenger operation known as Amtrak can *either* be run as a profitable business enterprise or be operated as a service to communities or individuals who can't support it as a business; *but it cannot be run as both* (unless the profitable routes are charged a premium at least sufficient to offset the losses incurred by the unprofitable routes, meaning that some riders would then subsidize the rides of others; the same applies to all mass transit services, public or private). A major reason that Amtrak requires continuing government subsidies to cover operating costs is that we want it to be a public service, to be there for people who otherwise would have no rail transportation. To the extent that we require it to be run like a business, we will require that it terminate unprofitable routes.

When it comes to education, it seems to me you can make money on some of the kids all of the time and on all of the kids some of the time, but you can't turn a profit on all of the kids all of the time. And in business, the object is to make money and not to lose it, to cut your losses. In a business model, as I understand it, this would mean cutting the unprofitable kids or using them as loss leaders (offered at a loss to attract customers who purchase items on which a profit is made). Low achieving kids wouldn't be good loss leaders. That is, they wouldn't attract people to the school. So I think low-achieving students are likely to be avoided by schools whenever possible.

Fifth, what businessperson of sound mind would agree to a contract specifying the nature and quality of outputs when he or she is given no control of inputs? Or, are schools going to be able to select their students, refuse students they deem not helpful in achieving their bottom line? Who will get the students who are particularly difficult to teach? Will education of these difficult students receive a premium, and, if so, from whom? Or will particularly difficult-to-teach students be expected to achieve less? Or, in the argot of business, will these students be the equivalent of "as is," "day old," "scratch and dent," "pre-taught," or other euphemisms for damaged goods? People proposing a business model of education often seem to lose sight of the differences among students. They also seem to forget that private schools run as a business have some choices about whom to try to educate. As William Raspberry noted:

> The thing we forget about "school choice" is that it's the *schools* that have the choice. Private schools routinely turn away kids they think won't fit their programs. . . . I do think it might be helpful to remember that in school failure, as in athletic failure, the problem often involves distribution of talent, distribution of resources and distribution of leadership all at the same time.[36]

Business may be good for producing goods and many services, but that does not mean that business is good for producing everything imaginable (anymore than governments or public agencies are good for producing everything). Those of us who are interested in making sure that education is good, even for those who are likely to be seen in the business world as defective parts, inferior raw materials, or expensive mistakes, tend to see education as a function best kept in the public domain, except as a private option for families of means and those willing to have the education of their children controlled and subsidized by religious organization.

In chapter 1, I recalled Richard Cohen's irritation with the Chase bank slogan, "The Right Relationship Is Everything" and his frustration with private business that serves its customers very poorly. He wrote in his understandable pique at the lousy attention of large corporations to their customers, "It ain't business. It's personal."[37] The problem of bad customer service is so common and such a pervasive experience of contemporary American life that on April 9, 2001, National Public Radio's *Marketplace* devoted a substantial portion of its program to the issue. Nearly everyone, it seems, has been driven to distraction by customer "service" that is incompetent and, sometimes, rude in addition.

In chapter 1 I also mentioned the fact that "*Jim, it isn't the phone company!*" has become a standing joke among my colleagues. My experiences with the phone company parallel those of Richard Cohen with a bank and Michael Kinsley's with a cable company.[38] Whenever I become agitated by incompetence or intransigence, I can bet that certain colleagues will bring up the phone company, playing on my long-standing battle with our local "service provider." I do not use my own personal experience alone to make my point—an art of the stupid that I described in chapter 2—but merely share a personal experience that I know is similar to others' and that has become the basis for considerable ribbing.

"*Jim, it isn't the phone company!*" derives from my near apoplexy at our local service provider's inability to provide me one bill per month for three phone lines, to use the phone number I had had for over 10 years as my primary number for billing purposes, and to link my three phone numbers for billing purposes. The last straw came when my wife was in Europe, we had a big snowstorm, and the phone company cut off my phone because, they claimed, I had not paid my bill. But I had paid the bill, and had cancelled checks to prove it. I had received from the phone company on the same day of the month—and for several months in a row—both refund checks and late payment notices for the same amount. Naturally, the way businesses are typically run today, I was unable to talk to any actual person about my plight, even after spending interminable periods on hold listening to the phone company explain to me how wonderful they are. So, on that snowy day when my phone had been disconnected, I stormed into the phone company's lo-cal offices. I was assured by a real (and really nice) person that things had been "fixed." They had not been. It took several more months, more calls to other states, another visit to the local office with paper trails in hand to get things fixed—sort of. I had been threatened by a collection agency for nonpayment, although it was the phone com-pany's own inability to communicate among its various offices and functions that was the problem. My wife and I considered turning the matter over to an attorney. But that seemed to us very likely only to fur-ther complicate and prolong matters and make any settlement more costly in a variety of ways, regardless of other considerations.

Then there was our out-of-state, long-distance "service provider." One month we stopped getting bills from the company. After a couple of months, we got an "overdue" notice, along with threats to cut off our service and turn collection over to a bill collection agency. I did pay an overdue amount by credit card to keep our service going, but I could not get the company to send us a bill. When I finally got a real person on the phone to inquire, she could not tell me how much money I owed. She said the company was having trouble with its billing system. No kidding! After another month or so of the same run-around—we're sorry, but we can't tell you how much you owe, and we're still work-ing on our billing system—I cancelled my long-distance account with that company. I don't want "service" from a company that can't gener-ate a bill or even tell me how much I owe. But—you've probably guessed it—problems awaited me when I tried to add long-distance service with our local "service provider." After requesting that long-distance service be added to our bill—but not being provided the long-distance service—I finally got an actual person on the phone. And this person assured me that the company had no record whatever that I was a customer of theirs, notwithstanding my protestations that I'd been a local customer for many years, including long-distance service until fairly recently. And this person assured me that she had no record of ever having long-distance service connected with our phone number—a number that we had had for over 10 years!

A few months after our adventure with the phone company began, we discovered that we were not listed in the phone book. My wife's calls to the phone company offices were met with rebuffs. Our primary number was still not the number by which we would have been listed had we been included in the phone book, she was told, meaning that the number listed would have connected with a fax machine. Furthermore, she was not allowed to request any changes, as she is not listed as responsible for the account.

A year and a half after our saga with the phone company began, I continue to be afraid to try to pay my phone bill by electronic banking, as my experience has been that the phone company's payment center (in another state) does not communicate well with its billing office (in yet another state) so that even if I order payment of the bill on the day I receive it my electronic check is not credited to my account in time to avoid a late payment notice. I wonder, is this the fault of our bank (which is another, separate story of business snafus) or the phone company or both? Furthermore, we have an unlisted number, not by our choice but by the phone company's choice. Frankly, I do not know to whom to turn next, as the incompetence of the phone companies I have dealt with seems boundless.

Which brings me to this observation, one I'll bet is shared by many readers of my story: Private businesses are often as abusive, incompetent, intransigent, and difficult to negotiate as any government agency I have dealt with. In fact, in my experience government as often as not has served me better—more reliably, efficiently, and competently—than private business. The profit motive may be good for a lot of things, but it's not good in every case. Unbridled, it often becomes abusive of individuals. Many of those who complain most about government are those who are the first to complain about private businesses charging what the market will bear, just doing what businesses do. Or they express resentment of businesses that "take advantage" of people by producing inferior goods and services. They want a government that is there for them—but only for them, apparently. They want a government that will protect them from business without regulations that anyone sees as "burdensome." Many of them complain of government largess, although they had government jobs all their lives and live on government pensions. They do not recognize the childishness of their attitudes.

None of this is to suggest that government is never inefficient, abusive, or wrong. It sometimes has been; it sometimes is. But, run schools like businesses? Not a smart proposition in my estimation. Doesn't get my vote; won't solve the problem.

But wait! Although I think running education like a business in *every* respect, particularly its focus on the bottom line of profitability, would be foolish, there are *some* ways in which business uses information that make sense for education, too. Doug Carnine has pointed out how the scientific and business communities use information about reliable solutions to problems. Education has a history of refusing to recognize and use reliable data to improve its practices.[39] This is quite unlike the approach of scientists and business people. As Carnine points out, in science and business—usually—something may be "innovative," but if it's tested and found not to work it is abandoned. In education, people tend to cling to ideas based on philosophical ideals or ideology regardless of data.[40] Not very smart, I think, and in this particular case—obtaining and using reliable data—I think taking our cues from good business and scientific practices would be much smarter.

GOOD EDUCATION MAKES A GROUP OF CHILDREN MORE HETEROGENEOUS

One of the most fatuous ideas of education reformers is that good education will homogenize the population, that students will become more uniform in their abilities. Laurence Lieberman recounted the idea in his commentary on the death of special education in *Education Week*.[41] Lieberman refers to the philosophy of homogenization—the idea that all children are the same and, therefore, should be given the same education and be expected to achieve the same outcomes. This idea of homogenization is described in the quotation of Ysseldyke et al. in "Denying That Students with Disabilities Have Different Needs Isn't Smart" above. If taken seriously, it leads inevitably to the death of special education, as Lieberman points out and as I have imagined in the hypothetical press release I included in the said essay.

The idea that good education homogenizes the population is captured in slogans about having "the same high expectations for all children" and similar sentiments. It is a foundational idea in the standards movement, which seeks to produce greater uniformity or homogeneity among students' performance, to set a floor level of achievement and try to make sure that every student gets to it. It is contained in the slogan "No child left behind." And it was an assumption of Benjamin Bloom, in the 1970s, that good learning conditions would make children very similar in their abilities and motivation.[42]

But education that does not stifle the progress of the fastest learners—education that encourages each student, whether fast or slow, to learn as fast and as much as possible—will inevitably have the effect of increasing the differences among students. Such education will inevitably increase the spread of attainments, increase the variance in the distribution of outcomes. That is a mathematical certainty. Richard Feynman had it figured out: "For instance, in education you increase differences. If someone's good at something, you try to develop his ability, which results in differences, or inequalities."[43]

But denial abounds in rhetoric about education, including denial of the fact that good education increases differences. A philosophy of homogenization that presents education as an equalizer is considered politically advantageous. Understanding why education does not homogenize the population unless it hampers the achievement of the best students or excludes the low achievers may require consideration of normal and skewed statistical distributions. Thinking about statistical distributions—what they are, what they mean, what is possible, and what is probable—helps us understand not only why good education increases the discrepancies among students but also why special education is a good idea. Special education here refers to extraordinary education for both students who have disabilities and for gifted students—both those under the extreme left and those under the extreme right "tails" of a distribution.

A statistical distribution actually represents a mathematical function, but as a practical matter it is simply a smoothed curve of a histogram. A histogram is a bar graph showing the number of people (or items or events) obtaining each score or value on a scale. The graph, whether a histogram or a smoothed curve, could depict the scores of a small sample or a large one, a biased sample or a purely random sample. To the extent that the graph represents a large random sample (technically, of means or averages), it usually tends to approximate a "normal" curve or distribution with the shape often referred to as a "bell curve." Figure 4.1 is a bar graph (histogram) and an associated smoothed curve to illustrate a hypothetical distribution of test scores. Actual distributions of many types of measurements of large samples look a lot like the close-to-normal (but not precisely normal) statistical distribution shown in figure 4.1.

Every distribution has a range (highest to lowest score) and a standard deviation, which is an index of the variability or "spread-outness" of the scores. Figures 4.2 and 4.3 show two distributions, one with a comparatively smaller standard deviation (figure 4.2, scores more bunched up) and one with a comparatively larger standard deviation (figure 4.3, scores more spread out). A small standard deviation is associated with a high degree of sameness in measurement, a high degree of similarity or *homogeneity* in the sample on whatever was measured. A large standard deviation is associated with a low degree of sameness in measurement, a high degree of *heterogeneity* in the sample. The degree of spread-outness or variability in a group of students is a very big issue in education—the degree to which heterogeneity or homogeneity is desirable or undesirable in grouping for instruction and the degree to which good education produces more heterogeneity or more homogeneity as an outcome.

Every set of measurements produces a distribution, but some statistical distributions are clearly not normal (symmetrical) by a long shot. The *shape* of a distribution can change, but certain features of it cannot

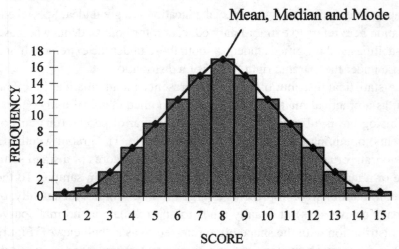

Figure 4.1. Histogram (bar graph) and an associated smoothed curve illustrating a near-normal distribution.

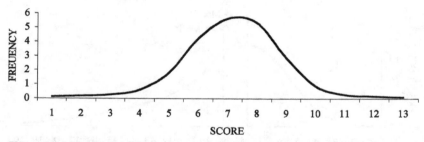

Figure 4.2. Distribution illustrating a relatively small standard deviation (bunched-up scores).

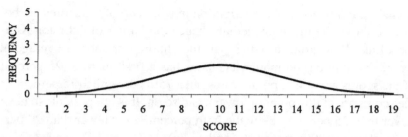

Figure 4.3. Distribution illustrating a large standard deviation (spread-out scores).

change. Every distribution has a *mean* or arithmetic average. This is just the total of all the scores divided by the number of scores. Every distribution has a middle score or *median*. Half of the scores are always above the median, and half below. It is possible to have more than half the scores above the *mean* (the arithmetic average), but it is *never* possible to have more than half the scores above the *median*. Every distribution also has a *mode*, the most frequent score, which is always the highest point on the curve. A "normal" distribution is symmetrical, and the mean, median, and mode are all the same value—lined up exactly in the middle, as shown in figure 4.1.

Figure 4.4 shows a positively skewed distribution in which more than half the scores are below the mean (i.e., the area under the curve to the left of the mean is greater than the area to the right of the mean—remember, the median is the middle score, so any deviation of the mean to one side of the median puts more than half of the group under the opposite side of the mean, but not of the median). However, it is important to note that it

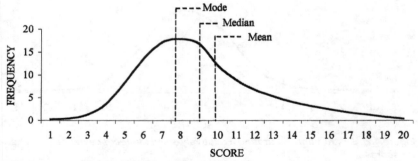

Figure 4.4. Distribution illustrating a positive skew.

is *never* possible to have a distribution in which *all* of the scores are below or above the mean or median (hence the humor of Garrison Keil-
lor's Lake Wobegon, in which "all the children are above average").
Every distribution, no matter its shape, has a first quartile (25 percent
of the scores are at this point or lower), a 75th percentile (75 percent of
the scores are at this point or lower), and so on. It is not possible to have
fewer than 25 percent below the 25th percentile (or fewer than 20 percent below the 20th percentile, and so on).

Notice that in figure 4.4 the distance from the median to the highest
scores is greater than the distance from the median to the lowest scores
(i.e., the highest scores are more extreme in their discrepancy from the
median than are the lowest scores). That is always the case when more
than half of the scores are below the mean. The opposite is true, too.
The only way to have more than half the scores *above* the mean is to
have larger differences between median and lowest scores than between median and highest scores. Extreme scores (greater in their distance from the median) have the effect of pulling the mean away from
the median in the direction of the extreme, such that a few extremely
high scores will put more than half of the scores below the mean. Remember, in a distribution with a positive skew (an elongated right tail),
more than half of the individuals measured will necessarily be below
the mean; with a negative skew (an elongated left tail), more than half
of the individuals will fall above the mean.

The features of distributions I have described are mathematical phenomena that can't be wished away or overthrown by any ideology or
political orientation. The questions for education policymakers are

simply these: First, what can be done to distributions of scores on out-come measures? That is, what are the *possibilities* for changing aver-age score and the shape of the distribution? Second, what is the *proba-ble* outcome of any given policy—the effects on the average score and the shape of the distribution? Third, what do we *want* to happen to the shape of the distribution of any given outcome, given the possibilities and the probable effects of a policy?

Most people would like to see the average score improve, whether it is the mean or the median. This is possible, and it is probable, too, if most students are taught better, as Siegfried Engelmann has shown.[44] But many people also want to decrease the discrepancies between high scorers and low scorers—that is, to shrink the variance (dispersion or spread-outness), to make the population more homogeneous. The only way to do this, though, is to totally neglect if not inhibit the learning of the fastest students while pulling out all the stops to help average and low achievers or, alternatively, simply to not include the low perform-ers. A distribution like that shown in figure 4.4, in which more than half the scores are below the mean, is very likely to be achieved, I think, if we simply speed up the learning of all children. This might not be the final outcome of really good education for all children if we approach a right "wall" or limit of progress. "Wall" is a concept of Stephen Jay Gould's that I take up again later. For now, however, let us assume that a distribution like the one shown in figure 4.4 is very likely to be achieved if the fastest learners are allowed to progress at their usual rate of learning, at least until they approach a limit or wall.

To understand why a distribution like that in figure 4.4 is likely to be achieved if we simply speed up all learners, it is necessary only to un-derstand the concept of rate of progress. You could imagine cars, horses, planes, or trains moving at different speeds (rates), or you could just think about the fact that students learn any given thing at different speeds. For any given skill or topic, some learners are faster than oth-ers. Some are a *lot* faster than the average, and some are *a lot* slower. Most students are approximately average (within a standard deviation or so of the mean). For whatever reason, the fastest learners pick up the information or skill in a very short period of time and with very few tri-als; the slowest learners take a long time and many trials to learn the same thing, if they are able to learn it at all (a few children can never reasonably be expected to read). The *rate* of acquisition of knowledge or skill involving any performance approximates a normal distribution.

If you start with a normal distribution and allow the students (or cars, horses, planes, or trains) to proceed at different rates, then they spread out with time. The longer they go at that rate, the more spread out they get. This will produce a positive skew *until some of those going at the top rate reach the upper limits of the possible and many others begin approaching this "wall."*

So, if you start with a normal distribution of knowledge or skill and give equal attention to helping students learn, the differing rates at which they learn will inevitably produce a positive skew (something like figure 4.4) *at first*. It is not difficult to understand why some people won't like the first results. For one thing, the standard deviation will be greater than in a normal distribution, which means that we have increased the discrepancies between high and low achievers—we've then done just the *opposite* of homogenizing student performance. Furthermore, the positive skew of the curve will mean that more than half of the individuals will be below the mean (remember, it's impossible to have more than or less than half of the individuals in a distribution below the median, as the median is the middle score). Other possible scenarios might change the shape of a distribution of scores and other considerations we must make. First, with good teaching, many of the slower learners may speed up—increase the rate at which they learn. In fact, Engelmann has described how and why this speeding up of slower learners will occur when excellent instruction is provided for them. The increasing rate of learning of slower learners will obviously have the effect of decreasing the positive skew of the curve *over what it would have been had they not speeded up*. Then, too, the faster learners could slow down, which is something I think we should try to keep from happening (and we most certainly should not slow them down deliberately).

Second, we must consider what Gould refers to as the "walls" of a distribution—extremes beyond which we simply cannot go due to our limitations or beyond which any human being is very unlikely to go.[45] In education, the left wall is defined by children who are unconscious or whose consciousness is in doubt. They have profound cognitive limitations, and usually profound physical disabilities as well. Next to the left wall are those who are apparently conscious but respond only to intense stimuli and are able to learn only the simplest of motor skills (movement of some kind) after many trials. Gould's "full house"—the whole distribution, excluding none—in education encompasses all living children, and it is therefore not possible, if we speak of *all* children, to detach the left tail from the left wall or to move the wall. This is one reason that good education will increase, not decrease, variance in the population. There may be a right or upper wall in education, too, although I don't think we know exactly what or where it is. And I think we're probably so far from it that we needn't worry much about reaching it anytime soon. In sports, as Gould points out, we now seem to be near or against an upper wall—finding the absolute limits of human performance. Any increments of improvement in many sports are minute. If we were to find such a wall in education, then it might be possible to produce a negative skew that would put more than half of the population above the mean—an eventual distribution approximating the one shown in Figure 4.5. But we'd still end up with more variance in the population than we currently have, simply because we can't detach education from the left wall (unless we exclude low performers altogether, which I hope we won't do, and which is currently illegal in the United States).

Different contingencies produce predictably different results or distributions. If we could lop off the left tail of the distribution of educational outcomes—simply ignore kids who are retarded by any

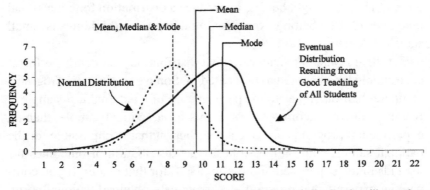

Figure 4.5. *Normal distribution and a negatively skewed distribution illustrating the possible (hypothetical) results of effective instruction of all students.*

reasonable definition—then we'd have a different situation. And if we could choose to educate only those who reach a high criterion of performance to begin with, then we'd have a new ballgame altogether. In fact, we'd have a new ballgame if we didn't have to include kids with disabilities. Please understand, I am not suggesting that we do this; in fact, *I think remedial and special education for kids whose achievement is lagging is extremely important to keep and enhance*. It's worth considering, though, that a lot of the "all children" rhetoric of school reform doesn't include Gould's "full house."

When researcher Ron Edmonds said in the 1980s that we could, if we were actually interested in doing it, successfully teach all children and that we already know more than we need to accomplish the task, he surely wasn't including all children with disabilities.[46] And when Diane Ravitch comments that "The promise of liberal education was that all children would study the same knowledge that had once been available only to elites," she clearly isn't including severely mentally retarded kids in her "all."[47] As I mention elsewhere, "all" is sometimes clearly not meant to be taken literally, to mean "each and every." "All" taken to mean "all those we believe are able" and "all" meaning "each and every" take us to different ballparks.

Gould argues that baseball has improved, although .400 hitting has disappeared, because the standard deviation of batting averages has shrunk.[48] You have to be a better player these days than in the past to get on a major league team. Suppose we could decide to educate only those kids who already excel in learning (we might call them major leaguers)? Then we might be able to produce a distribution for educational outcomes like the batting averages Gould describes (high means, small standard deviations).

But there is also the matter of what distribution a student's performance should be compared to or located in. Some experimental programs compare their outcomes to the performance of a national test sample.[49] If you compare outcomes to test norms for a national sample, then an experimental program *can* have a distribution that is impossible for the national sample—and impossible for the distribution of outcomes for the kids in the experimental program itself, for that matter. If you compare an experimental program to a previously obtained national norm, then it is possible to have more than half the experimental students above the median of the national norm, fewer than 20 percent below the 20th percentile, and so on. It's just important to remember the source and nature of the distribution to which we want to compare students. Just suppose that we improved education dramatically, such that nearly all students performed a lot better than they did in some past year. That kind of improvement is, indeed, possible and, I think, a good objective. But eventually someone would want outcome measures to be "re-normed" to reflect the *current* national distribution. Alas, all the mathematical certainties about distributions will apply to the new norms.

Of course, it is possible to deny realities that we see as unpleasant. Some people may deny that some students learn at higher rates than others or complain that rate of learning is only a construct. Some may deny that the outcome of students' learning at different rates for a given period of time inevitably puts more than half of the group below the mean. Some may simply deny that such observations make any difference or say that differences in rate of learning are merely a result of unfairness in measurement or instruction or both. If things were really fair, they argue, then differences in rate of learning wouldn't exist or, if they did they wouldn't matter to teachers or policymakers. And some may suggest that all students are exceptionally fast at learning something or complain that we place too much value on being fast at learning particular things. I think it's important to recognize differences in learning rates for particular knowledge and skills. And I think some things are especially important for students to learn as fast as they can (reading, writing, calculating, social grace, for example). Learning these things is particularly important because they bring the student additional opportunities to learn. I also think raising the average (mean and median) score on good tests of academic achievement is a good idea—as long as we take care to give equitable treatment to exceptionally fast learners (those gifted in a particular area of learning) and exceptionally slow learners (those who have disabilities) and understand what will happen to the distribution of outcomes if we do that.

Giving equitable attention to exceptionally slow learners means providing extra teaching, excellent teaching, and, in some cases, a different curriculum, as I discuss further in the last chapter. Good teaching of exceptionally slow learners will not detach the lower tail of the curve from zero, but it will result in fewer students falling in the very low ranges of performance. Neither special education nor any other strategy for addressing the needs of low achievers can put fewer than 20 percent at or below the 20th percentile of the distribution in which they perform, but effective special education can put fewer students below the point on the distribution marked by two standard deviations below the mean. That is, really good teaching can scrunch up the lower part of the distribution. When special education for students with disabilities is practiced well, it pushes up the bottom of the curve and lessens somewhat the discrepancies between many low achievers and the typical or average achievers (as defined by the mean) *compared to what it would have been had special education not been provided*. It is important to recognize that actual discrepancies between the slowest learners and the average may stay the same or even increase if all exceptional students are given equitable treatment, but without special education for students with disabilities the discrepancies would be even greater.

Giving equitable attention to exceptionally fast learners means providing extra teaching and, in many cases, an accelerated curriculum, as I discuss further in the last chapter. Such special education for gifted students will extend the upper tail of the curve somewhat and lift the upper reaches of the distribution. It will place more already advanced students even further above the average, spreading out the scores and increasing the discrepancies between the highest achievers and the lowest. It will also place a larger percentage of students below the mean (remember, you can't have fewer than half below the average as defined by the median of the distribution in which performance is measured).

An important point to remember here is that I have been discussing distributions of outcomes *for particular areas of performance*, not what might be called "general intelligence." Furthermore, I am not suggesting that the abilities represented by these distributions are innate. It is possible for a given student to have disabilities in particular areas of performance (movement and math, for example) and to be gifted in another (perhaps in language or reading). As my colleague Dan Hallahan and I have pointed out, some students are gifted in multiple areas of performance (math and music, for example).[50] Others are extraordinarily slow learners due to disabilities in multiple areas (language, reading, and math, for example). Some are neither disabled nor gifted in any particular category of performance. Denying that students differ in what they have learned and the rate at which they are capable of learning in particular areas of performance, however, is simply an evasion of reality. These differences in learning hold whether the performance in question is baseball or paleontology, mathematics or magic tricks, car repair or economics, and so on. This does not mean that the differences in rate are immutable, either.

Another important point about distributions is that means—averages, whether for schools or states or groups of students—have distributions with the same properties as distributions of scores for individuals. (In fact, you may recall that a truly "normal" distribution is a distribution of means.) Alas, this means that "achievement gaps" in which some schools and some groups are below others will be with us *always*. These gaps cannot be closed, although it is possible for means (for schools or states or groups, for example) to trade places in a distribution and for distributions to have smaller or greater standard deviations (spread-outness). But the gaps will be there for someone, as surely as the time in New York, NY, will be different from the time in Los Angeles, CA. (I realize that we could, if we wished, just declare the time in the two locations to be the same and that we could just declare all mean test scores to be equal, but in both cases we'd be denying some pretty important realities.)

At a practical level, attempts to make means for children reared in poverty and social disadvantage equal to the means for children with economic and social advantage may be doomed to failure (unless needs of children already scoring at or above the mean are largely ignored). Schools cannot change our entire society or revolutionize home environments, and home environment plays a large role in academic achievement. The rational consideration of distributions, including the distribution of means, suggests to me that such laws as the *No Child Left Behind Act* and associated rhetoric are detached from reality. This does not mean that we should give up on improving education, simply that we need to get real about what is possible.

Homogeneity among students can be achieved only by really bad educational practices—neglect or suppression of the performance of the gifted or of those with disabilities, for example. Or homogeneity can be conjured—touted as a goal of "good education" derived from ideology and based on denial. Achieving homogeneity among students is, in my view, a stupid idea. So are the ideas about how homogeny might be achieved through good education. This is why in 1981 I suggested that we value two outcomes:

> First, differences between the initial performances and the current performances of individuals in educational settings, with maximization of these differences being the goal for each person; second, differences between the performances of individuals that are the natural result of effective education, with as much concern for maximizing the performance of the most able as of the least able students. That would be a good augury for the human condition and for special education.[51]

HETEROGENEOUS GROUPING FOR INSTRUCTION IS A TERRIBLE MISTAKE

It is not a great distance from believing that good education will make children more homogeneous as a group to believing that heterogeneous grouping for instruction is appropriate. *Hetero*geneous grouping, the "in" or popular idea, means assigning students randomly to classes rather than grouping them according to what they have learned. Jeanie Oakes of UCLA is perhaps the leading advocate of heterogeneous grouping for instruction.[52] The opposite—*homo*geneous grouping—is equated with "tracking" in the minds of many, and anti-tracking statements are supported by many educators and noneducators who comment on schooling. Homogeneous grouping is thought to be inequitable because it has often resulted in students of given ethnic identity, socioeconomic status, or gender being grouped together. Advocates of heterogeneous grouping suggest that homogeneous grouping (assigning students to classes based on what they have learned rather than assigning them randomly) is discriminatory and, at best, ethically questionable. After all, if education results in students becoming more similar to each other in what they know, then we should be able to take a group of dissimilar children and turn them into a homogeneous group—or, at least, keep them from getting more unlike each other in what they know about what we're teaching. We should, according to this logic, begin with a heterogeneous group—a group of very dissimilar students. We can then give them all similar experiences and, thereby, produce similar outcomes for them so that we achieve equity. Teaching all students the same way, according to some, is the way to achieve equity. Or, some suggest, we can meet all the differing instructional needs of students in a heterogeneous group through some sort of peer tutoring or differentiation of assignments—"differentiated" education. The idea is often that students should work together to solve problems in cooperative learning groups, in which each student contributes his or her special expertise.

Predictably, perhaps, advocates of heterogeneous grouping argue that there is no such thing as a homogeneous group—that there are always differences among students that require special accommodation. In this matter, the argument often parallels that regarding any other thing that is a matter of degree. The postmodern way of dealing with doubt is to argue that any doubt at all is sufficient to overturn a proposition. That is, there is no such thing as "beyond reasonable doubt" simply because any doubt at all about an assertion or accusation or proposition discredits it completely. Were I being tried for a crime, I'd want a jury composed of people who think like this, as any doubt at all would be sufficient to exonerate me, never mind the preponderance of evidence. But the point here is this—those who argue for heterogeneous grouping may deny that the *degree* of homogeneity is crucial and argue, therefore, that teachers must be ready to teach groups as heterogeneous as may occur by random assignment or, even, purposeful assignment to achieve maximum heterogeneity. Well, as a former teacher of students of elementary age, as a current teacher of university students, as a student of music (and other things), and as one who has studied education, this argument is nonsensical to me.

As I discuss later, neither common sense nor reliable data suggest that students are most effectively and humanely taught in heterogeneous groups; both common sense and reliable data do suggest that groups as homogeneous as we can reasonably make them are much more effective and humane. Teacher Patrick Welsh describes how the heterogeneity of talent and motivation among his students makes teaching them all well a very difficult if not impossible task.[53] And here I digress to personal experience in heterogeneous and homogeneous groups for my music instruction.

Several years ago, at age 55, I first went to a summer jazz camp. I'd only picked up the upright bass about six months earlier, never having played anything but piano for a few years as a child and never having played in a musical ensemble. I was assigned to a combo consisting of several young musicians (the oldest was probably about 18). As I recall, our group consisted of a drummer, two piano players (who shared numbers), a couple of sax players, and a couple of trumpet players. Our instructor, probably about age 40, was a very competent bassist and teacher—warm, encouraging, good-humored, attentive. He soon saw that I didn't really know how to hold my instrument and pull the strings properly, so he gave me some individual attention right away. In fact, he devoted about the first 10 minutes of our hour to helping me just get the hang of those extremely fundamental skills. The other combo members were waiting, obviously anxious to get on with playing tunes. One, a boy of about 16, eventually said to our instructor, "Hey, Rich, we paid our money for this camp too, and we're not doing anything." Rich did what I'd recommend a good teacher do. He went across the room to speak with the kid as privately as possible and said something along these lines very quietly and directly: "I don't want to hear anything like that from you again. He needs my help right now, and if he can't play the bass, then we can't have our combo. I'll help you, too, and I'll make sure you get your money's worth, but right now I need to help him." Never mind that the teacher was warm, supportive, competent, sensitive, and that other kids in the combo later said to me to ignore what that kid said, they wanted me in the group, the damage was done. I was humiliated (before the kid spoke, actually, by my own mismatch with the group). I wanted out.

Fortunately, Jamey Aebersold and the other people running the jazz camp realized that people need to be on about the same level for instruction in music theory or combo playing. Some things, like listening, can be done in heterogeneous groups, because everyone is working independently. But for instruction, well, you need homogenous groups or things don't go well. Aebersold and his instructors told us that if we were not able to keep up with a group, find a lower level; if we found what the group was doing too easy, move to a higher group. Their knowledge led them to understand that learning to play music is not going to be much fun if you aren't matched up with people whose level of competence in playing approximates yours. This didn't mean that people differed in their inherent worth, just that people have the best time learning to play with others who are on about the same level. I found a group of beginning bassists, all learning to play along with a CD. They were learning the basics from another extremely competent, supportive instructor. It was a good lesson for me. And when I hear people talk about the wonders of heterogeneous grouping I want to hand them an instrument they don't know how to play and put them on stage with a fine orchestra.

Back to the issue of equitable treatment. I think that achieving equity in education (fair treatment of students regardless of their ethnic origins, gender, or socioeconomic status) is critically important. The only question for me is how to achieve it most certainly. I think a careful analysis of the problem shows that heterogeneous grouping on performance—the popular idea about equity—is dead wrong. It is, I think, a silly proposition that inevitably results in the perpetuation of inequities. James J. Gallagher notes that heterogeneous grouping just doesn't make common sense. In sports, in music, in every walk of life in which we are serious about teaching students well, we group them homogeneously by what they've learned. Gallagher asks, "Do we improve the skills of our Olympic swimmers by asking that they take time to teach nonswimmers how to swim?"[54]

What is needed to achieve substantive equity—not ostensible equity, in which fairness is judged by who is in the class, but fairness in instruction and opportunities to learn—is homogeneous grouping for instruction. Homogeneous grouping for instruction means that the students in an instructional group are all on about the same level (that is, they've all learned the particular subject to about the same level).

Effective School Practices, a journal focused on promoting reliable instructional practices, devoted an entire issue to the topic of heterogeneous grouping. As Bonnie Grossen noted, "Heterogeneous grouping has come into vogue in America."[55] She summarized the situation well in the opening paragraphs of a subsequent issue of *Effective School Practices*:

> Heterogeneous grouping is often regarded as "the way" to remedy educational discrimination. As the last issue of *Effective School Practices* indicated, heterogeneous grouping is only a superficial solution to the problem of educational equity. Equity involves much more than simply providing all students with a seat in the same classroom. In this issue, we further develop the idea that discrimination is not erased by simply providing the same instruction to all children, especially if the "same" instruction assumes a rich, supportive home environment as North America's currently most popular reforms do.[56]

The reasoning of those who are proponents of heterogeneous grouping seems to be that low achievers are stuck with bad teachers, low expectations, lower-level curricula, and poor outcomes; therefore, if they share teachers, expectations, and curricula with higher achievers they will achieve at a higher level. Well, it doesn't really work that way. And it never seems to occur to those who advise heterogeneous grouping that a better strategy might be to use homogeneous grouping for instruction but provide good teachers for the low achievers—teachers who would take students at the level they are and provide excellent instruction on tasks at which they can be successful. There is no point that I can see in "challenging" students by putting them into instructional groups where they are clueless, but that's what happens when all kids, regardless of their skill level, are placed in the same class. Some reformers will say that the good teacher will adapt instruction for the full range of students, but that is malarkey if the goal is to provide maximum, effective instruction for all students. A teacher can't possibly instruct all kids well when he or she has to contend with many different instructional levels at once.

Siegfried Engelmann has described why public schools virtually never use really effective instruction: There are objections to individual instruction and to homogeneous placement for instruction. But, if instruction is to be really effective—produce mastery and acceleration, which are outcomes reformers ostensibly are after—then students have to be placed in homogeneous groups for instruction. Engelmann suggests that placement should be made using four criteria, so that a student should be able to:

1. Get at least 70 percent correct on what's being taught.
2. Get at least 90 percent correct on what's being reviewed (what's assumed to have been mastered).
3. Go through a lesson in the anticipated amount of time and not need a lot of added practice.
4. Get nearly 100 percent correct at the end of a lesson.

Clearly, many low achievers who are placed in heterogeneous groups for instruction do not come close to meeting these criteria on the material being taught. The fact that they are in a class with high achievers does little or nothing to help them learn and is, for many, a humiliating experience. Engelmann comments further:

Homogeneous grouping is preferable because it provides motivational features and challenges not possible in the one-on-one setting. Also, it is far more cost efficient. The major problem in maintaining groups is to

assure that the composition of the group is consistent with the four placement criteria. It is not legitimate for a group to have four children placed
appropriately and two who are being dragged through the lessons (with
extra firming and practice). The two lower children do not meet the
placement criteria and should be placed in a lesson range that is more
commensurate with their abilities.[57]

A lot of people have said it before, but it bears repeating, given the
popularity of heterogeneous grouping: In the end, especially when
you're trying to find a job or get admitted to a program of higher learning, people don't care who you sat beside in school. They care what
you know and can do. Yes, they may want you to know how to get
along with people who are different from you, but that won't matter
much if you can't do the job. Ultimately, if you can't do the job, then
others different from you are likely to abandon you socially if not reject you.

"Tracking" is inequitable if it means a system in which a student
is stuck in a track regardless of his or her performance—assigned to
a homogeneous group regardless of what he or she has learned. But
that is not the kind of grouping Engelmann or other responsible educators suggest. Instructional groups should be homogeneous on the
particular material being taught, and students must be moved to another group higher or lower on the skill in question if their performance indicates the desirability of such a change. The criteria for
placement have been spelled out by others (see the four criteria
above from Engelmann).

An education system should be "forgiving," in that mistakes made by
students or teachers should not disqualify students from further educational opportunities. My impression is that the American system is in
many ways forgiving, and that homogeneous grouping for instruction
like that described by Engelmann is flexible, not a rigid system creating educational "castes." Particularly for post–high school education,
America provides many opportunities to change paths.

No amount of "detracking" will improve equity for anyone unless
instruction is improved for the students in question. A simple reality
check on education reform leads any reasonable observer to conclude that higher expectations alone will do virtually nothing at all
to help students achieve at higher levels.[58] Furthermore, the only
way to make instruction maximally effective for all students is to

teach them in homogeneous groups. Yet, heterogeneous grouping is touted as the solution to equity. Go figure!

Deformed Education: Our tenth grader, Laura, had an interesting assignment: to write a hypothetical news story about a sequence of events involving a controversial local police action. Her English teacher, Ms. Smith, told everyone in her class to get all the information they could about the incident, then take the perspective of a particular person in the community and write the story from that person's point of view. We thought this would be a really valuable and interesting assignment. It was something Laura really got into.

However, we are not happy with the way the assignment was handled later in class discussions. We had assumed that Ms. Smith would help students see that different people have different perspectives on what happened or may have distorted the facts, but that she would also help them understand the importance of finding out just what *did* happen. To our dismay, she took the position that all of the stories were equally valid, equally true. She told Laura that the truth depends on who writes it and that there may be no actual truth to be found. This left Laura rather upset.

But even more upsetting to her and to us is what happened with other students in the class. According to what we hear from Laura, this kind of thing happens routinely. The school Laura attends believes that "tracking" is morally wrong and ineffective, so the kids are all in groups of mixed ability—"heterogeneous groups," the school people call them. Well, Laura was supposed to discuss her story in some sort of cooperative learning arrangement with three other kids, her group. But, according to Laura, one of the other kids in her group didn't write anything at all and spent the whole time sleeping. Another wrote a couple of incomprehensible sentences and didn't participate much. The third wrote a couple of short paragraphs, but she couldn't even read Laura's story.

Laura had read newspaper accounts and even interviewed a couple of people to write her story, which would have filled a couple of newspaper columns. To her credit, she wasn't just upset because she didn't have anybody in her group capable of actually reading and discussing her story. She also was upset because the other students weren't getting anything out of the assignment. Sometimes we think she'd be better off if we home schooled her.

NOTES

1. Kauffman (1992).
2. St. Pierre (2000).
3. National Center on Education and the Economy (1989, p. 9).
4. Ysseldyke, Algozzine, & Thurlow (2000, p. 67).
5. Fitzgerald (1945). See www.quotationspage.com; see also *Columbia Quotations*.
6. Broder (2001a, p. B7).
7. Kinsley (2000a).
8. Kinsley (2000a, p. A25).
9. Kinsley (2000b, p. A27).
10. Hirsch (1996).
11. Sokal & Bricmont (1998), Koertge (1998); see also McKerrow & McKerrow (1991).
12. Krauthammer (2000).
13. Wassermann (2001, p. 32). Humorous misinterpretation of Heisenberg has even found its way into film noir. The defense attorney's strategy in *The Man Who Wasn't There*, a 2001 movie by the Coen brothers, is a black humor send-up of misunderstanding of the Uncertainty Principle.
14. Wassermann (2001, p. 35, 14).
15. Gould (2000, pp. 342–346). Physicist Steve Reynolds provides the following example about how the Uncertainty Principle could actually be applied to the measurement of a pitched baseball's position, given that we are also measuring its speed. "If the radar gun at a baseball game measures the speed of a pitch to be, say, 91.3 mph, at that instant there is an irreducible uncertainty, according to Heisenberg, in our knowledge of the location of the baseball (along the direction from pitcher to catcher). Let's say the uncertainty [of the radar gun] in the speed measurement is 0.1 mph. For a typical baseball, the corresponding minimum uncertainty in position is about 0.000000000000000000000000000001 inches (10^{-30} in). This is a billion billion times smaller than the radius of a single proton, and is obviously unimaginably smaller than any real uncertainties we would have in measuring the position of anything, even an atom. Similar numbers come out for any macroscopic objects. Heisenberg's Principle has ABSOLUTELY NO practical application to macroscopic objects!!!"
16. Elkind (1998a).
17. Glanz & Overbye (2001, p. A1).
18. Glanz & Overbye (2001, p. A12).
19. See Engelmann & Carnine (1982), Walker, Colvin, & Ramsey (1995).
20. E.g., Rhodes (1987).

21. Kauffman & Lloyd (1995).
22. Stainback & Stainback (1991, p. 328).
23. Bartholomew (1974, p. 47).
24. Dupre (1997).
25. Bateman (1994, p. 516).
26. Semmel, Gerber, & MacMillan (1994, p. 485).
27. Kauffman & Lloyd (1995).
28. Gallagher (1994, p. 528).
29. Ysseldyke, Algozzine, & Thurlow (2000, p. 67); see also Ysseldyke, Algozzine, & Thurlow (1992, p. 64) for the same statement in an earlier edition.
30. Gartner & Lipsky (1989, p. 20).
31. See Kauffman (1999d).
32. Kauffman (1999–2000, pp. 64–65).
33. See Hirsch (1996), Tanner (2000).
34. Sarason (1990, p. 72).
35. Wilgoren (2001, p. B5).
36. Raspberry (2001a, p. A6).
37. Cohen (2000a, p. A23).
38. See Cohen (2000a), Kinsley (2001).
39. See Becker & Gersten (2001), Carnine (1993, 2000), Hirsch (1996).
40 Watkins (1996).
41. Lieberman (2001).
42. See Ravitch (2000, p. 416).
43. Feynman (1985, p. 281).
44. See Engelmann (1997).
45. Gould (1996a) also discusses skewed distributions and their meanings.
46. See Ravitch (2000, p. 416).
47. Ravitch (2000, p. 50).
48. Gould (1996a).
49. E.g., Engelmann (1997).
50. Hallahan & Kauffman (2000).
51. Kauffman (1981, p. 21).
52. Oakes (1985, 1992).
53. Welsh (2001).
54. Gallagher (1993, p. 42).
55. Grossen (1993c, p. 5).
56. Grossen (1993b, p. 1).
57. Engelmann (1997, p. 184).
58. Broder (2001b).

CHAPTER 5

Misleading Statements

"What is known about the education of students labeled as handicapped? First, separate special education does not work. It does not do so by any measure of assessment—learning, development of self-esteem and social skills or preparation as student, worker, or citizen."

—Alan Gartner and Dorothy Lipsky, inclusion advocates

SPECIAL EDUCATION AND MULTICULTURAL EDUCATION ARE OFTEN MISCONSTRUED

Popular but misleading statements about education and its reform are particularly likely to be made about two aspects of contemporary schooling: multicultural education and special education. This is not to say that either multicultural education or special education is a foolish or failed enterprise. In fact, I think quite the contrary is true. Nevertheless, some of the things said and some of the positions taken about these aspects of education are in my opinion outrageously illogical and hurtful of the causes they represent.

Both multiculturalism and special education can be practiced well. Both are, in my opinion, necessary aspects of a good system of public education. Nevertheless, both are especially prone to misunderstanding, in part because they are topics about which emotions run high. On these topics, emotion often overwhelms careful thinking. Both are often taken to mean particularly wretched and indefensible educational practices. And, in truth, both are very often badly practiced.

Unfortunately, multicultural education and special education are not the only topics about which high-profile writers and speakers frequently make misleading statements. Standardized testing and teacher education also come in for a large measure of twisted rhetoric. I think these topics—multiculturalism, special education, standardized testing, and teacher education—are the ones about which I see the most confusing statements and about which people are most likely to be mislead by popular rhetoric. Here, I take up only a few such statements.

DANGER LURKS IN COMMENTING ON SPECIAL OR MULTICULTURAL EDUCATION

Multicultural education and special education are dangerous topics, in that anyone who questions the dominant and politically or professionally sanctioned view (i.e., the "politically correct" or "professionally acceptable" view) will be seen as an enemy. True believers who hold "correct" views and use "correct" language will be publicly approved; those who don't will be reprimanded, tutored, corrected, and "rehabilitated." Even those who hold "correct" *views* but use *language* that is not judged to be entirely "correct" may be subjected to intense criticism (I refer here to *ideological* correctness, not to *grammatical* correctness). Thus people are misled into believing that multicultural education and special education are supported only by those whose language is approved, who use the "correct" words and phrasing. The unfortunate result of insisting on linguistic and cognitive purity is that potential allies are turned away.

I myself have been told that for my sins of wrong language I should make apologies to numerous groups and that such would be important for my "long-term and short-term recovery." I'm sure many others have had similar experiences, but I'll tell you mine. My most reprehensible language sin against multiculturalism was co-authoring, with a colleague, who was then also my journal co-editor, the following sentence in our first editorial: "We will seek to attain diversity of ethnicity, gender, and other differences among our contributors and reviewers while holding uniformly high expectations of competence."[1] Although we expressed what we thought were clear commitments to both competence and diversity (of ethnicity and gender and other differences unrelated to competence) in our editorial decisions, we made the "error" of link-ing the concepts (diversity and high expectations) with the word "while." Some of our readers then raised suspicions that we did not really believe we could do both and that we thought ethnic minorities and women represented threats to excellence. Neither those suspicions nor any like them were in our thinking, but that was of no consequence. Our subsequent management of the journal seemed to us to reflect the nonsexist and nonracist sentiments we had expressed in our first editorial.[2] Needless, perhaps, to say, we heard from none of our critics about any action we took—for example, appointing more women and ethnic minorities to our editorial board, reporting that we had published substantial percentages of articles authored or co-authored by women and ethnic minorities (for the latter, we had to ask the gender and ethnicity of our authors, as in many cases we did not know).

Unfortunately, for our peace, we also used the words "desirable diversity" and "defensible difference" in our initial editorial, thereby opening ourselves to additional charges of wrong language or wrong thinking—seeing some diversity as undesirable and some differences as indefensible.[3] Our thinking was corrected with repeated explanations to us that *all* diversity is to be valued, that *all* differences are desirable, that we simply did not understand multiculturalism and demeaned those who strive to attain diversity and welcome all differences. Our explanations that people can be diverse or different in many different ways, some of which are unacceptable, were unacceptable to our critics, who did not see the irony in condemning us for saying something of which they disapproved while lecturing us that all diversity is to be valued. We pointed out that to us racism and sexism and white supremacist rhetoric are types of diversity or differences that we think are unacceptable. We were told that our explanations made matters worse. I think this is why scholars like Robert Conquest talk about the destructiveness of ideology, about the horrors of the Idea.[4]

Our unintentional linguistic "gaffes" created a firestorm of protest, in part because we offended some of our readers in yet another way in our first editorial—by affirming our belief in positivism and a scientific understanding of our field. This, too, our accusers said, could be interpreted as racist and sexist. Of course, not a single one of the roughly 50 university faculty members around the country and in Canada who wrote to our professional organization to complain of our language and beliefs, which they described as implicitly racist and sexist, bothered to discuss our "sins" with us before launching their attacks. I am accustomed to controversy in academe, to point and counterpoint, to hot argumentation, to what E. D. Hirsch, Jr. has called the rough-and-tumble debates of people about scientific issues. However, I admit that I was not prepared for the attempts to remove us as editors for our linguistic transgressions. We were very sorry to offend anyone's sensibilities, and we printed an apology, after much discussion with and conflicting recommendations from various critics of our words. Still, we continued to receive criticism from those whose linguistic standards we had violated. I would characterize the criticism as personal and vitriolic, not a matter of disagreement on an intellectual issue. But personal attack seems to have become the tactic of those who give greater allegiance to power than to truth and believe that power makes truth.

I suppose people's fear of personal attack and retribution is one of the reasons Kurt Schmoke, a Yale University trustee and former Baltimore mayor, commented:

> I worry that the term [reparations] itself will achieve symbolic status and that the symbol will divide those who believe targeted investments must be made to help eliminate the lingering harmful effects of slavery. It troubles me that a litmus test may be developing that judges people solely on the basis of their response to the question, "Are you for or against reparations?" I can envision a time in the near future when energy will be expended, fingers will be pointed, and questions will be raised about the legitimacy of leadership revolving around the response to this loaded question. This would be an unfortunate turn of events.[5]

Schmoke's comments recall for me the loaded question that many educators are asked today: "Do you support diversity?"

When accusations are tantamount to the assumption of guilt, then it is understandable that people will be afraid to speak out. Gao Zhan, a Chinese-born scholar at American University who was accused of spying for Taiwan by the Chinese government and imprisoned in China, put the problem this way: "Fear, silence and indifference join hands in the making of tyranny. The more we fear threats of retribution from an oppressive tyranny, the more relentless and ferocious the tyranny becomes."[6] Rabbi Robert Marx said something similar in his interview with Studs Terkel: "Silence is not inaction. It is doing something: silence is *acquiescence*. When you acquiesce to injustice, you are contributing to it.[7]

More than the accusations that I personally may encounter, I fear the silence that fear of such accusations may coerce from those who would otherwise speak out. The silence of many rational intellectuals has allowed radicals to stunt the growth of civil society in some nations of the world. Mona Eltahawy has described how silencing verbal opposition is counterproductive, but—and this is the even more important point—*failure to speak up for rationality, democracy, and other values brought by the Enlightenment only ensures that irrationality and repression will become dominant.*[8]

Fortunately, other Americans have shared observations similar to those Rick Brigham and I made about diversity. And some of them do not have our European ancestry. Orlando Patterson wrote:

> There are limits to cultural tolerance, a lesson the 20th century has repeatedly taught us. There are, among some cultures, deeply held convictions—about women and their bodies; about races; about children; about authority; about lawbreakers, the sick, the weak, the poor and the rich—that we absolutely deplore. The fact is, we need absolutes. Where a plurality of cultures exists, we need an overarching set of values cherished by all. Otherwise what begins as multicultural harmony inevitably descends into balkanization or chaos.[9]

There is considerable danger inherent in any discussion of multicultural education that does not meet the approval of the group that claims to know the "correct" way of thinking and the "correct" words and the "correct" combinations of words in sentences such that nothing can be said to be uncivil. This kind of incivility, which my colleague Hal Burbach and I referred to as the GOP (Group Offense Patrol) is, unfortunately, sometimes promoted in the name of civility in schools.[10] But, as I discussed in the previous chapter and describe further in the next, self-contradiction is frequently found in postmodern texts. And as I discuss further in this chapter, multiculturalism in education is sometimes defended with postmodern language. So we were not surprised to read an email message to our professional organization from a self-described "philosopher of science"—he did not deign to copy us, much less to write us a direct message, but a friend sent us a copy—saying that the only interpretation he could make of our editorial was that it carried racist and sexist overtones. He made this statement even though he embraces the postmodern notion that no text has a plain or single meaning. He also stated that our views of science are primitive, hardly reaching the standards expected of high school students, and suggested that we take a basic course in the philosophy of science.

We were both amazed and amused by this man's statements. First, his other writings put forward the notion that a text says nothing but what the reader brings to it, which might be taken as an indication that his own racism and sexism were showing, not ours. But his type of cognitive self-entrapment is common among those who embrace antiscientific thinking, regardless whether they call it postmodern, deconstructivist, or hermeneutical.[11] Second, he made his judgment based only on our very brief comments on science and positivism, a kind of shoot-from-the-hip response that philosophers generally deplore.

Special education, too, has its reformist and postmodern "truth squads" who patrol the field for possibly offensive words and for "incorrect" positions on issues. Much of this has to do with the correct use of "inclusionary" language and rhetoric. I have found that anyone suggesting that some students need special classes or special schools runs the risk of being called a "segregationist." People run the risk of castigation for using a label like "mentally retarded" rather than the more acceptable "person with mental retardation," which is judged to be preferable because it puts the "person first." I discussed what I think are the actual effects of "person-first" language or labels in chapter 3. Some have embraced euphemisms like "person with cognitive challenges" or "person with differing cognitive abilities." It is difficult for me to confront the fact that someone actually won a prize of $50,000 for coming up with the term "person with differing abilities," which was supposed to be terminology for referring to disabilities without creating social stigma. Who is *not* a person with differing abilities? Of what value is the terminology if it includes everyone? Some people object to the "R" word (retarded or retardation), apparently supposing that if it is stricken from our language, we will have done something marvelous. They suggest that the R word be replaced with the "DD" term (developmental delay or developmental disability), seeing it as more acceptable and less damaging. It seems, according to the *Inclusion*

Daily Express for June 5, 2001, that the provincial government of Ontario, Canada has expunged the term "retarded" from its legislation.
Apparently, the Ontario government considers "retarded" similar to a
racial slur.[12]

There is much to say about the language by which people are judged
in certain fields of education. These judgments and the reprimands that
go with transgression may be painful to those who offend, particularly
if they do so unwittingly. But there are more substantive issues in
which people are misled, and these deserve the bulk of our attention.
What multicultural and special education are assumed to encompass,
for example, are matters of great importance.

FOCUSING ON CULTURAL DIFFERENCES
CAN LEAD TO RACISM AND OTHER EVILS

Among the most misleading of statements about multicultural education today are those based on the assumption that culture is well defined and that multiculturalism must focus on differences among cultures. The assumption that differences among ethnic groups are more
important than commonalities is in my judgment pernicious, divisive,
and the opposite of what multiculturalism should represent.

"Multicultural" can be defined in a variety of ways. The definition is
particularly problematic because "culture" is not easy to define. Moreover, there are obviously many dimensions of culture and many degrees of enculturation. Usually, the term refers primarily to racial or
ethnic cultures. Sometimes it is used to refer to gender and sexual orientation, or to social class, religion, disability, and so on. But, a reasonable person must ask, what is encompassed in the "and so on?" For
example, is there, actually, a "culture of poverty?" Under what conditions is social class a more important facet of enculturation than, say,
ethnicity? If, as many recognize, there is great diversity of characteristics within a given ethnic group or gender or any other cultural marker,
then how does one define "culture" to account for these within-group
variations? How can one be sure that he or she is aware of, understanding of, and accommodating of *all* cultures? Is there an "American
culture," and, if so, what defines it? And just what does the buzz-phrase
"cultural competence" mean? These are some of the questions I and my

colleague Dan Hallahan have raised in our introductory text in special education.[13] We do not pretend to know the answers ourselves. Neither are we convinced that anyone else knows the answers. Perhaps answers to these questions will never be widely agreed upon.

Even more problematic is the attribution of characteristics by "cultural" group, usually meaning ethnic or racial groups or genders. One's apparent or supposed group affiliation (e.g., male, white, heterosexual, Christian, etc.) is assumed to give one special dispositions, sensitivities, understandings, values, and so on. But that assumption is neither accurate nor fair. As Michael Shermer observed about combating racism, "It is always the individual that matters, not the group; and it is always how individuals differ that matters, not how the groups differ. This is not liberal hope or conservative hype."[14] And even if it is a fact of evolution that *individual* variation is more important than group variation, it is the shared humanity of every individual that is more important still.

Many people speak of multicultural education, but very few actually check out any hypotheses by obtaining data on the performance of teachers or their students using a rigorous research design. Alfredo Artiles and Stan Trent have noted the danger in rhetoric without reliable empirical data to support given practices: "We contend that it is dangerous to continue discussing and implementing multicultural education policies in teacher education programs (including special education teacher education) if they are not based on sound empirical evidence."[15] Yet, most of the material written about multicultural education is merely opinion; it does not include data that can be checked out in any scientific way. If we lack scientific evidence, the danger is that superstition, folklore, and pseudoscience will become the basis for action. Low levels of scientific evidence make fertile ground for prejudice. But, as I have become acutely aware, "scientific" is now regarded by some as a culturally biased and therefore deeply suspect concept.

Science and reason in the Enlightenment tradition represent, to some, a distinctly white European, male, heterosexual epistemology, and these ideas are therefore assumed to be inherently discriminatory against people of all other identities. But as Roger Wilkins stated in *Jefferson's Pillow* about the American ideals of freedom and democracy laid down by the white fathers of the nation, "All of this was grounded in their energetic, even passionate embrace of Enlightenment ideas about the power of human reason."[16] True, the founding fathers were flawed human beings whose weaknesses are denied by many myths, and true also that many Africans in America, whether free or slaves, understood the power of these ideas. As Wilkins points out, these Enlightenment ideas have been embraced by people of every color and give possibility to work for social justice for people of any description. The ideas of freedom, dignity, democracy, and other human rights—including the reason and scientific evidence that support them—belong to everyone, regardless of their "race" or other identity.

Among the most egregiously misleading statements about multicultural education, in my opinion, are those putting the focus on differences rather than the commonalities among people who differ in ethnicity, social class, gender, religion, and so on. However, much of the literature on multicultural education highlights the ways in which groups of students are different, how they need "teachers who look like them" as role models. Nevermind the fact that without segregation by their external differences students can never be assured of having a teacher who looks like them—shares their gender or ethnicity, for example. The messages we are sending to each other, and indirectly, at least, to children, is that external appearance is the critical factor in a good role model. To suggest that color or gender or ethnic identity is more important than other characteristics—fairness, responsiveness to others, intelligence, or professional competence, for example—is one of the worst mistakes we could make in multicultural education. Why not teach children that they can see—in fact, *must* see and imitate— good role models who are of a different hue or gender or ethnic group?

To my way of thinking, finding the good in others who differ from us and finding the characteristics we share are the more important aspects of multiculturalism. It is not that differences are trivial, but if they are not trumped by what we have in common, then I see no hope for a peaceful multicultural society. In various parts of the world today, multicultural societies have come apart and people have committed horrible atrocities because of a focus on differences—usually religious or ethnic differences, not differences in hue or physiognomy that are readily apparent. Commonalities and similarities are lost altogether or deemphasized, trumped by what is not shared. The other person's difference in color or religion or personal heritage or tribe or place of origin is assumed to make him or her an essentially different human being, and the focus on that difference is used to justify mistreatment.

This is the ugly history of racism—teaching that a difference in ethnic identity is more important than human commonalities, telling a story that people of a certain description are alien creatures, not like us, not fully human. It is an old story that underlay slavery in America. It is a story too common today. Whether the reference is to "mud people," "sun people," "ice people," "white devils," "blood suckers," "infidels," or others whose appearance or heritage is different from that of the self-aggrandizing racist, the effect is the same—a dehumanizing caricature. As I stated in a guest editorial about caricature, science, and exceptionality,

> Racism is one of the most pernicious caricatures. It is the simultaneous aggrandizement of one skin color or hue or ethnic origin (i.e., hyperbole about a sameness) and belittlement of another color or ethnicity (i.e., overstatement of a difference), the intent being to obscure human similarities that transcend color and ethnic identity and, concurrently, to deny important differences among individuals in ability, performance, or character that are not determined by color or ethnicity.[17]

William Julius Wilson discusses how finding commonalities is essential for the mutually beneficial advocacy that I think is the foundation of true multiculturalism:

> Although it is important to acknowledge the racial divisions in America so they can be meaningfully addressed, the incessant attention given to these gaps has obscured the fact that blacks, whites, Latinos, Asians and Native Americans share many concerns and have important values and aspirations in common. . . . Social psychological research on interdependence reveals that when people believe they need each other they relinquish their initial prejudices and stereotypes and join programs that foster mutual interaction and cooperation. This does not mean group differences should not be acknowledged.[18]

Today's preoccupation with diversity may be understandable, given America's history of ill treatment of ethnic minorities. If it is pushed to an extreme, however, then the focus on diversity becomes another example of the art of the stupid, a good idea—welcoming and promoting diversity in such personal characteristics as gender and ethnicity among those in various societal roles—driven into the ground by excess. When people express the view that *all* diversity is to be tolerated, if not encouraged, then in my opinion we have crossed the line into ideology, a mindlessness that is truly destructive. Unfortunately, I know some people, including university faculty members, who do in fact express this view. Any good thing can go sour (perhaps we should make an exception for good whiskey). Celebration of diversity without exception is, in my view, multiculturalism gone sour. So is the idea that human differences are more important to highlight than are human commonalities. Obsession with difference and the tendency toward rage preclude the building of community, as William Raspberry noted in his commentary on a sermon of Nathan D. Baxter, the dean of Washington's National Cathedral.

> Baxter, who recently published a collection of his sermons and personal reflections called "Visions for the Millennium," believes the use of rage and anger as tools to motivate the majority—no matter how justified the rage and anger may be—"makes it impossible for us to fulfill our larger humanity, makes us lose sight of the commonality that lies behind community."[19]

My own view is that multicultural education means helping students acquire important abilities regardless of their personal identities (i.e., students learn academic and social skills without differentiation by ethnicity, color, gender, or other externally identifying characteristic), teaching things that are useful to students, teaching students to respect and value the good features of every culture and oppose every culture's undesirable aspects, and teaching by precept and by example that every student is a valued and respected person but not every view is positively regarded. Furthermore, I think multicultural education can succeed in making the world a better place by increasing substantive equity among people if—and only if—it emphasizes the common humanity of all people. We can have respect for our forebears and our cultural heritages without becoming cultural sycophants, glorifying our "race" or gender and fawning over the members of "our" group who attain power or notoriety.

Pride in something we did not choose and cannot change—our ethnicity, for example—is, in my way of thinking, the ultimate conceit. It is the core of cultural chauvinism and misguided attempts to instill self-esteem. By pride I mean the feeling of privilege or superiority, or the assumption of special sensitivities, entitlements, or immunities to human failings. I think it is good for all of us to love and respect and cherish our origins and other aspects of our identities, such as gender. I do not think it is good for us to assume that our identities make us good people or better people than those of other groups.

I fear the rise of a new racism in our country. The racism inherent in slavery, the segregation known as Jim Crow rules, the "final solution" to the "Jewish question," and all other forms of mistreatment and discrimination against those known or thought to be racially different from the dominant racial group was based on the idea of racial specialness, privilege, and superiority, not just the racial inferiority of the oppressed group. What I see emerging is a new racism, mimicking that of the old but clothed in the language of race-biased or race-based epistemology and other notions that ideas, realities, understandings, and interpretations of the world are peculiar to one's color or ethnic origins. The new racism, like the old, suggests that if you aren't of the _____ race (black or white or Jewish, for example), then you are necessarily _____ (racist or criminally inclined or biased or unintelligent, for example) and can't or don't or won't understand the knowledge and ways of other "races." Never mind that the whole notion of race is deeply suspect, if not totally discredited on scientific grounds. That oppressed peoples should adopt the characteristics of their oppressors is, perhaps, understandable, if not predictable. But that fact makes the new racism no less horrific to me than the old.

In chapter 7, I describe in more detail the aspects of multicultural education that I think make sense.

GLORIFYING DIVERSITY WITHOUT QUALIFICATION IS A TRAGIC MISTAKE

In multicultural education today the notion that no diversity can be unacceptable is apparently widely held. But there is tragicomic irony in the suggestion that *all* diversity is to be accepted and treasured. Moreover, as I have already described, I have been called racist for expressing the idea that diversity of some types is evil, not good, not welcome, the opposite of multicultural, the embodiment of racism. Racists are apt to claim they are just different, just hold different views on human beings, are just part of the normal and honorable diversity of citizens. "Well," I've been corrected and lectured, "Racism is *not* diversity. *Diversity* refers to only good things. Unacceptable diversity doesn't exist, and you demean all of those who are diverse by suggesting that some diversity is not welcome." My disagreement with the view that all diversity is to be cherished is, ironically, considered racist, giving racists the protection of an infatuation with diversity.

Certainly, diversity in many personal characteristics is to be accepted and valued. But not every diversity in behavior or opinion is to be given equal treatment. For one thing, accepting all diversity of behavior or ideas invites diversity that is clearly malevolent, even in the opinion of at least some of my critics (e.g., opinions of racial or gender inferiority or superiority or the veneration of certain children or the subjugation and abuse of people or the intimidation of political opponents because it is acceptable in the individual's culture). Furthermore, it is a strange quirk of this argument that *all* diversity is to be accepted—*except* the diversity represented by the argument that some diversity is unacceptable.

To say that something is "culturally based" does not justify, beatify, or condemn it. Yet certain ways of knowing or thinking or behaving are beatified or condemned simply because they are assumed to belong to a given culture or ethnic group or to one gender or to a sexual preference. When behavior is said to be justifiable simply because it belongs to a culture, then the culture of institutional racism can't be challenged effectively. I wish racism were more of a relic in the United States than it is. I wish South Africa's cultural tradition of racial atrocities were more of a relic than it is.[20] In a culture in which anti-Semitism is normative (as it was and is in the Nazi subculture) racism can't be overturned by appealing to its cultural norms. If the dominant cultural viewpoint is assumed to condemn or beatify policy or behavior, then we can heap equal condemnation—or adulation—on totalitarianism and on our American ideal of social justice.

Some cultural practices, beliefs, and mores are, I think, bad or good independent of who practices them or what the majority of people comprising a given culture believe. We often read about or watch on television atrocities committed by people of various colors and nations of origin. Some sociopolitical movements are defended on the basis of tradition or culture, including acts ranging from the brutal treatment or butchery of women or persons differing in skin color or tribe or place of origin or religion or sexual orientation to butchering one's political opponents. Those who claim to value all cultural diversity do so at considerable risk of embracing human degradation, which is not peculiar to persons of any conceptual orientation, sexual orientation, color, gender, religion, or place of origin.

True, slavery is a horrid blot on our nation's history, as Roger Wilkins pointed out in *Jefferson's Pillow*.[21] Those who follow the news know that in some nations of the world today there is still slavery. Not metaphoric slavery, but literal slavery, in which people "own" other people as their property. Slavery is a tradition that, mercifully, no longer is tolerated in America. But in other nations of the world, tradition sometimes includes other forms of brutality. Writing in the *Washington Post* in August 2001, Molly Moore described the horrors of "honor killings" in Turkey, in which girls or women are killed by males in their families who feel "dishonored" if a female family member is raped or engages in behavior of which they disapprove.

> Last April, two sisters age 12 and 14 and their 17-year-old cousin were allegedly shot dead by male relatives because they were seen socializing with boys. The extended family had moved to the outskirts of Istanbul from the eastern province of Bitlis five years earlier.
>
> "They were children; they were very young," said Ismail Kaya, a relative not implicated in the killings. "They [the accused] are young too. One of them is only 17. I feel sorry for everyone."
>
> Kaya added, however: "This is our tradition. Tradition has to be followed."[22]

Certainly, most members of Turkish society do not condone such killings. And such killings are not peculiar to Turkish society. In a case involving an Egyptian gynecologist who murdered his wife, a state's attorney said, "The motive here was a cultural one . . . that his wife, in his words, disgraced the family."[23] Most Egyptians do not condone such murders, nor do most Muslims hold the radical beliefs that led to the atrocities of September 11, 2001.[24] However, in every nation, including the United States of America, there are radical groups that use a holy writ or their cultural tradition to justify horrible acts. The point is this: cultural tradition, like the one that allowed slavery in the United States, is sometimes vile and needs to be changed. The fact that a practice is embedded in cultural tradition does not mean it is desirable, defensible, or should be considered merely culturally different.

Ellen Goodman explained how we risk destroying our own cultural value of gender equality if we insist on respecting other people's values just because they hold them.

> One woman stationed [in Saudi Arabia] who purports to be comfortable with the rules [requiring military women stationed there to live as second-class citizens] said, "When in Rome, do as the Romans do." But how far does that go? To feeding the lions? . . . It [the forced second-class status of military women stationed in Saudi Arabia when they leave the military base] raises questions America faces in the larger world. What happens if we disrespect our own values out of respect for others?[25]

In my view, one's gender or color or nation or continent or family of origin and so on does not determine how competent one is as a thinker, how sensitive one is to others, the keenness of one's intuition, or how good or valuable one is as a person. True, some contend that there is a female way or an ethnic way (assume whatever ethnic group you will) of knowing or thinking. Surely, women compared to men or the members of different ethnic groups often receive different treatment under the same circumstances or for the same behavior, and this is the basis of much injustice in the world. But what does people's sex or skin hue or place of origin tell us about them, particularly about what they know or how they think? Not much, if anything, as far as I can tell, although I find in the literature on teaching the opinion that certain ethnic groups are inherently more culturally sensitive than others or that white teachers are simply stuck with the inferiority or the inherent privilege and domination that stick to their whiteness. Christine Sleeter expressed this opinion: "Preservice students of color bring a richer multicultural knowledge base to teacher education than do White students. Students of color generally are more committed to multicultural teaching, social justice, and providing children of color with an academically challenging curriculum."[26] Norma Ewing stated in her discussion of the power and privilege that she maintains are inherent in whiteness:

> It [whiteness] is not something that can be "turned in" or renounced but is routinely "cashed in" or used as collateral every day—in the classroom or on the playground, workplace, bank, supermarket, department store,

real estate office, or any other milieu in which cross-racial academic, social, economic, or political interactions occur. It is not something whites have the option of not taking or giving up ever in their lifetime. White privilege is readily apparent to those to whom privilege was not granted . . ., but asking those with white skin to recognize their "invisible knapsack of unearned assets" . . . is like asking fish to notice water and birds to consider air.[27]

I am aware that whites have been and often continue to be granted what are called "privileges." I do not accept such "privilege" as fair or just. I understand that I do not need to worry about racial profiling or redlining or many other indignities that people of color may suffer. I understand that one of my colleagues at the University of Virginia, Stan Trent, was questioned by police because of his color and that this will not happen to me because I am white. I understand that my wife was educated in white schools because she and her relatives did not reveal the ethnicity (American Indian) of her great grandmother; had they, she would have been considered "colored" and denied the education she received. I will not, because of my whiteness, experience the unfairness related to color that people in our society too often practice.

As far as I can figure out, "white privilege" consists of certain freedoms. The shame of our society is not that anyone has these freedoms but that anyone is denied them. They are freedoms that everyone can and should enjoy, regardless of their color. The solution is not to deny them to anyone but to extend them to all. I will guess that those whose work I quoted above agree.

That America was in many ways founded by white male privilege is something Roger Wilkins made very clear in *Jefferson's Pillow*. But Wilkins also makes clear that the flawed but great men who founded our nation gave us the promise of the Enlightenment idea that all people should be free. The promise of Enlightenment ideas is the extension of freedoms formerly reserved for white males to women and non-whites. It is a promise only partially fulfilled. And many people with white skins, including many males, are more than a little aware of these facts—far more aware of them than are birds of air or fish of water.

I do not accept as fair or just the stereotyping of any people, white or any other color. The comments I quoted above suggest to me an unbearable whiteness of being, not fairness or justice. To me, they seem to be merely the old and reprehensible white supremacy rhetoric imitated or turned on its head. But I find the face of racism is no less ugly because it is upside down. (And, lest deconstructionists try to turn this statement into a message that racism "right-side-up" is somehow morally right or correct, I wish to say as unambiguously as possible that in my view racism is evil no matter which way it might be turned.)

I applaud those who refuse to accept the attempted imposition on them of inferior status because of their color. I myself will not accept the attempted imposition of racism on me because my skin is white (well, more red, actually, but I would be classified as a white European-American in current categories). Although I may be aware of and deplore what has been called "white privilege," I am not obliged to accept it as morally right any more than someone of another color is obliged to accept subservience because he or she is not white.

Do skin color or ethnic origins imbue some with special sensitivity and prevent others from understanding or being sensitive? Casual observation of what has happened in many nations of the world ought to reveal the falsehood of such a racist proposition. From Northern Ireland to Bosnia to the Middle East to Rwanda and to anywhere else in the world, including America, we can find hatreds and conflicts between and among various ethnic groups. And sensitivity to the feelings of others is found among all of the peoples of the world. No one can change his or her ancestry, but most people are capable of changing their attitudes and behavior. That is why we have education, and that is why we need good multicultural education. (I describe later in this book what I mean by *good* multicultural education.)

Demographic characteristics specify only gender or color or geopolitical ancestry. In my view, the assumption that all or even most members of a group defined by ethnicity or sex think or know or perceive in a certain way and not in another is racist and sexist on its face. The argument that certain phenomena or ideas (e.g., scientific methods or principles; ostensibly race-biased or race-based epistemologies) should be suspect or discredited or embraced because they were discovered or invented by a person of particular gender and ethnic origin is, to me, sexism or racism at its rankest.[28]

Donna Britt captured the essence of the idea that people's preferences and ideas cannot be classified by their ethnicity in her commentary on the music people like:

"You can't say all black people like this or that. We listen to *everything*." So do millions of other Americans. More of us than ever realize that the inner grace required to create Beethoven's Fifth—or Ellington's "Take the 'A' Train," or Smokey Robinson's "Ooo Baby Baby"—isn't about color but about heart, a quality inherent to every group God made.[29]

I suppose some people may be concerned that if we allow diversity of any type to be disapproved of, then we'll risk disapproval of all diversity and welcome only conformity. It is the old "slippery slope" argument that I mentioned in an earlier chapter. We either embrace an Idea (an ideology), or we allow people to make judgments, in this case about diversity that is acceptable and diversity that isn't. Of "multiculturalism" that puts no diversity out of bounds, I want no part—particularly if it is multiculturalism that says the only unacceptable difference in thinking is the idea that some diversity is not ok.

IDEAS DO NOT BELONG TO
RACES, COLORS, ETHNICITIES, OR SEXES

The postmodern proposition that words do not refer to any underlying reality has enormous potential for evil, as I discuss further in chapter 6. Some people use this postmodern argument to defend multicultural education, but they do so, in my judgment, at the high risk of cultural suicide.

The idea that words *are* reality—that text or power *creates* reality simply by naming it—is behind many silly and misleading statements in education. But the basic idea that misleading others through the denial of underlying reality and supposing that words create the world is the basis for irony and humor in fields other than education. For example, the comic strip Dilbert (drawn by Scott Adams) for November 26, 2000, has the boss trying to overcome Dilbert's observation that the boss's project isn't feasible and that words don't change the underlying reality. First, the boss proposes "working" the numbers, then "massaging" the numbers, and finally "fiddling with" the numbers. Dilbert tells his boss that it's impossible to make something possible by hallucinating new numbers. But hallucinating is an apt description of what some misleading statements about education ask us to do.

Sometimes particular words are deliberately avoided and others are substituted to create a different image, to make a bitter pill seem more palatable. This is particularly the case in political life, where image seems to be more important than substance. Some of us can recall the Reagan era tactic of calling catsup a vegetable for purposes of enhancing at no cost the perceived nutritional value of school lunches. I suppose it is understandable at some level that U.S. Representative Henry Hyde would wish to describe his own sexual escapades (when he was older than 30) as "youthful indiscretions." One can understand the liberal sentiments that prompt a government to expunge "retarded" from all of its official language, as the Ontario, Canada government did, even if it is a useless exercise. President Clinton's argument about the meaning of the word "is" and his contention that he did not have sex with a woman because he did not have vaginal intercourse with her deserve public contempt. Word games do not change the underlying issue. If the four cases in point that I have given are not examples of misleading the public, then I do not know what "misleading" means.

Favoring image over substance—a way of misleading people's thinking—is becoming a familiar tactic in education, too.[30] Perhaps it is understandable that President George W. Bush and his Secretary of Education, Rod Paige, would like to avoid the word "voucher" to describe their education proposals. But that does not change the nature of their plan. They hope, obviously, that the words will lead to public approval of something that the public seems to oppose in substance.

I hope the warning about the cul de sac of postmodern ideas is taken seriously by people who share my concern for fair treatment of those who have been discriminated against. In America, the discriminated-against includes women, ethnic minorities, and people with disabilities. Postmodernists often cite Michel Foucault and Jacques Derrida in defense of their enthusiasm for radical doubt and the end of what they consider the tyranny of science and scientific thinking. They believe Foucault's and Derrida's ideas will bring greater equity and social justice. But, as others have noted, the way to equitable treatment is exactly the opposite of that suggested by Foucault and Derrida. Noretta Koertge stated, "I continue to believe that science—even white, upper-class, male-dominated science—is one of the most important allies of oppressed people."[31] Alan Ryan noted in "Princeton Diaries":

It is, for instance, pretty suicidal for embattled minorities to embrace Michel Foucault, let alone Jacques Derrida. The minority view was always that power could be undermined by truth. . . . Once you read Foucault as saying that truth is simply an effect of power, you've had it. Those with power have "truth" on their side, and the old radical hope that we can undermine power with truth is incoherent. But American departments of literature, history and sociology [and, I would add, education] contain large numbers of self-described leftists who have confused radical doubts about objectivity with political radicalism, and are in a mess.[32]

Ryan comments further on the erosion of rational arguments combined with liberal sentiments in contemporary universities. As he puts it, "the number of people who combine intellectual toughness with even a modest political radicalism is pitifully small."[33]

Mira Nanda writes as a non-Western scientist about the unwelcome "gift" of postmodernism to the third world. She and others are not satisfied to achieve some sort of rhetorical or imagined cognitive equality among various groups. She explains eloquently how postmodernism works to thwart the very values it says it holds and how science offers far more hope and better strategies for achieving substantive equality. Among her statements are these:

How is the post in postcolonial related to the post in *post*modern science critiques? My answer is simple: the postmodern elements of the constructivist science critique strengthen the *pre*modern elements of post-colonial societies.

So the reason that we—the dogged advocates of scientific temper in non-Western societies—must reject the privilege of having our traditional knowledge considered at par with science is clear: the project of different and equal sciences for different people completely negates our project of science for all people. We prefer our much maligned universalistic project because we are not interested in a supposed cognitive equality of different cultures but, rather, in substantive equality for all people in terms of healthier, fuller, and freer lives. We prefer the cold, objective facts of science to the comfortable, situated knowledge of our ancestors for the simple reason that we refuse to subordinate what is good to what is ours.[34]

I think that the same reasoning applies to women, ethnic minorities, the poor, and others with histories of discrimination in the United States and other developed nations of the world. The idea of "epistemological" racism or sexism is, in my view, both silly and destructive of substantive equality for reasons that Nanda and others have given. ("Epistemological" refers to the way people come to know things; the postmodern assumption is that people have different ways of knowing what they know depending on their sex or ethnic identity.) Compare Nanda's observations with those of James Scheurich and Michelle Young, who suggest that because scientific knowledge has been constructed primarily by white males "the resulting epistemological racism, besides unnecessarily restricting or excluding the range of possible epistemologies, creates profoundly negative consequences for those of other racial cultures with different epistemologies, ontologies, and axiologies."[35] Who is advantaged, and who is disadvantaged by the rejection of knowledge and methods of inquiry on the basis of the color or gender of those who created these tools for achieving equity?

Do Scheurich and Young not understand that to see racism everywhere is tantamount to seeing it nowhere? If racism is assumed to "saturate" American life or to be pervasive, we lose focus on the specifics of it. If it is assumed to be present in every interaction, then we have difficulty discriminating what is unavoidable from what must be avoided. The paranoia and terror created by the assumption that skin color makes one racist and that racism lurks everywhere reminds me more than a little of fundamentalist religion and the idea of original sin, or Senator McCarthy's way of dealing with communism. That communists were a real threat to the nation is likely true; that Senator McCarthy's approach to the threat was both abusive and counterproductive is hardly questionable. I cannot be approving of what I see as mangled thinking in such comments as these:

> Our point here, then, is that in the U.S., to be White (no matter what your political or moral commitments are), to go through daily life with White skin privilege (a kind of long-term White affirmative action), is, to some degree, to be a White racist. . . . The two of us, for example, see ourselves as *both* anti-racist *and* White racists. This, we argue, is the contradictory, ambiguous reality of Whites doing anti-racist work. The two of us are *both* inside White racism, deeply and unconsciously affected by it, *and* working against it—both within and against.[36]

I do not see any value in the kind of breast-beating or self-loathing that comments like these suggest, although I do see the value in being angry about and taking action to remedy specific acts of racism. I think racism is loathsome, but I do not assume that my color or anyone else's makes me, or them, a racist or an anti-racist or someone who is immune to racism. No matter who says it—black or white—the assumption that one's skin makes one racist, or particularly this or that on some moral dimension, is, to me, both racist and revolting. As Roger Wilkins noted, "Just as self-love can be enriching beyond understanding (as, for example, in the case of George Washington), self-hatred can be the most destructive of human feelings."[37]

But sentiment is no substitute for sense. And neither common sense nor scientific sense is owned by or exclusive to those who discovered or invented it, any more than is music or art or literature or technology. Jazz may have been invented by black musicians, but to suggest that it can be understood or practiced authentically only by blacks is, in my judgment, as racist as the view that J. S. Bach or W. A. Mozart can be understood and interpreted authentically only by whites. We do not assume that because the light bulb was invented—at least we usually suppose so—by a white male, light bulbs are legitimately used or understood only by white men; or that if a black female invented the light bulb, then light bulbs or the idea of them is black or female. Noretta Koertge noted, "Well-meaning moralism is no substitute for intellectual integrity."[38]

I fear that the gravitation toward "race-biased epistemologies" or "race-based epistemologies" and other postmodern ideas actually traps those who embrace such nonsense in a second-class status. It ensures that they will remain in a world that favors totalitarianism and resists Enlightenment ideas. I fear that the elevation of differences in sex and color and ethnic identity over our common humanity will bring new and more vicious stereotyping, drive wedges between groups based on sexist and racist ideas, and be used to justify the inhumane treatment of people based on personal identities over which they have no control. "Multicultural" practiced this way promises a serious coming apart.

CRITICAL THEORY DOES NOT
REPRESENT CRITICAL THINKING

"Critical theory," like postmodernism, is difficult to pin down. Sometimes it targets a particular problem, as in "critical race theory." It ap-

parently refers to critiquing a culture "by examining larger political, social, and economic issues and [focusing] on oppression, conflict, struggle, power, and praxis."[39] "The central theme that runs through these
and other conceptualizations of critical theory is a focus on interrela-
tionships between society and its institutions and issues of race, ethnicity, gender, and social class."[40] James M. Patton has described how
critical theory applies to special education:

> These critical, or conflict, theorists hold that education, and, thus special
> education, grounded in structured power relationships, is designed to
> serve the interests of the dominant social, political, and economic classes
> and to place African Americans in a devalued position. As such, the struc-
> tures, processes, assumptions, and beliefs of the dominant classes are
> deeply embedded in the special education knowledge base and its knowl-
> edge producers, thus undermining its theory, research, and practice.[41]

Critical theorists typically rely heavily on Marxist or neo-Marxist
views, an important point in trying to figure out what "critical theory"
means. Critical theory should not be assumed to reflect analytical
thinking in the sense of applying scientific concepts or principles or
logic to the solution of problems. It appears to be more a political view
of the evils of power and the necessity of evaluating "truth" as an expression of social power than a way of finding reliable solutions to
problems and communicating them unambiguously. As far as I can figure out from trying to read critical theory, it makes no substantive contribution to the ostensible objective of identifying the powerless and
helping them participate more effectively in societal decisions.

A comment of Alan Sokal and Jean Bricmont is pertinent here:

> If intellectuals, particularly those on the left, wish to make a positive
> contribution to the evolution of society, they can do so above all by clar-
> ifying the prevailing ideas and by demystifying the dominant discourses,
> not by adding their own mystifications. A mode of thought does not be-
> come "critical" simply by attributing that label to itself, but by virtue of
> its content.[42]

To me, it is important to figure out how race and gender and social
class are related to power and to work toward making sure that power
does not come from these things. That is, I think my general view of

things could be best described as "liberal," in that social justice is a very important if not the most important objective we can achieve. But social justice is a very important objective in much "conservative" thinking, too. The question for me is this: How do we find the most reliable route to the greatest possible social justice? If we want what Mira Nanda calls *substantive* equality or social justice, not merely philosophical or rhetorical equality, then I think critical theory offers little or no help. It only accuses those who hold power of having it illegitimately, but does not mark a path toward obtaining it by legitimate means. It is not very helpful, in my opinion, to insist on the proportional representation of various groups in making decisions regardless of their knowledge, under the assumption that no one, actually, is an expert or has expert knowledge, only the power to "make" knowledge.

But the critical theory view tends to put proportional representation in decision making ahead of anything else. It tends to discount knowledge that might be called "common" in its scientific origins in favor of personal identity (e.g., ethnic origin, gender, social class). Consequently, critical theorists tend to ignore or trivialize scientific understanding as a tool for achieving social justice. Paul Gross made the following observations about science and social justice:

> How did they [liberal politicians since the 18th century] accomplish that [realize the goals of greater social justice]? Why, by identifying true (or nearly true) universals, such as the common origins, physiologies, aspirations, and feelings of all humankind, *and refuting the false ones*, such as the divine right of kings, natural slavery, and the general inferiority of women. Yes, by some scientists, and at various times, science has offered false universals, but those have been overthrown *only by better science*. And without reaching for true, or better-approaching-true commonalities, we would have only the idiosyncrasies of tribes, including those of whatever tribe you or I happen to belong to.[43]

Critical theory, like so much of postmodern thought, seems to confuse having or asserting power with obtaining it through truth. That is, critical theorists seem to assume that power makes truth, not that power resides in truth. It is perhaps understandable how the confusion occurs, as some people have attempted to make truth through assertion of their power, as often has occurred in totalitarian states or religions. Some devotees have believed that truth is thus made. But equating power with truth has not succeeded in the long run, as more reliable or more nearly universal truth is eventually uncovered by careful empirical studies or scientific inquiry.

Critical theorists often make the mistake of assuming that because a truth was found by someone of given ethnicity or gender or social class that it is either sanctified or tainted by the discoverer's personal identity. This is, I think, the very heart of racism, sexism, and classism—to call into question or to excuse from question the truth of a finding or proposition because of the identity of its maker.

There are those who see power as corrupting. "Power corrupts, and absolute power corrupts absolutely." This may be a defensible proposition if one assumes that power makes truth—that the truth is whatever those in power say it is, that it is made up to suit the powerful. It seems hardly defensible, however, if truth gives someone who knows it a certain kind of power. If power both makes truth and corrupts the person who has it, then I am not sure just how one can morally justify the pursuit of power, or even the sharing of it with someone else. After all, who wants to argue for a fair share of corruption? But if truth brings intellectual power, which may or may not lead to political power, then I can understand both the moral and the practical reasons for wanting to pursue truth to obtain intellectual power. Power derived from truth has nothing to fear but hatred of the truth. However, when we assume that truth is made by power, then the truth really doesn't matter, just the power to make it, and the powerful fear both the truth and others who make it up as they wish. The powerful postmodern guru is rightfully paranoid.

I have been called racist and sexist and a believer in scientism (the belief that science yields *all* answers). I have also been said to be *unconsciously* racist and sexist, as my observable actions don't seem to substantiate the charge of conscious racism. I don't think I am any of these, but no proof has been required of my accusers; the truth of it is thought by some people to reside in the power to make the accusation.

Now it is manifestly true that words can be used to mask the truth or promote untruth. However, we can assert this only if we assume that truth exists outside of the words that are used ostensibly to "create" it. Roger Wilkins commented on the U.S. Supreme Court's Dred Scott decision of 1857, which held that black men had from the beginning of the nation been viewed only as property and are, therefore, property.

"Things can be defined that way, but human beings are terribly hard to pin down with mere words, particularly in a society in which words are used to redefine the truth of active existence."[44] It is worth noting that the Dred Scott decision can rightfully be excoriated only if we assume that active existence is more accurately described by some words than by others. To counter Dred Scott, we must assume that the realities of existence are independent of the words used to describe them. Likewise, the truth that all people *should* be equal in their rights before the law—but often, still, are not in fact—can be affirmed only if we assume that reality is not simply made of words. As Wilkins observes further, "In a superficial sense, [George] Mason and [James] Madison had succeeded: the words *slave* and *slavery* did not sully the nation's basic charter. The founding fathers had their fig leaf of decency. But the underlying reason for their reticence—their *shame*—endured.[45]

But, again, some contemporary writers maintain that "truth" is only a construction, and if someone of their color or gender or sexual preference or social class does not construct it, then it is suspect—for them, at least. There are many "truths," these critical theorists claim, and none deserves privilege over another. There is no common truth that applies without reference to personal identity. We are, then, back to this: We can have no common knowledge, no common understanding, as every group constructs a different truth according to its identity.

I wonder whose truth will "win" in any given contest. Depends, I suppose, on whether the people with political power believe that truth is constructed willy-nilly by one's personal identity. We have seen the view that truth is made by power played out in various nations of the world, and the results have not been the enhancement of human kindness or equality or personal freedom. Such views of truth seem inevitably to foster inhumanity; they did, they do, they will.

FULL INCLUSION DEMEANS SPECIAL EDUCATION AND MANY OF THE STUDENTS IT SERVES

I turn from multicultural issues to issues of exceptionality and special education. A major controversy, if not the central issue in special education since about 1985, is whether children with disabilities are best educated in special classes and schools or in regular classes in their neighborhood schools.[46] Some of us have maintained the position that although inclusion in general education in regular schools with support from special educators may work well for *some* students, such inclusion is neither feasible nor effective for *all* students.[47]

Alan Gartner and Dorothy Lipsky have condemned special education's structure as well as its results and advocated the inclusion of students with disabilities in regular classrooms in their neighborhood schools (i.e., in the schools the students with disabilities would attend if they had no disability). In their zeal to reform special education, they have made what I think are some very misleading statements. Among the most misleading is this one: "There is no compelling body of evidence that segregated special education programs have significant benefit for students."[48] Another is this one:

> What is known about the education of students labeled as handicapped? First, separate special education does not work. It does not do so by any measure of assessment — learning, development of self-esteem and social skills or preparation as student, worker, or citizen. Its failure is costly in several currencies — in dollars, in public confidence and, most importantly, in students' lives.[49]

This line of argument is not peculiar to Gartner and Lipsky. A substantial number of special education "reformers" since the 1980s have condemned special education that is not "integrated" or that represents something less than "full inclusion." For example, Maynard Reynolds commented, "There was no evidence in the past and there is no evidence now showing that removing disabled children from the mainstream and putting them into special classes or schools is an advantage for them."[50] I believe that these statements are false, that the information we have does not support them, that they have been used to mislead many. I and my colleague Dan Hallahan have provided some contrary arguments in a book we edited in 1995, *The Illusion of Full Inclusion: A Comprehensive Critique of a Current Special Education Bandwagon*. Other colleagues have provided additional critiques of the statements of Gartner, Lipsky, and others.[51] At the same time, the proponents of the full inclusion of students with disabilities in general education maintain that inclusionary or "integrated" programs are known to "work."

This is an old, sad, frustrating story in which the "anointed" see the heavenly lights of full inclusion and the "benighted" do not, as Ken Kavale and Steve Forness describe the inclusion debate.[52] The details of the arguments on both sides have become, at least to me, wearisome in the extreme. But let me pose this question: What evidence would be credible, or, to use Gartner and Lipsky's term, "compelling," that special classes have not all failed or that so-called segregated placements (special classes or schools) provide benefit to some students? If we consider anecdotal or "qualitative" evidence, then surely we can find some supporting the value of special classes and special schools. If we consider experiments—actual scientific tests in which outcomes for students are measured—then we find evidence to support the value of "segregated" placements for some students with disabilities. To my knowledge, no *experimental* evidence has been published supporting the value of full inclusion for *all* students with disabilities.

In my judgment, the claim that full inclusion in regular educational classes and schools benefits all students, regardless of the nature of their disability, is based on nothing more than wishful thinking, political posturing, and misleading rhetoric. Consider, first, some anecdotal or qualitative evidence of the value of special classes and schools.

Courtland Milloy described a special school—Chelsea School in Silver Spring, Maryland—where students with learning disabilities were said to "thrive." Milloy says of this "segregated" (by disability, not by color) special school: "Nearly half of Chelsea's student population is black—including debate team captains Hughes and Reynolds. Count them among the lucky ones. About 90 percent of the school's graduates go on to college."[53] This doesn't square with the quotation above from Gartner and Lipsky or with others' conclusion that separate special education simply doesn't or can't work.

I made repeated observations in the special classroom of two award-winning special education teachers who taught a special self-contained class for children with emotional and behavioral disorders in Charlottesville, Virginia. Subsequently, I worked with these teachers, Jeanmarie Bantz and Jenn McCullough, to write a description of their class and its perceived value as revealed in interviews done by an independent researcher.[54] Contrary to the views expressed by those who say that "segregated" special classes and schools do not work, we found considerable reason to believe that this class was successful. Here are some summaries of statements made to an interviewer by other school personnel in which the special class was located:

- None of the respondents felt that these students could be served in the general education setting. Seven out of 12 believed that these students would end up in an alternative setting. The other five believed that even if they were placed in a general education setting, they would spend their time out of the classroom or not learning. About half of the respondents stated that the learning that occurs in the self-contained class could not be replicated in another setting.
- The respondents stated that the self-contained environment allowed the teachers to provide a highly structured, individualized education that addressed the unusual needs of the students. Additionally, they believed that the self-contained setting provided an internal support system for the teachers and staff.
- Most respondents felt that without this placement these students would not be able to learn, nor would their specific emotional/behavioral needs be met. Further, the amount of time, energy, and resources these students demanded would place an excessive burden on the general educator and ultimately affect the education of students in the mainstream classes.
- The respondents overwhelmingly identified consistency, structure, individualization, and strong educational practices (both academic and behavioral) as the backbone of this successful class. In addition, they noted that the unique dynamic of the teachers and paraprofessionals enhanced the effectiveness of these characteristics.

In 1996, one of my students, Betty Hallenbeck, and I edited a special issue of the *Canadian Journal of Special Education* on the value of special placements for students with emotional or behavioral disorders.[55] Our contributors included authors from Australia, England, and the United States. All provided descriptions of special classes or special schools in which students with disabilities *did* thrive, *did* improve academically and socially—*did*, in fact, the opposite of what proponents of full inclusion claim can't be achieved in a "segregated" program. The English authors provided a particularly vivid and poignant description of how a special school "worked" for a girl who could not cope with a large school, and it calls into further question Gartner and Lipsky's statements that there is no compelling evidence that separate or "segregated" programs "work" or provide benefits to children:

> Pauline entered the school bedraggled. Tall and slender, she hobbled in more like a wounded crow than a graceful swan. This was Pauline's first day in a special school for students with emotional and behavioral difficulties. She was now 14 years old.
>
> In the small special school of 40 students, Pauline found peace. She learned to trust again—first adults, and then fellow students. She became an active participant in classroom learning experiences, no longer the peripheral onlooker. Her capacity to care for others became clear, and she befriended many isolated individuals.[56]

What I have described so far is merely anecdote, not evidence from experimental studies. Suppose we were to examine all of the empirical evidence, including experimental studies? Several detailed reviews of research and policy find no basis for the claims of those who promote the notion of full inclusion.[57] Being "pulled out" into special classes has, in fact, been shown to be very helpful academically and socially for some children in experimental studies.[58] As Doug and Lynn Fuchs have summarized, special classes *can* work, and their research demonstrates that they can produce better results than placement in general education. Moreover, the so-called research on full inclusion is fraught with methodological weaknesses so great as to make it useless.[59]

But, for now, set the matter of research aside and consider the argument that many full inclusion proponents expect to be taken seriously—that special education has many effective strategies and techniques for working with students who have disabilities, but the reason special education is both morally wrong and ineffective is that these methods are used in the wrong place. The idea that what is wrong with special education is *where* it is practiced seems to me a laughable notion, one that is furiously illogical as well as contrary to the best research information we can muster. It also is curiously at odds with federal law—at least federal law at the beginning of the twenty-first century.[60]

Yet, as some have put it, "'place' is the issue," and proponents of full inclusion seem to agree:

There is nothing pervasively wrong with special education. What is being questioned is not the interventions and knowledge that have been acquired through special education training and research. Rather, what is being challenged is the location where these supports are being provided to students with disabilities.

Special education needs to be reconceptualized as a support to the regular education classroom, rather than as "another place to go." Recent research suggests that what is wrong about special education is the stigma and isolation that result from being removed from the regular education class for so long. We now have the effective strategies to bring help to the student rather than removing the student from the enriching setting of the regular education class.[61]

So, if we just change the place at which special education is offered it will be effective? We have the means for teaching all students with disabilities in regular education classes? I can hardly believe that people suggest something so irrational and contradictory of the best studies we have. But they do, and in the process many use the ploy "recent research suggests" or a similar phrase without citations (or with citations of sources that would not pass most referees as reliable research evidence). E. D. Hirsch, Jr. describes this ploy—saying that research suggests something that it does not—as a hallmark of the romantic, progressive education tradition.[62] It is a trick frequently used in the inclusion literature.

Consider just one such instance. Alan Gartner and Dorothy Lipsky, as well as other proponents of full inclusion, use a "meta-analysis" (a now frequently employed statistical summary of many experimental studies) of Conrad Carlberg and Ken Kavale to support their contention that special education offers "little or no benefit for students of all levels of severity placed in special education settings."[63] True, if all children are lumped together, then the data analyzed by Carlberg and Kavale do show a small difference in favor of placement in regular classes. However, the data also show a large, distinct advantage for special classes for students with learning disabilities (LD) or behavior/emotional disorders (BD/ED). This finding—much better outcomes with special classes for certain types of children—is omitted from statements of full inclusionists about research. Likewise, the results of other meta-analyses showing better outcomes for special classes have been ignored by proponents of full inclusion.[64]

But data contrary to the full-inclusion ideology is simply ignored. In fact, full-inclusion rhetoric has become so dominant in the literature and such a powerful political force that I have made up hypothetical "news releases" about the death of special education and how the event might be described. Here's a sample:

Special Education's Conversion Experience:
All Things New and Wonderful

WASHINGTON, D.C.: A former special education teacher says he has found a new faith and, because of it, he has become a new person. He describes how special education recently went through a total transformation. "It has been born again, converted from a place to a service," as he describes it. The old has passed away, and all things are new, he says. According to his account, special education found redemption by rejecting its old self, which included the evil practices of identifying, labeling, and pigeon-holing children in what was described as a "continuum of alternative placements." What he calls the "good news of inclusion" has washed it clean of its past wrong practices.

"I'm not even tempted to think of removing a child from general education anymore," said another teacher. "Actually, we don't talk about special education or general education anymore. We just talk about education, period, and teaching and learning, and it frees us from all our old habits. For me, alternative placements might as well not even exist, and I'm just so happy to be included in what we used to call general education and to have all of our students in the same classrooms that I want to tell everybody I meet how wonderful it is. All of the old barriers and distinctions are down, and all of us just work on the same things in the same place together, because there's really no difference among kids or teachers or classes or schools as far as we're concerned."

Today, a new organization was formed to replace the old—some say tainted—special education advocacy groups. Promise Keepers to Kids (PKK) is described in its literature as "a professional collaborative upholding the promise to educate all kids together, no exceptions."

"We don't label kids or teachers, we just teach them," said a PKK official. Apparently without thinking of the irony of her statement, she went on, "Unlike the special educators of the past, we aren't labelers. We are simply teachers who keep our word to educate every child."

Said another, "It feels so good to know we're doing the right thing, even if the so-called evidence says it isn't working. We don't care that much about test scores and other questionable measures of outcome or progress, because we know what real progress is. *Real* progress is doing the right thing, not separating someone out because they're different."

A member of Congress who has been active in special education's conversion added, "Under the old system, half of the students in our schools were below average, and that's intolerable. It doesn't have to be that way if we're serious about reforming our thinking and doing what's right."[65]

Perhaps many readers will think that I have written hyperbole. But it might be good to keep in mind that Robert Worth, writing in *The Washington Monthly* in June 1999 described special education as a scandal that "wastes money and hurts the poor" and as the "road to hell." This and other full-inclusion rhetoric that describes special education as a failed enterprise is not substantially different in tone from the rhetoric that led, eventually, to the demise of Aid to Families of Dependent Children.[66] And one might be advised to know that in a film portraying the wonders of full inclusion an educator makes this statement about inclusion: "It does work, and that's great. But even if it didn't work it would still be the thing to do, because it's right."[67]

Finally, some researchers, having studied what happens in "inclusion" (whether described as "full" or not), have concluded that special education is no longer what it was, not because it is too "separate" but because it has lost its focus on instruction. As researcher and teacher educator Naomi Zigmond put it:

> Special education was once worth receiving; it could be again. In many schools, it is not now. Here is where practitioners, policymakers, advocates, and researchers in special education need to focus—on defining the nature of special education and the competencies of the teachers who will deliver it.[68]

Instruction, not place, should be the central issue in special education. Place is important because it constrains what instruction can be offered, but it is a secondary consideration by logic and by law.

Deformed Education: My husband and I were delighted when our mentally retarded daughter learned to tie her shoes, tell time, and read—all previously impossible skills for Annie that she mastered in a self-contained special education class. We were more than a little nervous when the small school system Annie attends decided to go to a full-inclusion program when she entered middle school, but the teachers were very reassuring. Annie's homeroom teacher said, "We believe that all children can learn," and he seemed so confident that he wouldn't have to "lower the educational standards for Annie," that my husband and I thought that it just might work.

By the end of September, Annie's backpack was coming home from school with only the remains of her lunch. There were no books, no homework assignments, and no papers or work from her classes. When we had a conference with her teacher, he seemed defensive, said that the books were too hard for Annie, and that he was an advocate for a flexible curriculum, and that Annie was "improving." However, he couldn't show us how much improvement she had made or in what areas. He finally said that it was important for children with disabilities to remain in the class with their nondisabled peers for social reasons. The other kids would provide positive role models for Annie.

But even though no one in Annie's class has ever been mean to her or bullied her, she doesn't seem to have any friends in the regular class and complains about being lonely. My previously happy child who loved school weeps every morning and begs not to go to school. Not only that. She isn't learning anything either, except the implication that she's dumb and odd. Why would anyone want to sell out a child like this?

TEST BASHING IS PART OF THE "PROGRESSIVE" RHETORIC THAT THWARTS PROGRESS

Standardized testing has become the Great Satan of education in the minds of some, a "monster" that must be put out of schools. For example, Alfie Kohn condemns standardized testing—not just certain tests or the misuse of tests, but standardized tests as tools—and calls for civil disobedience to eject them from public schools altogether. His suggestions for fighting standardized tests include not only civil disobedience by educators but printing bumper stickers with slogans such as "Standardized Testing Is Dumbing Down Our Schools."[69] Like most slogans in education, this one, too, in my opinion, is vapid. Standardized testing can, indeed, be stupid or be used stupidly, but I doubt very seriously that it is the ogre responsible for dumbing down our schools. And rejecting standardized tests can only deprive parents, teachers, school officials, and governing bodies of an important tool in monitoring students' performance.

Amy Biancolli said that she has come to one firm conclusion about schools and testing: "Widespread standardized testing is an evil that the American educational system should avoid at all costs."[70] Apparently, she feels certain that standardized testing will make students concerned only about what's on the tests and suppress their inquisitiveness about everything else. She notes that in the United Kingdom—specifically, in Scotland—where standardized testing is routine, students seem to be less ready to ask questions. So, the conclusion is that no worse calamity could befall American education than "widespread" standardized testing? News flash: Standardized testing is already widespread in the United States, although it is also haphazard.

Now it is undoubtedly true that some standardized tests are poorly made or misused, as are many teacher-made tests and other forms of "alternative assessment" such as portfolios. In fact, *any* form of assessment of which I'm aware can be (and has been) crudely made and badly used. So, why the seething hostility toward "standardized" testing? The answer is not simple, but I think much of the outrage over standardized tests is prompted by fears of comparisons of various individuals and groups who take the tests. Furthermore, educational theory has become, to some, a matter of religious conviction in which evidence doesn't matter. Too many educators—and, as well, too many people who are not educators—embrace "progressive" theory that relies on pet phrases and terminology for its defense of educational "quality" that tests are said not to be able to measure. These "reformers," who actually hold educational theories originated nearly a century ago, call for "real learning" that standardized tests are assumed not to be able to assess. For example, Alfie Kohn regularly uses the jargon or patois that E. D. Hirsch, Jr. has identified as part of traditional education's "Thoughtworld."

> Most of us have pet projects, favorite causes, practices and policies about which we care deeply. These include such issues as multiple intelligences, multi-age classrooms, or multicultural curricula; cooperative learning, character education, or the creating of caring communities in

schools; teaching for understanding, developmentally appropriate practice, or alternative assessment; the integration of writing or the arts into
the curriculum; project- or problem-based learning, discovery-oriented
science, or whole language; giving teachers or students more autonomy,
or working with administrators to help them make lasting change. But
every one of these priorities is gravely threatened by the top-down,
heavy-handed, corporate-style, standardized version of school reform
that is driven by testing. That's why all of us, despite our disparate agen-
das, need to make common cause. We must make the fight against standardized tests our top priority because, until we have chased this monster
from the schools, it will be difficult, perhaps even impossible, to pursue
the kinds of reforms that can truly improve teaching and learning.[71]

Kohn and others who take a position against standardized tests also
often raise the specter of uniformity across schools and states, which
they see as being overly rigid. Even such politically conservative opinion writers as George F. Will suggest that America probably should not
have a standard examination for high school graduation or a national
curriculum.[72] Perhaps it is inevitable that people of nearly all political
persuasions will figure out some day that math and reading and much
of what we need to know about science and geography and the United
States government is not really different in different places. People
might figure out that uniformity of expectations and curricula and testing might actually be beneficial in a society in which children move often to different localities or states. But it may take decades for people
to arrive at these conclusions.

All the more reason, in my opinion, that standardized testing has a
valuable role to play in measuring students' progress. Of course, as I've
already suggested, one argument against standardized testing is that
comparisons of schools and states—perhaps of individuals as well—
are insidious. No one is to be "left behind." And, as I pointed out in
chapter 4, any measure of progress—but most obviously a standardized
measure—produces a distribution that by nature finds some to have
performed better than others; for any measure that is not simply
"yes/no" or "pass/fail" or in some other way a truncated range, there is
a bottom fourth (first quartile) as well as a top fourth (or any other percentage of the sample one wishes to examine). So alternative assessment procedures that obscure if not obviate comparisons seem, to

some, a godsend. Such alternative measures can help maintain the fiction that all students are excellent or give the misimpression that nobody is actually behind. The "progressive" idea seems to be that an "authentic" assessment will show that everyone and everything is cool—nobody can fail.

For some purposes there is no good substitute for the test that is standardized and can be failed—normed on a large sample of test takers by which we want to judge the achievement of individuals and groups. It is easier to shoot the messenger that brings unwelcome tidings than to confront the differences among individuals and groups that tests may reveal, as E. D. Hirsch, Jr., has suggested. And it is easy to overlook the advantages of standardized tests while describing the tests themselves as monsters to be driven from our schools.

Some scholars have pointed out that the current popularity of standardized testing is really based on public concern about standards or accountability. The standards of performance that a state or school adopts are nearly always linked to a standardized test, and for this reason some writers refer to "test-linked standards."[73] We do, I think, want to know how a student's performance compares to others' and to be able to compare average student performances across schools and states. It is only through such comparisons that we can address some problems, including the problem of how well we're doing and the problem of equity. Nevertheless, some people seem to be in favor of accountability—but without knowing how students are doing on any standardized test. To them, standardized tests seem to be a way of holding people responsible for teaching a standard curriculum, which they find anathema.

Mary Anne Raywid has voiced a familiar complaint: "One problem with the vast majority of tests, of course, is that they are curriculum-based."[74] Well, it seems to me that we do want curriculum and testing to be aligned. That is, we want to teach what students are going to be tested on and to test what we teach. In fact, curriculum-based assessment is what some of us are after. It makes no sense to test students on things they haven't been taught, and it makes good sense to base assessment on the curriculum.[75] The curriculum could determine what is tested; the tests could determine what is taught. But, either way, it only makes sense for the two to be in sync. In fact, one is not likely to be developed without the other: Testing and curriculum *should* influence each other. To me, it makes little difference which comes first, as long as what is taught is really important stuff for students to learn. I suppose the question actually becomes what we think is important for students to know. Another way of putting it is to ask whether we think there is a common core of knowledge that most students should learn. I think there is this common content that most students should be expected to master, and I see no reason not to check up on how well we're doing it—to test it with a standardized instrument.

Others, particularly E. D. Hirsch, Jr., have described eloquently how having a core body of knowledge or core curriculum increases equity among groups of students differing in ethnicity or social privilege—or, at least, opportunities for achieving such equity.[76] Standardized tests were invented, at least in part, to be fairer to students without social privileges—to focus on a student's performance rather than his or her genetic or social heritage that brought privilege in spite of what a student could do. Standardized tests *can* be used to increase equity if they measure important knowledge and if all schools and individuals are provided the resources needed to allow them to attain a reasonable standard. Standardized tests *can* be used to improve the clarity of schools' objectives and focus on instruction. Standardized tests *can* be used to allocate resources more efficiently, and they *can* be used as a common metric—a common, readily understood language of measurement—for communicating educational outcomes.[77]

Please notice that I have *not* suggested that *all* students should learn exactly the same thing or be taught exactly the same way. I suggested that *most* students would benefit from a standard, core curriculum. Mary Anne Raywid gets *this* right: Some students are not going to be successful in the regular, general curriculum that may be right for the majority of students. I think it's essential that we provide alternatives for those students who cannot reasonably be expected to learn the core curriculum and be tested on it, as I suggested in chapter 4 and elsewhere in this book. But, of course, here's the problem: Who should decide, and on what basis, that an alternative to the core curriculum is a better choice for a given student? Here are some givens, in my opinion: First, the decision should not be based on the student's ethnicity, gender, or social privilege. Second, the decision should be based on the student's estimated ability to learn the core curriculum. Third, there are no perfect decision makers. Any decision making scheme we can devise will produce some false positives (students thought to be able to learn the core curriculum but who cannot) and false negatives (students who are thought to be unable to learn the core curriculum but who can). The goals should be to make as few errors of judgment as possible in either direction and to correct errors as soon as they can be detected by changing the student's curriculum. But don't miss this given: Assuming that any core curriculum should be studied and mastered by *all* students simply guarantees a very large number of false positives. For a substantial number of kids and a significant percentage of the student population, it's not in the cards. The majority of the students I'm referring to have disabilities of one kind or another, although some of those with disabilities can and should learn the standard—general, core—curriculum.

Standardized tests, like every other human invention and some natural phenomena, will be abused. That is a given. We are well advised to recognize abuses without proscribing the use of the instruments that are abused, to use instruments responsibly. Obscuring or hiding differences on good standardized measures merely locks in place the social inequities that anti-testing forces say they oppose. We cannot address inequities that we will not admit are real and important. George F. Will has reiterated the observation that an elite will rule any society.[78] Our only choice is *which* elite will rule. Personally, I prefer a ruling elite defined by knowledge and competence in the core of what our society considers important, not an elite defined by money or genetic heritage. The SAT (Scholastic Aptitude Test) was invented to prevent the economically elite from having unfair advantage in college admissions and making sure that elite colleges are open to students who can perform well academically but are at an economic or social disadvantage. I think we have yet to invent a better or more reliable way than standardized testing of finding out fairly what someone knows. The fact that some test questions are bad and that some people use scores unwisely should not be used as an excuse for bashing the very notion of standardized testing.

Every educational policy has a downside as far as I know, standardized testing and test-linked standards included. It is possible to narrow a curriculum unreasonably in efforts to prepare students for tests, and this is true for standardized tests or any other kind of assessment. It is possible to define good teaching simply as that which maximizes test performance—standardized tests or any other type of assessment. It is possible to use standardized test performance to devalue those who do not score well on them, but the same is true for any type of assessment—kids can be devalued because their performance is judged to be inferior, not up to expectations, not acceptable. And standardized tests or any other type of assessment can preclude certain opportunities for students who fail to meet expectations. Any kind of assessment of performance—standardized test or any alternative—can create anxiety in the person being assessed. Alternatives to standardized tests, such as "portfolio assessment" in which a student's work is judged in some way, have their downsides, too. They are cumbersome, extremely time-consuming, and present problems of reliability, validity, and comparisons across individuals and groups.

If our schools are being "dumbed down," I doubt that it's because of standardized tests. Much more likely, I think, is that the dumbing down is a result of fumbled thinking about issues in education, including mindless rhetoric that misleads people's thinking about the tools we use to assess educational progress. And make no mistake about this, either: *Standardized testing cannot take the place of the type of frequent teacher monitoring or assessment that is an essential part of good teaching.* Imagining that standardized testing provides sufficient early warning for failing students is similar to imagining that reporting tornado damage provides sufficient early warning of severe weather. Standardized tests can assess instructional success or failure long after the fact, and for that they're important, but they can't be relied upon to guide the instruction of individuals.

And what is the predictable consequence of demonizing standardized testing, the appeal to drive this "monster" from our schools? For all the misuses and abuses of standardized tests, such as evaluating teachers and schools based simply on such test scores, the important and useful information such tests can offer will be suppressed. Marc Fisher put it succinctly:

> One day, we will look up and see how we have crushed our schools, and tests—which when used properly have lifted the educational fortunes of many poor and middle-income children—will end up the culprit, and the

pendulum will swing to the other extreme, zipping right past the happy medium.[79]

Too bad the Alfie Kohns of the world make a living trashing useful tools because some people use them poorly. It's a good thing we don't trash people because they think or write poorly.

Some who write about education policy see the advantages of good standardized testing but suggest "criterion-referenced" tests that set "benchmarks" of performance.[80] Sometimes, these individuals even suggest that an advantage of such criterion-referencing is that the test does not rely on norms, that students' performance is simply compared to the criterion, not to other students' performance. This is quite a misleading interpretation of "criterion" or "benchmark." A reasonable person would, I think, have to ask something like this: How'd we come up with this criterion or benchmark?

A criterion or benchmark can be pulled out of the air or be based simply on someone's opinion of what a student should know at a particular age. But "pull-them-out-of-the-air" criteria are ultimately seen as arrogant and unworkable. Eventually, people come to their senses and inquire about what most students know at a given age. The criterion is then set based on a comparison to what most students can do. Otherwise, it is unreasonably high or unreasonably low.

People I think should know better than to refer to criterion-referenced tests as not comparative or non-normative. They're right in only a very restricted way—a student is judged to perform acceptably or not based only on comparison to the criterion or benchmark of performance. However, a reasonable person has to ask where the criterion comes from, and this inevitably takes us back to a normative sample or normative comparison. Witness the difficulties various states or school districts have in deciding on a "cut point" or benchmark on a standards of learning test. If the criterion is something that too few students can reach, then it's abandoned as unreasonable (and for good reason). If the criterion is something just about every student reaches without difficulty, then it's abandoned as too low (and with good reason). A criterion-referenced test does force the issue of manufacturing failure (just how much is enough, desirable, or too much?). But here's something I think you can go to the bank on: If a criterion is set that results in what is deemed a reasonable rate of failure and a few years down the road we find that nearly every child is passing it, we will see efforts to raise the bar because the benchmark is now judged too low.

Criterion-referencing might be a good idea. That is, it might be a good idea to set a standard that we think merits promotion to the next grade or graduation or the need for remediation. But nobody should be fooled into thinking that the criterion isn't based on some comparison to a normative group. And nobody should be fooled into thinking that every last student will reach whatever criterion is set. Some students will fail to reach the benchmark unless it is set at zero, and some will find reaching the benchmark ridiculously easy. That's one of the reasons we need special education.

MOST TEACHERS ARE POORLY
TRAINED, BUT SOME ARE TRAINED WELL

"But if you could choose to have your child taught either by Socrates or by a freshly minted holder of a degree in education, full of the latest pedagogic theories and techniques? Socrates, please."[81]

This quotation of George F. Will hides his keen intellect and writing skill behind a grotesque facade. I—and, I suppose, many others as well—wonder why he squandered his powers on the construction of such an ugly misrepresentation of realities and choices. Some of the other points Will makes in the essay from which this quotation is drawn are defensible. He argues reasonably that a few federal dollars (i.e., a very small fraction of the cost of schooling) are not likely to bring much change in public education. He rightly notes that teaching to the test is not too bad an idea if you have a good test, as preparing students to perform (i.e., demonstrate the competence reflected by a good test) is what we expect of education.

But the quotation above, ending one of Will's columns, does not represent good thinking, in my opinion. Coming up with similarly silly questions and answers isn't hard. Try this: If you could choose to have your newspaper stories written either by Mark Twain or by a freshly minted holder of a degree in journalism, full of the latest theories and techniques of literary criticism and reportage? Mark Twain, please. Such comparisons between a glittering figure in his or her field and the average performer are, I think, not terribly logical. And broadsides,

whether aimed at schools of education or the press or most other enti-
ties, tend to sink a lot of good performers along with the bad. I do think
that many schools of education are near worthless and many of the currently popular ideas about education—which have been popular for
nearly a century, as E. D. Hirsch, Jr. and Diane Ravitch point out—are
silly. But there are important exceptions. The exceptions are an important part of the reality, too. They are part of what Stephen Jay Gould
refers to as the "full house" that must be considered.

Will's license with reality is not really the issue, as the context of his
statement is a "thought experiment" in which purely hypothetical con-
trasts or choices are made. Such "experiments" are a well-worn and
useful part of the art of the stupid as well as of the brilliant. But I suppose it is fair to assume that the literary device Will used in his column
was intended to make a point, not merely to entertain. No one, I think,
would be so silly as to suggest that a person might actually have the
choice of Socrates himself as a teacher of his child. So, what is the
meaning of Will's remark? What is his point? I suppose there are several alternatives, none of which I find to be made convincingly by his
poke at schools of education and the latest pedagogical techniques
without distinguishing the good from the bad.

Perhaps Will meant to suggest that Socrates had some extraordinarily admirable characteristics as an educator and that the teacher of his
child should be like the ancient Greek in significant ways. Socrates' apparent wisdom and extraordinary skills in the use of language and questioning are among his considerable assets as an educator. Perhaps these
characteristics enamor Will of the idea of a Socrates-like character
teaching his child. However, I suppose many people might not like the
idea of their child being taught by someone who leaders in their society believe needs to die, as was true of Socrates. Many people, if not
most, I think, don't want their kids taught by martyrs, regardless of the
martyr's intellect. But the nature of Socrates' death is, perhaps, beside
the point.

Let us return to Will's presentation of a 1934 "thought experiment"
suggested by someone else. This unnamed (by Will) "critic of American schooling" asked whether an ill person, if given the miraculous
choice, would rather be treated by Hippocrates or by a young graduate
of the Johns Hopkins University School of Medicine.[82] The choice

most people would make, Will surmises (and I concur), would be the recent medical school graduate, who could be expected to have a much better grasp of scientifically based treatments and resources than did Hippocrates. The recent medical school graduate would have the advantages of modern information, technologies, and techniques, which overshadow the sagacity of the ancient Greek physician. In the "thought experiment" involving Hippocrates and the recent medical school graduate, Will seems to be comparing wisdom to practical knowledge (two virtues that are not mutually exclusive) or comparing primitive understanding to contemporary scientific knowledge. Either way, Will seems to be casting aspersions on all of today's education graduates. He seems to compare contemporary knowledge of education and educational practices unfavorably to ancient practical knowledge or wisdom in matters of teaching.

I suppose Will might have been suggesting that someone with Socrates-like wisdom would be preferable to a recent teacher education graduate. Depending on just how close to having the wisdom of Socrates the teacher would have to come, Will would be excluding both himself and very nearly all of the rest of us as well. Never mind. Let us assume that Will meant to say that he would prefer to have his child taught by a very smart person, such that a reasonable number of living human beings could qualify. Fine, but the idea raises several questions: Does the smart person have to know anything about teaching, other than the Socratic method? Are no recent graduates of teacher education programs smart enough to teach Will's child? What are the latest pedagogic theories and techniques? Might the pedagogic theories and techniques that one acquires in *some* education schools help a smart person teach better? (I suppose one could ask about what is taught in *some* medical schools, too.) And so on.

Will says, "Socrates, please," as if a certain generalization is safe: Smart person using intuition beats education school graduate nearly every time. Not safe at all. The Socrates choice reveals not merely arrogance but ignorance of the demands of teaching and the availability of scientific information to guide it, at least on the more basic, foundational skills level. Are we to assume that being smart about one thing— physics or English literature, for example—means that the person will be smart about something else, such as teaching? Not if research on teaching and learning like that reviewed by E. D. Hirsch, Jr., and Lester Mann is to be believed.[83] Hirsch strongly and repeatedly makes the case that proficiency in one area of learning does not readily generalize or transfer to another. Hirsch notes that a person with formal training in logic, for example, does not necessarily think logically about all problems he or she encounters in everyday life. Mann notes that for nearly every teaching strategy, even those that fail miserably overall, there is *some* transfer of training, though not enough to warrant confidence that the transfer will be significant. Furthermore, "Socrates, please" seems to ignore the considerable difference between the students of Socrates—almost assuredly a highly privileged and select group of students—and those served by today's American schools, which include those of every description, including some with very limited cognitive abilities. Would it not be wise to consider the probable differences in the teachers' classes?

A fair question for me is what I would prefer and why. Were I to make the choice for any child I cared about, I'd say, "It all depends on the ed school grad and what's to be taught to whom." In my experience—maybe because I'm a faculty member at a fine university with a teacher training program that recruits a lot of very intelligent students—a lot of smart people go into education. Our undergraduate Curry School of Education students at the University of Virginia compare favorably on test scores to those in the College of Arts and Sciences—actually, they come out of the College of Arts and Sciences. Still, would I really like to have a stupid person teaching a child? No, thank you, not really. But there are, in my opinion, people of very modest intellect doing lots of things besides teaching or professing in fields other than education. And some of these are doing quite well in their professions. Moreover, some of them are columnists. (No, I do not believe George F. Will is one of the not-so-bright ones; he is very smart, but I sometimes disagree with him.)

Then there's the matter of what is to be taught, and to whom. What is to be taught is a matter of considerable importance insofar as a teacher's training and experience are concerned. Who is being taught is of no small consequence either. Socratic questioning might be the best way of teaching essay-writing to an adult whose wit is comparable to George F. Will's, but it takes no great wit to see that it is a decidedly inferior way of teaching basic reading or math skills to someone of about normal intelligence, regardless of their chronological age.

Some of the theory and practice of education are testable and intellectually demanding, not fluff. Siegfried Engelmann, Doug Carnine, E. D. Hirsch, Jr., and Barak Rosenshine, for example—as well as many others who have pioneered and researched effective instructional practices—have described not only *how* to teach effectively but *why* effective practices work.[84] Furthermore, skill in teaching is *not*, contrary to the assumption of many, merely intuitive. To the extent that teachers simply follow their intuition instead of carefully tested, scientific practices, they typically fail. When medicine begins to rely more on the intuition of its practitioners than scientific data, it, too, fails miserably.[85] Human intuition is often misleading in teaching, just as it is in other applied sciences.

Now, it is manifestly true that too many students in education schools are not as intellectually able as we would like. But that is not peculiar to schools of education; it is true in the programs of higher education in every discipline, and it is a greater problem in some colleges and universities than in others. It is also without doubt that too many students are taught theories and practices that are worthless or worse, as E. D. Hirsch, Jr. has explained. But, again, this problem is not peculiar to education schools.

I am unhappy that so many of my professional colleagues in education teach "progressive" ideas about education and give an enthusiastic welcome to postmodernism. Again, my unhappiness is shared by many of my colleagues in colleges of arts and sciences, some of whom see their discipline turned to rubbish by intellectual dereliction. Programs in the arts and humanities as well as in many professional schools present laughable ideas and courses. Education schools need to clean up their act; so do other schools in our universities. The preparation of teachers is not merely a function of schools of education, as prospective teachers receive a substantial measure of their education in other schools or departments in institutions of higher education.

I suppose that George Will and many who agree with him about education may entertain the notion that college and university students in the arts and humanities (as well as their professors, presumably) tend to have a mental sharpness, a level of intelligence and practical knowledge of things, that will make them acceptable teachers — better teachers, at least, than those graduating from education schools. Well, what kind of mental sharpness is evidenced by the postmodern intellectual mush that Will has described so piquantly?[86] It might be worth remembering that the intellectual foppery bemoaned not only by Will but also by many others has its origins in the arts and humanities.[87] It has found a ready home in American universities' colleges of arts and sciences and only comparatively recently has begun flooding into schools of education. It is a most unwelcome flood to many of us in education. And it is now the unhappy task of many of us to disabuse these students of postmodernism when they come to us from colleges of arts and sciences for their preparation as teachers. Those who believe that any college graduate — but especially a graduate in arts and sciences — reliably makes a good teacher might want to think again about the warm reception and nauseating "refinements" that the blatant nonsense called postmodernism has had in higher education *outside* colleges of education.

So, what is the kindest thing we can say about the end of George F. Will's commentary, with reference to its value in guiding careful, logical, informed thinking about education? This, I think: It's unhelpful in most respects. But I'll grant you this: pick at random a graduate of an education school, and the chances are high you'll get someone poorly trained. But, come to think of it, if I were ill and by some magic had the choice, I just might prefer treatment by Hippocrates to treatment by *some* contemporary medical school graduates. Depends on the illness and the graduate. Richard Cohen put it succinctly: "the only true answer to life's questions is, always and without fail, it depends."[88] I think the smart person doesn't pick at random a mechanic or doctor or anyone else who provides a technical service. Ignorance and stupidity do not recognize the boundaries of professions. Neither do insight and competence.

NOTES

1. Kauffman & Brigham (1999, p. 6).
2. See Kauffman & Brigham (2000b).
3. Kauffman & Brigham (1999, p. 6).
4. Conquest (2000); see also Kernan (1999).

5. Schmoke (2001, p. A15).
6. Zhan (2001, p. B4).
7. Terkel (2001), p. 135.
8. See Eltahawy (2001).
9. Patterson (1993, p. C2).
10. Kauffman & Burbach (1997).
11. See Hammersley (1998), Kernan (1999).
12. See Reynolds (2001).
13. Hallahan & Kauffman (2000).
14. Shermer (1997, p. 248).
15. Artiles & Trent (1997, p. 277).
16. Wilkins (2001, p. 126).
17. Kauffman (1997, p. 131).
18. Wilson (1999, p. 21).
19. Raspberry (2001c, p. A19).
20. See Associated Press (2000).
21. Wilkins (2001).
22. Moore (2001, p. A14).
23. Snyder (2001, p. A1).
24. Eltahawy (2001).
25. Goodman (2001b, p. 25); see also King (2001b).
26. Sleeter (2001, p. 95).
27. Ewing (2001, p. 16).
28. See Kauffman (1999c).
29. Britt (2000, p. B5).
30. Kauffman (1993); see also Kernan (1999).
31. Koertge (1996, p. 413).
32. Ryan (1992, p. 21).
33. Ryan (1992, p. 21).
34. Nanda (1998, pp. 289, 299, italics in original).
35. Scheurich & Young (1997, pp. 8–9); see also Scheurich & Young (1998).
36. Scheurich & Young (1998, p. 31, italics in original).
37. Wilkins (2001, p. 109).
38. Koertge (1998, p. 256).
39. Schwandt (1997, p. 22).
40. Imber (1997, p. 15).
41. Patton (1998, p. 27).
42. Sokal & Bricmont (1998, p. 209).
43. Gross (1998, p. 48, italics in original).

44. Wilkins (2001, p. 51).

45. Wilkins (2001, p. 63, italics in original).

46. See Crockett & Kauffman (1999, 2001).

47. E.g., Brigham & Kauffman (1998), Kauffman (1995), Kauffman & Hallahan (1995, 1997), Kauffman, Lloyd, Baker, & Riedel (1995).

48. Gartner & Lipsky (1987, p. 375).

49. Gartner & Lipsky (1989, p. 26).

50. Reynolds (1989, p. 8).

51. E.g., Kavale & Forness (2000), MacMillan, Gresham, & Forness (1996).

52. Kavale & Forness (2000).

53. Milloy (2001, p. B1).

54. Kauffman, Bantz, & McCullough (2002).

55. Hallenbeck & Kauffman (1996).

56. Carpenter & Bovair (1996, pp. 6–8); see also Kauffman (2001, pp. 465–466).

57. E.g., Forness (2001), Kavale & Forness (2000), MacMillan, Gresham, & Forness (1996), Semmel, Gerber, & MacMillan (1994), Singer (1988); see also Kauffman & Hallahan (1995, 1997), Huefner (2000), Yell (1998).

58. E.g., Marston (1987–88), O'Connor, Stuck, & Wyne (1979); see also DuPaul & Eckert (1997).

59. Fuchs & Fuchs (1995), Fuchs, Fuchs, & Fernstrom (1993); see also Fuchs & Fuchs (1988).

60. Bateman & Linden (1998), Crockett & Kauffman (1999, 2001), Dupre (1997), Huefner (2000), Yell (1998).

61. Blackman (1992, p. 29, italics in original).

62. Hirsch (1996).

63. Gartner & Lipsky (1989, p. 13); see meta-analysis of Carlberg & Kavale (1980).

64. E.g., Stage & Quiroz (1997); see also DuPaul & Eckert (1997), Forness (2001).

65. Kauffman (1999–2000, pp. 67–68).

66. See Edelman (2001).

67. Goodwin & Wurzburg (1987).

68. Zigmond (1997, p. 389).

69. Kohn (2001, p. 353).

70. Biancolli (2001, A23).

71. Kohn (2001, p. 350).

72. E.g., Will (2001d).

73. Brigham, Tochterman, & Brigham (2000), Hess & Brigham (2000).

74. Raywid (2001, p. 584).

75. E.g., Choate, Enright, Miller, Poteet, & Rakes (1995), Deno (1985), Fuchs, Deno, & Mirkin (1984), Fuchs, Fuchs, & Fernstrom (1993), Howell, Fox, & Morehead (1993).

76. Hirsch (1987, 1996).

77. Hess & Brigham (2000).

78. Will (2001d).

79. Fisher (2001b, p. B1).

80. E.g., Rotherham (2001).

81. Will (2001b, p. A21).

82. The critic was William C. Bagley, whose case against progressive education is discussed at length by Diane Ravitch in *Left Back* (2000).

83. Hirsch (1996), Mann (1979).

84. E.g., Engelmann (1997), Engelmann & Carnine (1982), Hirsch (1996), Rosenshine (1997).

85. Satel (2001).

86. E.g., Will (2001c).

87. See Kernan (1999), Koertge (1998), Sasso (2001), Shattuck (1999), Sokal & Bricmont (1998).

88. Cohen (2001c, p. A31).

CHAPTER 6

The Unintelligible

"To this end, I believe that our responsibility is to keep educational research in play, increasingly unintelligible to itself, in order to produce different knowledge and produce knowledge differently as we work for social justice in the human sciences."

—Elizabeth St. Pierre, educational researcher

UNINTELLIGIBLE STATEMENTS CAN BE AMUSING

If religion is the last refuge of the scoundrel, unintelligibility is surely the last refuge of the quack. Not that there is much difference between the scoundrel and the quack or their refuges. The important point here is that when the evidence supporting a quack treatment is questioned, the quackery can often be sold by a flurry of mumbo-jumbo. Neologisms and grammatically correct but nonsensical sentences sometimes convince those who want to believe the con. Quackery has a long and interesting history in medicine. Quackery in the social sciences and education has kept pace with, if not surpassed, that in medicine.[1]

Most people understand that medical quackery was prevalent in the nineteenth century and find it funny. In "Those Extraordinary Twins," Mark Twain pokes fun at the "medical science" of his era with the following mumbo-jumbo of a fictional physician:

Without going too much into detail, madam—for you would probably not understand it anyway—I concede that great care is going to be necessary here; otherwise exudation of the oesophagus is nearly sure to ensue, and

this will be followed by ossification and extradition of the maxillaris su-
perioris, which must decompose the granular surfaces of the great infu-
sorial ganglionic system, thus obstructing the action of the posterior var-
ioloid arteries, and precipitating compound strangulated sorosis of the
valvular tissues, and ending unavoidably in the dispersion and combus-
tion of the marsupial fluxes and the consequent embrocation of the bi-
cuspid populo redax referendum rotulorum.[2]

The fictional physician in Mark Twain's story intended to be unintelligible to Aunt Patsy as well as to anyone else, and we recognize that
he throws real words together with neologisms to provide a pastiche of
knowledge (a jumble of words that imitates a style but reflects silliness
rather than knowledge), which is part of the charm and humor of the
story. Everyone reading Mark Twain's story knows that the pastiche is
for laughs, but things are different now. Today, postmodernists are often deliberately unintelligible but without being so for laughs (and in a
later essay I return to the notion of pastiche). Postmodern unintelligibility is, however, no less laughable than that of Mark Twain's fictional
character. Consider the following excerpt from a book on postmodernism and education:

> The reduction of possible interpretations to the demands of "basic lan-
> guage" or the increased surveillance of unauthorized interpretations
> through the imposition of a metalanguage create [sic] definitively favorable
> conditions for "consensus." In other words, once we learn the right use of
> language (as put forth through the performativity principle of capitalist
> technoscience or a universal normativity), the "true" meaning behind the
> proliferation of second-order meanings will shine forth. With only "correct"
> meanings in circulation, consensus would be "natural.". . . In order for the
> discussion to go further, to take different directions, to open it up to "the
> event," dissensus or paralogy must be introduced. However, within the do-
> main of performativity (which both "basic language" and metaprescriptive
> norms enforce), paralogy would be reduced to mere innovation of contents
> within the ordained form. If paralogy is understood as the invention of new,
> imaginative moves not prescripted by the norms, then paralogy is directed
> at the forms themselves. The intent of paralogy is the creation of new id-
> ioms (forms and expressions) for thought. Paralogical moves ensure that
> any metanarratives do not terminally congeal into totalitarian imperatives.[3]

Pomposity is funny, as I pointed out in chapter 2, whether it is purposeful or not. So is illogic. Both can also be tragic, but only if they are

taken seriously. The tragicomedy of unintelligible discussions of education is that such discussions are seen as serious.

THE GIBBERISH CALLED POSTMODERNISM IS NOT HELPFUL TO EDUCATORS

The unintelligibility of some of what is currently being said about education and educational research is not due to a lack of intelligence. It is, rather, a failure, sometimes deliberate, to make sense with language and to make sense of the world. It calls to mind Philip Roth's description in *American Pastoral* of a young person whose behavior has become incomprehensible to her father, if not to nearly everyone else.[4] Her intelligence seemed to be intact, yet her "logic" reflected no power whatever to reason. In short, she was mad. I am not suggesting that all of the people who say unintelligible things are mad, although to me there is a lack of reason, which might be considered one sign of madness, in some of the vapid and unintelligible statements people have made about education, language, and other matters.

Perhaps the most blatantly and proudly unintelligible jargon of the current era is that of the "postmoderns." As we shall see, "postmodern" is itself an unintelligible term in some respects, as those who embrace postmodern philosophy claim that they themselves are not able to define it. In a parody of postmodernists' complaints on a television talk show, Mark Leyner began, "Recently, the University of Virginia [now Stanford University] philosopher Richard Rorty made the stunning declaration that nobody has 'the foggiest idea' what postmodernism means. 'It would be nice to get rid of it,' he said. 'It isn't exactly an idea; it's a word that pretends to stand for an idea.'"[5] If I understand postmodernism, then the joke—the spoof—is that postmodernists argue that words do not really represent anything other than other words, which means that "postmodern" itself is meaningless.

"Postmodern" is a vague term that leaves me asking, "Are we all postmodern now?" because it seems to encompass virtually any assertion someone might make.[6] Perhaps we could all be defined by someone as postmodern, although some of us do not buy the strange and unintelligible language or assumptions about language that go with postmodernism. Try this for starters: "Philosophers have shown that words and sentences do not represent ideas or objects. They are rather connected to other words, other sentences—their derivation is not to [sic] the world."[7] In other words, Roger Shattuck's notion of a real world is untenable. It is a fake, consisting only of words that have no "derivation to the world" (i.e., if I can interpret Smith, words have no *reference* to the world, at least not to a real world, because they are not *derived from* any real world).

Roger Shattuck refers to the seeming "music" of postmodern prose as "cantata style" and "intellectual song."[8] It has a captivating cadence, although it is not intelligible. It is a style, a cadence, a song not terribly difficult to learn, as long as you are not concerned about meaning or decipherability or you are, in fact, determined to avoid intelligibility. In one of the great spoofs of the last century, Alan Sokal imitated the postmodern style, stringing together words and sentences in grammatically correct but meaningless fashion, and submitted his nonsensical essay to a journal called *Social Text*.[9] The editors of *Social Text* snapped it up, apparently unable to tell the difference between Sokal's parody and the "real thing" (whatever the "real thing" may be).

I cannot figure out what postmodernism really is, as it seems to have no anchors in the real world and no practical applications (except to justify, well, whatever). As George Sugai has suggested, postmodernism is a distraction, not an advancement.[10] David Elkind is surely one of the most intellectually capable apologists of postmodernism. However, in rejoining the criticism of Sugai and others he seems to play the now familiar trick of postmodernists—define postmodernism as something reasonable and not different from science as we know it (and, therefore, not really *postmodern*), then contradict that same definition. For example, in an article on postmodernism in the field of behavioral disorders, Elkind wrote that "A mixture of therapeutic techniques, a therapeutic *pastiche*, is quintessentially postmodern."[11] And in a rejoinder to his critics, he added, "Postmodernism is not a rejection of what we know; rather, it is the demand that we be selective and take what works from the past but not be bound by what doesn't work—a basic tenet of positivism."[12]

So, postmodernism means finding what works and what doesn't, just like positivism? I am confused, then, about how postmodernism differs from Enlightenment science, which has always taken what can be demonstrated to work and rejected what has been shown not to work, regardless how old or new it may be. This does not seem to be the postmodernism that others describe, which asserts that nothing can be shown to work or not to work.[13] Elkind continued, "Postmodernism, from architecture to science, is a pastiche of past and present, taking what is best from both."[14] When I try to make sense of this statement or make it square with what I know of science, I find that I can do neither.

Architecture is apparently the only area in which "postmodern" is relatively well defined. I don't know that any credible scientist buys into the notion of a "pastiche of past and present" ideas. My understanding of the word "pastiche" is that it is not an entirely flattering term and that it could hardly be applied to scientific endeavors. I believe it refers to the usually deliberate imitation of artistic, musical, literary, and perhaps architectural styles. Often, apparently, the imitations are considered questionable in quality and seem to reflect a lack of effort on one's own part. So, postmodernism is an imitation of something—but of what, and in what way? "Pastiche" may also refer to a potpourri, a hodgepodge, neither an original style nor a coherent assembly but a combination of incongruous elements.

It could be that I do not understand "pastiche." Could be that Elkind meant something other than "pastiche of past and present." Could be that Elkind himself does not understand postmodernism, and he could hardly be faulted for that. I can't help wondering what is *post*modern about taking the best ideas of past and present, as long as they are combined coherently, not a jumble of incongruous imitations, not a pastiche. Perhaps Elkind meant "eclectic," which denotes selecting what is best or true, regardless of its theoretical or philosophical leaning. But supposing that he did mean "eclectic," not "pastiche," there remains the problem of the basis on which various ideas are selected. What is the basis for the judgment that something "works" or is "best?" Personal testimony? It just feels right?

Sometimes I can find no reasonably objective or scientific basis for choice, and I suppose that the same goes for virtually any scientist. For some things, we simply have no reliable data to guide a choice between X and Y. So, then, personal preference or personal belief or religious faith might as well be the basis for choice. I think most scientists understand this. And in some areas of our lives we are justified in allowing personal choice without question, as I discussed in chapter 2. But what about the cases in which reliable data are available, and what about the pursuit of reliable data to find out what we can? In education and other areas of study, Sasso describes the postmodern way as flight from the knowledge that we do have, a choice that discounts what we know through science in favor of personal preference alone. Gary Sasso's description is consistent with the email exchange I had with a proponent of post-modernism in education (see "Postmodern Theory Harms People by Promoting Ignorance" following).

Oh, well, the postmodern way seems to be to feint, dodge, deny, con-fuse, be deliberately obfuscatory and self-contradictory—presumably because the world is full of things poorly understood and such are the steps to power. Postmodernists appear to believe "that writing trite and diffuse prose is a brilliant way to capture the trite and diffuse nature of modern life."[15]

But I'm afraid that the postmodern dog won't hunt, as some might put it. Others have detailed how the hodgepodge of ideas known as postmod-ernism is incompatible with science.[16] Scientist E. O. Wilson reminded us in his book on the unity of knowledge that in the real world order wins over disorder, clarity wins over confusion, intelligibility beats unintelligi-bility—not always immediately, but eventually and inevitably.[17]

Postmodernists seem to assume—in fact, some say directly—that people who "don't get it" are at fault.[18] They contend that postmod-ernists have no responsibility to use language in a way that is intelligi-ble to others who are not of postmodern bent. This view seems curiously at odds with other contemporary conventions in the use of language, in which "plain language" relatively free of the jargon or argot of a given profession—law, for example—is set as a worthy goal and is encour-aged or demanded. In many areas of our lives, we assume that if some-one cannot "translate" argot into plain, interpretable language, then ei-ther (a) that person does not really understand the matter he or she is talking about, but is merely repeating words that may as well be gib-berish (imitating someone's linguistic style, creating a pastiche or hodgepodge of words) or (b) whatever he or she is saying is, indeed, gibberish and cannot be translated into something understandable.

You may draw your own conclusions, but when I hear or read the as-sertion that I cannot expect postmodern ideas to be made intelligible to me until I learn to understand postmodernism, I get the distinct im-pression that I am hearing or reading gibberish and that there is cogni-tive rubbish to be disposed of. If it is not disposed of properly, or if it is mistaken for wisdom or understanding, this rubbish will surely poi-son the well of knowledge.

THE CONCLUSIONS DERIVED FROM
POSTMODERNISM ARE ABSURD OR BANAL

Postmodernism and deconstructivism defy definition, as I discuss further. So do hermeneutics, cultural studies, post-structuralism, post-disciplinary, antidisciplinary and a variety of other new-age cognitive peculiarities with different labels meaning roughly the same thing. Actually, post- or anti- just about anything is a common element in the postmodern lexicon. Some writers try to draw distinctions among such terms, but the distinctions are largely unintelligible to me, and, I imagine, to many.[19]

Beginning with the definition of what it is or isn't, the postmodern way is deliberately to confuse rather than to clarify or, at best, to suggest that clarity is neither attainable nor helpful. As Usher and Edwards put it, "Although it is customary to define what one is writing about, in the case of 'postmodernism' this is neither entirely possible nor entirely desirable."[20] As we shall see, unintelligibility is a basic and highly valued characteristic of terms used by postmodernists—and of the referents of these terms as well. For the sake of brevity and clarity in my own writing, I shall often refer to the general ideas of these terms as PD, as postmodern and deconstructivist are the most common terms used to describe the general point of view (or lack of point of view, perhaps). Here are the central ideas of PD as I understand it:

1. All truth and all knowledge are constructed according to social rules. These rules give someone power to identify truth or knowledge. Moreover, these rules have been constructed by oppressive power structures, mainly by white, European, heterosexual males, to protect their own power.

2. There are multiple truths, multiple realities, hence no one or best way of knowing anything. All "truth" is merely a text; the text or script can be rewritten to suit one's fancy or to manipulate power. That is, power comes from deconstructing or constructing texts. Power comes from what some PD enthusiasts refer to as "textuality."

3. No text has superiority or power over another; or, at least, no text *should* be seen as superior to or be allowed to have power over another. Truth and knowledge are merely social constructs that

can be deconstructed and reconstructed to suit one's desire for having power or giving it to others.

4. Rationality and intelligibility are not legitimate tests of truth, as rationality and intelligibility themselves are merely social constructs or texts reflecting white male, Western scientific biases and lust for power.

5. Any argument that arguments 1–4 are wrong is, itself, erroneous. PD views cannot be refuted on logical grounds or by any evidence, as these (PD) views of text and power are the bedrock of postmodern "theory" or "philosophy," which seems to be a text saying that no text is actually intelligible.

Postmodernists and deconstructivists suggest that my inability to make sense of their writing and speaking is a function of my inability to read and listen without my biases about intelligibility and rationality. My own discredited positivism, my preference for linear thought, my primitive views of science, language, rationality, logic, truth, and intelligibility are all wrong-headed. I do not make sense to them, apparently, precisely because I say that I can make no sense of *their* statements. They have seen the light of multiple realities, multiple truths, the construction of *knowledges* in all of their multiple and equally valid forms. I have not seen the light, simply because I insist that there is a "real" world—because I believe that for some real things, if not for many, there is only one verifiable way of knowing them. Moreover, I think that some language is unintelligible or irrational and, therefore, should not be taken seriously, should not be judged to represent scholarship, knowledge, or truth.

But postmodernists' deconstruction of texts is, when intelligible, banal. Robert Conquest described their work as follows:

At any rate, one thing obvious to adults is that, insofar as there is anything in the point that the effect of a poem or novel depends not only on the writer's intention but also on the reader's reception of it, it is so obvious as not to be worth saying; but that to make too much of it is to fall from the obvious into the inane.

In fact, to the degree that such things as the theses of deconstructionists and their heirs are not absurd, they are banal.[21]

Understandably, perhaps—though one wonders just why it is so— those who embrace PD insist that they make discriminations among texts. They do, apparently, believe that in some cases *A* is better than *B*. But, of course, they will not state—at least not in terms comprehensible to anyone whose views are not PD—what the criteria are for making discriminations among ideas or statements or deciding that *A* is better than *B*. There is one exception, of course: the PD view is superior to the outdated, positivist, scientific view because PD recognizes the truth that truth is simply made up. Never mind the cognitive dead end. Self-contradiction seems acceptable among proponents of PD.

I like Roger Shattuck's comment about PD gimcrackery versus the real world in which at least some of us live: "I hope that all intellectuals pull jury duty when they begin to abandon all hope for fact and truth and to embrace a socially constructed textuality."[22] I also admire columnist Colbert King's clear writing, including his unapologetic assumptions that (a) there are truths and there are lies about people and events and (b) we can discriminate between truths and lies. The fact that Dr. Tareq Tahboub wrote certain things about national security advisor Condoleezza Rice and about American women and children does not mean they are true. In fact, King claims that what Dr. Tahboub wrote in an Arabic-language daily paper was "full of lies and misrepresentations," and King presents the evidence to substantiate his claim.[23]

PURPOSEFUL UNINTELLIGIBILITY HELPS NO ONE BUT THE UNINTELLIGIBLE PERSON

Gary Sasso has written a wonderful critique of PD in special education. He describes "two kinds of ignorance: natural and willful (i.e., traditional and postmodern)." We cannot avoid natural ignorance, he says, a point I also have tried to make clear, and we must admit our own shortcomings about things we do not know. But willful or PD ignorance—the deliberate refusal to learn things relevant to one's own area of interest or study—is avoidable. The unintelligibility of PD prose and the deliberate refusal of PD proponents to make sense of the world by learning about it within a scientific frame of reference are difficult to overlook. Sasso comments,

If it can be accepted that the intellectual project of the Enlightenment is intent upon building a sound body of knowledge about the world we confront, then postmodernism defines itself, in large measure, as the antithetical doctrine. Such a project is inherently futile, self-deceptive, and worst of all, oppressive.[24]

As opposed to the Enlightenment, the PD project is not to make sense, simply because sense cannot be made (with the single exception, I assume, that sense is made of the assertion that it can't be made).

But, who am I to say what makes sense? For readers not familiar with the rhetoric of PD writers, some examples might be helpful. I provide a few quotations here from writers identified with PD "theory" or "philosophy," although there is, obviously, some danger in that. People associated with this point of view generally deny that postmodernism or deconstructivism (or other terms referring to the same sort of "thought") can be defined.[25] Often they deny that they themselves are postmodern or have postmodern views (what else can they do, given that no one can define what postmodernism is?). Some grudgingly accept someone else's use of a label for writing a particular essay but insist that their views can't be categorized or labeled.[26] I recall one instance in which I reviewed the manuscript (for possible publication in a professional journal) of a writer presenting postmodern ideas who replied to the editor (who rejected the paper for publication, and for good reasons) that he or she is not a postmodernist but a Gadamerian hermeneuticist.[27]

Following are some examples from PD writing. I suppose that the only way you can try to confirm whether these excerpts are peculiar lapses in texts that are mostly intelligible, are taken out of context, or are simply unfair portrayals of PD writing is to go yourself to the PD works and read them in their entirety. Perhaps you will be able to read the whole of these works without choking with laughter or rage—or both.[28] All three of these examples are taken from *Educational Researcher*, a publication of the American Educational Research Association.

Although the shift to cultural studies is relatively new, we can already discern from the characteristics of cultural studies what the implications will be for curriculum theorizing. Because of the cultural studies emphases on working on the cutting edge of theory and theorizing; taking the popular seriously; doing not only interdisciplinary but anti-disciplinary and even postdisciplinary work; undertaking praxis rather than theory or practice, and so forth, we are likely to see (indeed we are already seeing) a greater emphasis on curriculum theorizing that employs cutting edge theory and juxtaposes a number of theoretical discourses; deals with popular culture, the new media (taking up television and the World Wide Web rather differently than current dominant approaches), and a very expanded notion of pedagogy and pedagogical spaces; and utilizes an inter/anti/post-disciplinary approach.[29]

Elizabeth St. Pierre suggests that unintelligibility is just fine, in fact demanded. The problem, she suggests, is people who expect intelligibility. She cites other PD writers, Foucault, and Nietzsche to try to explain why no one can define postmodernism. Understandably, perhaps, she herself is unintelligible to me, and probably to many others, too. And apparently she is proud of it, having no intention of writing something intelligible to the likes of me and no aspiration to be intelligible to other educational researchers! She offers criticism of an earlier call for intelligibility in postmodern educational research:[30]

> For some reason . . . readers expect postmodernism to be readily accessible and coherent within a structure it works against. When it isn't, those who employ its critiques are often accused not only of being deliberately obfuscatory but also irrational and even nihilistic. . . . To this end, I believe that our responsibility is to keep educational research in play, increasingly unintelligible to itself, in order to produce different knowledge and produce knowledge differently as we work for social justice in the human sciences.[31]

Perhaps unintelligibility should be the rule for discourse about education or anything else, but I doubt it. However, PD is unintelligible only to those who are too lazy or stupid or ignorant or poorly trained to understand it, so the proponents of PD argue. Actually, PD is said to be fully intelligible, but only to those who have given themselves to it. Wanda Pillow explains:

> Many postmodern researchers forefront the necessity of making visible the myriad of ways such work is (un)graspable, (im)possible, (un)intelligible, (un)knowable, and provisional. This is not a failure of postmodernism—this *is* the work of postmodernism.[32]

When reading such PD (provide your own descriptor), I can't help recalling Mark Twain's pithy aside in his 1899 essay about Christian Science:

> (It is very curious, the effect which Christian Science has upon the verbal bowels. Particularly the Third Degree; it makes one think of a dictionary with the cholera. But I only thought this; I did not say it.)[33]

POSTMODERN THEORY HARMS
PEOPLE BY PROMOTING IGNORANCE

Twain had great fun with incomprehensibility, regardless of the source
of it. And I can't read his essay on Christian Science without laughing.
Laughter is, after all, the response we should have to things that don't
make sense, whether they are religion or, as I suggested some years
ago, reform statements made with great seriousness.[34] Twain (Sam
Clemens) wrote of Christian Science:

> For of all the strange, and frantic, and incomprehensible, and uninter-
> pretable books which the imagination of man has created, surely this one
> [*Divine Science*] is the prize sample. It was written with a limitless confi-
> dence and complacency, and with a dash and stir and earnestness which of-
> ten compel the effects of eloquence, even when the words do not seem to
> have any traceable meaning. There are plenty of people who imagine they
> understand the book; I know this, for I have talked with them; but in all
> cases they were people who also imagined that there were no such things
> as pain, sickness and death, and no realities in the world; nothing actually
> existent but Mind. It seems to me to modify the value of their testimony.[35]

Too bad that Mark Twain's mind is gone from this world, though I'm
grateful that his wit has been collected and published.[36] But I admire
Mark Twain for more than his wit. He also had a more finely tuned
sense of justice than most of his contemporaries, including a sense of
shame about slavery and racial discrimination. "'The skin of every human being,' he wrote, 'contains a slave.' He could at least make America flinch before it laughed."[37]

Another comfort is that a century later, Richard Feynman was having fun with the oddities of faith healing, Christian Science, astrology,
and other pseudosciences. As long as there are propositions that do not
add up, there will be people able and willing to poke fun. And as long
as we see the funny aspects of voodoo and its equivalents, there is hope
of making sense. As Feynman observed:

> There are, if you turn on the radio . . . you hear all kinds of faith healers.
> I've seen them on television. It's another one of those things that it ex-
> hausts me to try to explain why it's rather a ridiculous proposition. There
> is, in fact, an entire religion that's respectable, so called, that's called

Christian Science, that's based on the idea of faith healing. If it were true, it could be established, not by the anecdotes of a few people but by the careful checks, by the technically good clinical methods which are used on any other way of curing diseases. If you believe in faith healing, you have a tendency to avoid other ways of getting healed. It takes you a bit longer to get to the doctor, possibly. Some people believe it strongly enough that it takes them longer to get to the doctor. It's possible that faith healing isn't so good. . . . It's possible either way. It should be investigated. It shouldn't be left lying for people to believe in without an investigation.[38]

Pseudoscience and faith healing may make the humorist's day, but such claptrap has its dark side when it is not the butt of jokes. There is enormous potential for evil derived from the proposition that truth is merely constructed by social power, by text, by narrative, that there is no external and objective world to be apprehended. Robert Conquest and Roger Shattuck have commented brilliantly on the viciousness of this proposition from the perspective of history, literature, education, and the arts.[39] In an interview of Aleksandar Hemon by National Public Radio's Renee Montagne, Hemon described how one of his favorite former professors had started to use language in the service of Serbian aggression, denying massacres, concentration camps, and rapes, twisting truth into falsehood. He simply denied that Serbs were laying siege to Sarajevo, saying they (Serbians) were only defending themselves, and describing explosions of shells as only the traditional Serbian people's way of celebrating Christmas.[40]

For all their reference to social justice and oppression, those who embrace PD seem to ignore the malevolence it has already fostered or seem simply not to care. This attitude is most clearly exemplified by email messages I received in 1999 from a professor at another university explaining how and why postmodernism is a superior way of viewing the world and thus will become dominant. This professor suggested that postmodernists assume that it is simply impossible to determine the general effectiveness or ineffectiveness of any instructional or behavior management procedure. Hence, all we can say of any given method or procedure is that some people have found it helpful and others have not, and the only recommendation we can make is to try it if you want and see if it works for you.

We have little tolerance for such know-nothingism in medicine or the manufacture of consumer products, but we tolerate such nonsense in the education of children. To me, the PD attitude toward truth and knowledge is destructive of social justice (basic fairness) and cannot be otherwise, as it is the denial of any common truth, shared reality, demonstrable facts. Here is my response (in February 1999) to the professor who emailed me his description of postmodernism and its implications for special education. (I do not quote his letter, only my responses to his paragraphs, offering the gist of his statements in my parenthetical asides.)

(First, he suggests that he now understands my thinking, that I have mistaken postmodernism for a new type of science.)

> You have misunderstood my thinking completely. In no respect have I ever thought that postmodernism is a new brand of science that claims to be better than the old one. I have thought all along that "postmodernism" refers to the assumption that science is an unreliable way of finding out what is or what works, as is every other way of knowing anything. I am truly mystified by your statement that ideas drawn from postmodern philosophers might be used by special educators to support a given professional practice when you are working from the assumption that the effectiveness of practice cannot be determined. On what grounds would you support a practice if you are not able to attest to its effectiveness? [See my response to his subsequent argument that the general effectiveness of *any* practice cannot be affirmed.]
>
> If the "old" way of scientific verification of effectiveness is accepted by postmodernists, then we have no argument. If, as you seem to me to suggest above and below, effectiveness is simply unknowable, then you have said, in effect, that science is useless.

(He next states that no research paradigm can discover truth, that objectivity is not believable, that science has no particular advantage over other methods of investigation.)

> The ideas you state above seem to me strikingly similar to those of the sophists and Dadaists. The social/philosophical movements based on sophistry and dadaism weren't very successful or helpful, except that some of their proponents became quite well known and wealthy and their efforts were sometimes amusing or produced curiosities.
>
> My understanding is that scientists (excluding frauds, which exist in every field) have always understood that "truth" is tentative and that the

role of science is to seek always the closer approximation of truth, and that there are rules for judging what is closer to or further from truth, that objectivity itself is a continuously distributed variable (meaning that absolute objectivity may be unattainable, but that some methods or procedures are more objective than others). In other words, scientists live in a socially constructed world of relative and conditional truths, not absolute truths, but they do hold that some assertions (e.g., that the earth is not the center of the universe and that the sun does not orbit the earth) are very close to absolutely known facts and that others (e.g., that positive social reinforcement is important in teaching and learning) are very reliable principles that we ignore or deny at considerable peril.

(His next paragraph states that the effectiveness of facilitated communication [FC] cannot be determined. [FC is a postmodern pretense of communication with individuals having absent or minimal verbal skills. It involves "facilitators" typing out messages for autistic and retarded children and adults. FC has been thoroughly discredited by scientific studies. Stephen Jay Gould, the father of an autistic young man, describes it as a "poignant but truly unreasonable hope for communication" and "a 'harmless' sop to hope turned into a nightmare."[41]] My email correspondent states not only that the usefulness of FC cannot be determined but also that the general effectiveness of *no* professional practice can be determined! Therefore, he suggests, we should tell parents or others they might try a practice to see if they like it because we have no reliable basis for recommending for or against specific practices. Fact is, he says, some people like a given practice, some don't; some find a particular practice helpful, some don't.)

> I view the position about FC as you state it an abdication of both reality and professional responsibility. It seems to me you are saying, "Buyer, beware," in the sense of exposing parents and their children to knowable and known risks in the service of philosophical posturing. I find this morally repugnant. I do understand that very few, if any, of the interventions we might say are generally effective are effective 100% of the time. However, not to discriminate among degrees of effectiveness is, in my opinion, to throw baby out with bathwater. It is also to subject deliberately those we are supposed to serve to the vagaries of quack treatments and other abuses.
>
> But, perhaps you are right and nothing can be known, except through personal experience or testimonial. In which case, I don't know why I should believe you or any other person who holds a similar view.

(Finally, he suggests that science will fade from prominence and be replaced by postmodern perspectives and multi-paradigmatic inquiry. It has already happened, he intimates, in the publications of the American Psychological Association and the American Educational Research Association. We in special education are stuck with an outmoded scientific paradigm. Achieving social justice requires alternative paradigms, such as postmodernism, he believes.)

> Perhaps you are right about what will happen to the field. There are many instances in which large groups of people, indeed entire societies, have made very bad decisions that were antithetical to the achievement of social equality and the social good. I think it is worth remembering that scientific or common knowledge and its pursuit are among the best tools we have for fighting for social justice. I imagine that the parents and kids we serve are going to want functional assistance in learning, that they will ultimately condemn (and rightly, in my opinion) the academic puffery that does not provide us with better tools for solving problems. I think they will tell us—maybe they are telling us now, actually—"put up or shut up." As I understand postmodernism, it is a rejection of the idea of functional tools and a denial of our ability to know when something works better or doesn't work at all.

In early 2001, a professor promoting postmodernism in special education suggested in a university address (not at the University of Virginia) that people with views like mine are a dying breed. It seems the view of postmodernists is that they will lay claim to the world, that Enlightenment science is dead. Actually, postmodern views may already dominate in what E. D. Hirsch, Jr. calls the Thoughtworld.

Postmodernism seems to me to be a mulish, self-centered way of viewing the world. It is egoism without restriction. As I explained in a commentary on science and its alternatives, it recalls for me the Ogden Nash verse set to music by Camille Saint-Saens, "In the world of mules, there are no rules."[42]

Deformed Education: George Howard, a professor I know at a nearby university, read in the local paper that a neighboring school system had invested thousands of dollars to hire professors from a university in another state to teach their teachers to use cooperative learning with their entire school population, kindergarten through high school. The money was to purchase instruction for the teachers during the summer and ongoing workshops throughout the year. Every classroom was to be structured around cooperative learning.

After reading the newspaper article, George called the superintendent of this school system and offered to test the efficacy of the cooperative learning program at no cost to the schools. George had a large group of advanced graduate students who would assist him in this endeavor, and he thought that his offer would be a boon to the school system as well as of benefit to him and his students. Imagine his surprise when the superintendent said to him, "Absolutely, not, Professor Howard. We've invested a lot of money in this thing already. If it doesn't work, we don't want to know about it. Besides, no research is ever going to convince me that it works or it doesn't. We don't need research to tell us what's right."

George laughed immediately when the superintendent said this. He thought the superintendent was joking. Then he realized that there was dead silence on the other end of the line. He later said to me, "My God! Wouldn't you want to know whether an expensive program that required massive reorganization of your school system was effective? But the man was serious. He didn't want to know whether it worked and didn't think anybody could find out!"

FINDING COMMON KNOWLEDGE IS EXTREMELY IMPORTANT

The assertion that objectivity is simply unbelievable is a familiar complaint of postmodernists (as in the email exchange I discussed previously). However, this postmodern complaint is a straw person, as scientists recognize that their historical era, their culture, prejudices, and habits of mind all play a role in what they study and what they see. And scientists can be wrong. Nevertheless, science is a self-correcting system that ultimately places a premium on reliable data obtained with the least bias and the greatest objectivity possible. Although biases and preferences can't be totally eliminated, objectivity in science means subjecting them to particularly harsh scrutiny.[43] If someone with a different bias or preference cannot subject his or her preferences and findings to the same level of scrutiny and reach the same conclusion, then the matter is not settled in a scientific manner. Postmodernists seem to recognize that people have biases and preferences, but postmodernists do not subject these personal views to harsh scrutiny; they simply accept them as defining realities.

In his book about Benton Harbor and St. Joseph, Michigan, and the death of a young African American man there, Alex Kotlowitz notes how facts (truth, if you will) must be the anchor for building bridges across races and other divides. "As David Walker, Benton Harbor's police chief, bluntly told me, 'Facts don't mean shit. Perception is the truth.' And thus it becomes easy to dismiss one another's experiences."[44] Certainly, perceptions may differ, and they may be mistaken for facts or truth. But when perception is assumed to define truth—when no external world is assumed to exist outside of our perceptions, when objectivity is said to be unbelievable or impossible, when reality is assumed to be defined simply by creating a narrative or script—then, as Kotlowitz suggests, there is no basis for building bridges. People can't be brought together; they have only separate islands of perception and eternal suspicion, mistrust, and misunderstanding. The other person's experience is simply different, and there is no common ground to be found.

The alternatives to scientific knowledge offer, as far as I can tell, no hope of finding a common understanding of things that are central to social justice, fairness, or equity. Postmodernists seem to shut themselves off from the construction of common (scientific) knowledge. Without finding the common, we have two choices, both of which are unacceptable to me: avoidance or domination of those who are different from us—unless, of course, we simply don't believe that common understandings are what hold people together. So far as I know, attempts to teach tolerance without a foundation of common understanding hasn't worked out very well.

REMOVING POSTMODERN IDEAS FROM EDUCATION WILL BE DIFFICULT

Robert Conquest reports that he has found it easy to get across to his students the notion that Western culture—specifically its rule of law, freedom of speech, and political liberty—may be seen to have distinct advantages over other cultures. His dialogue with students does the trick, he says, and goes roughly as follows:

R. C.: So, we should treat all cultures the same?

Students: Right.

R. C.: Then I suppose we should advocate that notion—that is, we should support the idea that all cultures must be considered equal?

Students: Definitely.

R. C.: So, then, a culture that allows such equality, at least to the degree that it sees all cultures as equal, is superior to another one that doesn't?

Students: I see what you mean.[45]

I have no reason to doubt that Conquest can so easily get Stanford students to understand the straightforward reasoning to which he leads them. However, as Conquest himself suggests throughout *Reflections on a Ravaged Century*, many apparently bright people, including many university faculty members (who, one would think, should know better), swallow intellectual twaddle and call it both tasty and nutritious. They seem unable to see the self-contradictions in their own rhetoric or—as we have seen already in quotations of postmodernist writers—simply revel in their admitted obfuscation and unintelligibility. Consider how university-based postmodern "thinkers" defend their own and others' tripe. Or read critiques of postmodernism emanating from unconvinced university professors and philosophers of science.[46]

Columnist William Raspberry posed the rhetorical question, "Can it be that some educators are more attracted to elegant-sounding phrases than to approaches that actually improve learning?[47] The answer is obvious, but preferring elegant-sounding phrases to substance is not peculiar to educators; it is endemic in American political life and in advertising.

Economically successful enterprises may be built on the assumption that, as one seer put it, there's a sucker born every minute. University faculty recruitment often seems based on the same premise, as does the selection of school boards. Mark Twain saw too clearly, perhaps:

> All schools, all colleges, have two great functions; to confer, and to conceal, valuable knowledge.[48]
>
> In the first place God made idiots. This was for practice. Then He made School Boards.[49]

I do know some intelligent school board members, but I often marvel at the idiocy of some school boards' decisions.

POSTMODERNISM IS ABOUT POWER, NOT TRUTH

So, where does postmodernism in education lead? Ellen Brantlinger's 1997 article in *Review of Educational Research* illustrates for me how Roger Shattuck's notion is correct: Postmodernism patterned after the philosophy of Michel Foucault leads to the raw will to power. Education and educational research are always ideological, always political, so the postmodern argument goes, and science is merely politics by other means.[50] The issue is power. Robert Conquest stated, "A surprising number of midlife academics seem to have been trained in, or selected for, susceptibility to dogma. And most of these show one especial characteristic: an inability to believe that not everyone is driven by power lust."[51] Conquest goes on to describe the "mental blight" that has overtaken many contemporary English faculties that embrace postmodernism, a blight "carrying, separately or blended together, the pretentiously meaningless and the politically vicious."[52] This is much the same conclusion reached by others who have critiqued postmodern ideas.[53]

I have seen this view at work in higher education, including my own field of study, special education. Consider the matter of a letter written in the year 2000 to the president of the Council for Children with Behavioral Disorders. The writer, a professor at another university, requested that copies be sent to the entire Executive Committee of the organization. The letter protested the editorial policy of *Behavioral Disorders*, a journal I then co-edited with my colleague Rick Brigham. The letter writer attempted to explain how we (Rick and I) are unconsciously racist in our thinking and how no one's perspective (save that which rejects postmodern views) can be said to be wrong or irrational. The writer and others (as well as the 30 co-signers of another letter of complaint sent the Council for Exceptional Children, the parent organization of the Council for Children with Behavioral Disorders) apparently intended to force their will on the organization and on us as co-editors through political stratagems, such as complaining to higher organization officials without so much as copying us. Our impression is that they are not interested in discussion, simply political power. That is consistent with the rest of the postmodern rhetoric. It is consistent with my observation of what happens in organizations in which postmodernists gain a toehold.

POSTMODERN IDEAS ARE
OFTEN PRESENTED AS VIRTUES

The ostensible motives or objectives of those who at least embrace if not propound postmodern ideas are sometimes, if not often, laudable. Who would *not* want *democratic themes* to pervade school reform, as the subtitle of an article by Tom Skrtic, Wayne Sailor, and Kathleen Gee suggests?[54] One of the ironies of the postmodern movement is that its proponents propose objectives, such as democracy, that their very ideas undermine.[55] At the same time, the outspoken critics of postmodernism show how politically liberal ideals can be achieved most reliably by using the tools of Enlightenment science.[56] And while postmodernists paint traditional scientists as politically conservative, many if not most of these scientists express liberal political sentiments. Liberal scientists put flesh on liberal propositions, whereas postmodernists and those in sympathy with their perspectives mouth liberal platitudes without seeing the necessity of addressing just how liberal objectives can be achieved or liberal sentiments can be acted upon.

Whether those who write or say the unintelligible labor under the banner of postmodernism, the disjuncture between their unintelligibility and their admirable sentiments is often the same. For example, I find much of Paulo Freire's writing extremely dense and full of jargon, if not unintelligible. I estimate that I can decode only a rather small percentage of his sentences into something that is actually useful or applicable to working with children. For me, making sense of his paragraphs or large sections of his work is very challenging. You might try reading Freire's 1993 *Pedagogy of the Oppressed* or his 1998 *Pedagogy of Freedom: Ethics, Democracy, and Civic Courage* to see whether you fare better than I. Try the following:

> When we live our lives with the authenticity demanded by the practice of teaching that is also learning and learning that is also teaching, we are participating in a total experience that is simultaneously directive, political, ideological, gnostic, pedagogical, aesthetic, and ethical. In this experience the beautiful, the decent, and the serious form a circle with hands joined.[57]

Passages like this have a nice cadence, a sweet song, and admirable sentiment, but I cannot pretend to decode them. Freire appears to have taken a page from the book of postmodern prose stylists and applied it to writing about education. B. R. Myers has said of one example from contemporary fiction, "this [sentence] demands to be read quickly, with just enough attention to register the bold use of words. Slow down and things fall apart."[58] Freire and the postmodern theorists whose work I cite exemplify for me another observation of B. R. Myers: "The reader is meant to be carried along on the stream of language."[59] So it is for me. I like the sound of Freire; I cannot decipher his meaning.

Of course, I support ethical behavior, democratic ideals, and civic courage in education, ideals that are suggested by the title of Freire's book. I would like to teach in a way that encourages reflection, self-help, and resistance to oppression. And I'd like to help other teachers learn how to do the same. I know that Freire has many admirers and that his educational philosophy is seen by most of them as the best way of educating children who are poor. I think in all likelihood Paulo Freire was a very nice man, and a bright one, too. But I can make little sense of Freire's own writing or of commentaries on his pedagogy. I cannot, for example, make any sense of the following commentary by Peter McLaren:

> In all of Freire's teachings, the concept of truth becomes vitiatingly un-
> wound as the truth becomes linked to one's emplacement in the reigning
> narratives *about* truth. Of course, Freire's own work can be used against
> itself in this regard, and interpreted as an epiphenomenon of the narra-
> tives that create the textual effects of his own work.[60]

The task of educators, I think, is finding out how to support democratic ideals most simply, directly, and effectively. Others, like Mira Nanda, whose comments on the reasons for third-world rejection of postmodern views I mentioned in the last chapter, have shown why this is important—why a scientific view of truth is a far greater advantage to people who have been disenfranchised than is the postmodern construction of truth.

In Freire's work, I find that I can skim or surf to some general ideas, but I think these are ideas that others have expressed more clearly than he. Some of the general ideas have been around for a very long time: where there is no learning, there has been no teaching; methodological rigor and science are important; teachers must respect what students know and help them become critical thinkers; students will learn from their teacher's actions, not merely from their exhortations; racial discrimination is evil; it is important to reflect on one's professional practice. However, I cannot unravel the particulars of teaching in Freire's work. I find no fault with his sentiments, but sentiment alone does not make one an effective teacher.

Freire expounds at considerable length on the importance of "correct thinking," yet without explaining what "correct thinking" actually is (at least without explaining it in ways I can understand). Reading Freire leaves me wondering what teachers should do or be, other than be good people. Here is one example that puzzles me:

> What is important in teaching is not the mechanical repetition of this or that gesture but a comprehension of the value of sentiments, emotions, and desires. Of the insecurity that can only be overcome by inspiring confidence. Of the fear that can only be abated to the degree that courage takes its place.[61]

I am left with the impression that feeling good, thinking right, and being kind and confident are enough. But I doubt that, as much as I doubt that a good bedside manner is sufficient for a physician or good intention is all an engineer really needs. Maybe it's desirable, but without technical competence there is bad trouble ahead for the practitioner—and for his or her clients, too.

There is no reason I know of that good sentiments and technical competence must be in opposition, or that professionals in any field must choose one over the other. In fact, I think there is every reason to want and expect both a high level of technical competence and the sentiments we value most highly in teachers as well as in other professionals. Doug Carnine, among others, has pointed us toward the achievement of both.[62]

The world does have its paradoxes, but some assumed paradoxes actually make sense. Alan Sokal and Jean Bricmont have explained in their epilogue why and how the radical left has embraced postmodern doctrines and how postmodern obscurantism thwarts the achievement of democracy and other noble sentiments the postmodernists say they espouse.

> Those who wield political or economic power will quite naturally prefer that science and technology be attacked as such, because these attacks

help conceal the relationships of force on which their own power is based. Furthermore, by attacking rationality, the postmodern left deprives itself of a powerful instrument for criticizing the existing social order.[63]

At a time when superstitions, obscurantism, and nationalist and religious fanaticism are spreading in many parts of the world—including the "developed" West—it is irresponsible, to say the least, to treat with such casualness what has historically been the principal defense against these follies, namely a rational vision of the world. It is doubtless not the intention of postmodernist authors to favor obscurantism, *but it is an inevitable consequence of their approach*.[64]

Sokal and Bricmont appear to have been too optimistic about the intentions of postmodern authors. As some of the quotations in this chapter illustrate, at least some postmodern authors now appear to be deliberately and proudly obscurantist.

How, then, can liberal political ideals, especially as they apply to education, be realized? The answer is not through the nonsensical, irrational, antiscientific rhetoric of postmodernists but through the more traditional, staid, and provable, if not proven—conservative, if you will—methods of Enlightenment science to the problems of education. As Roger Shattuck and E. D. Hirsch, Jr. have noted, educational programs said to be "conservative" often produce more democratic results than those labeled "liberal."[65] Conservative here should not be interpreted to mean all of the education proposals put forward by those who are politically conservative. Rather, by "conservative educational programs" I (and, I believe, Shattuck and Hirsch) refer to the ideas that skills must be taught directly, that the content of education must include basic skills and knowledge known to be important for the student's later success, and that students must be grouped for instruction with others who are on approximately the same level in the subject matter being taught.

If intelligibility is not considered a virtue, then, to me, good sentiments are of no consequence at all and bad sentiments will surely prevail. That is, if things do not add up logically and empirically, then it doesn't make much difference what virtues one supports, as their collapse is predictable and vices will triumph. All it takes for irrationality and unintelligibility to triumph is for rational people to do nothing—fail to oppose the irrational intelligibly.

NOTES

1. Kauffman (1999a).
2. Twain (1894/1969, p. 288).
3. Bain (1995, pp. 7–8).
4. Roth (1997).
5. Leyner (1997, p. 11).
6. See Kauffman (1998).
7. Smith (1999, p. 131); see also Smith (2001).
8. Shattuck (1999).
9. See Sokal (1996), Sokal & Bricmont (1998).
10. Sugai (1998).
11. Elkind (1998a, p. 159, italics in original).
12. Elkind (1998b, p. 182).
13. I give more examples of that postmodern line of argument later in this chapter; see also Koertge (1998), Sasso (2001), Sokal & Bricmont (1998).
14. Elkind (1998b, p. 182).
15. Myers (2001, p. 114).
16. E.g., Brigham & Polsgrove (1998), Koertge (1998), Sokal & Bricmont (1998).
17. Wilson (1998).
18. See Kernan (1999), Myers (2001).
19. See Pillow (2000) and St. Pierre (2000) for examples of the word-salads in question.
20. Usher & Edwards (1994, p. 6).
21. Conquest (2000, p. 222).
22. Shattuck (1999, p. 94).
23. King (2001a, p. A29).
24. Sasso (2001, p. 179).
25. See Pillow (2000), St. Pierre (2000).
26. See Pillow (2000).
27. Gadamerian, presumably, because the views were patterned on those of H. Gadamer; see Gadamer (1959/1988). See Gallagher (1998) for further discussion of postmodern doubts about knowledge in special education.
28. For more postmodern writing, see Smith (2001).
29. Wright (2000, p. 7).
30. The earlier call for intelligibility in postmodern research was by Constas (1998).
31. St. Pierre (2000, pp. 25–27).
32. Pillow (2000, p. 22, parentheses and italics in original).

33. Clemens (1899 [1976], p. 378).

34. Kauffman (1992).

35. Clemens (1899 [1976], p. 383).

36. E.g., Library of America (1976, 1981).

37. Blount (2001, p. 81).

38. Feynman (1998, pp. 93–94).

39. Conquest (2000), Shattuck (1999).

40. National Public Radio (2000).

41. See Gould (1997b, pp. xi–xii), Jacobson, Mulick, & Schwartz (1995), Mostert (2001) for elaboration.

42. Kauffman (1999c).

43. See Feynman (1998, 1999), Gould (1997b, 2000), Gross (1998), Shermer (1997, 2001), Tolson (1998), Wilson (1998).

44. Kotlowitz (1998, pp. 257–258).

45. See Conquest (2000, pp. 218–219).

46. E.g., Koertge (1998), Sokal & Bricmont (1998).

47. Raspberry (2000a, p. A6).

48. Clemens (1899 [1976], p. 941).

49. Mark Twain—*Pudd'nhead Wilson's New Calendar*; Clemens (1897, p. 241).

50. See Brantlinger (1997), Giroux (1995), Smith (2001) for elaboration.

51. Conquest (2000, p. 220).

52. Conquest (2000, p. 221). See also Crews (2001).

53. E.g., Kernan (1999), Sokal & Bricmont (1998).

54. Skrtic, Sailor, & Gee (1996).

55. See Smith (2001) as an example of postmodern writing.

56. E.g., Gross (1998), Nanda (1998), Sokal & Bricmont (1998).

57. Freire (1998, pp. 31–32).

58. Myers (2001, p. 105).

59. Myers (2001, p. 108).

60. McLaren (1999, p. 50, italics in original).

61. Freire (1998, p. 48).

62. E.g., Carnine (2000).

63. Sokal & Bricmont (1998, p. 204).

64. Sokal & Bricmont (1998, p. 208, italics added).

65. Hirsch (1996), Shattuck (1999).

CHAPTER 7

Making Sense about Education

"Schools can be a vehicle for social change, but let us not overestimate the strength, actual or potential, of that impact. Far more powerful is the impact of society on schools, an impact that in recent decades has been as fruitless as it has been powerful. . . . Lest I be misunderstood: I am not advocating that the aims of education should include changing society."

— Seymour Sarason, psychologist

WE MUST MAKE SENSE ABOUT EDUCATION IF WE WANT TO IMPROVE IT

We have seen that there is much nonsensical talk about education, and it comes from many sources. For reasons that should be obvious to anyone who has read the preceding six chapters, postmodern and deconstructivist ideas offer no help in making sense. In fact, they are contrary to sense making. In my view and that of some of my colleagues, postmodernism is not merely impractical and dangerous in its implications but egregiously anti-intellectual.[1] Moreover, much of the popular reform rhetoric at both ends of the political spectrum, extreme right and extreme left, is vapid almost beyond belief. But merely pointing out intellectual folly begs the question of how to make sense of things in education. Therefore, I attempt in this last chapter to offer some suggestions and observations that I hope make sense. I offer a series of assertions and short accompanying essays of explanation that I hope will be of help in figuring out problems in education, including the problems inherent in providing appropriate education for students at the extremes of the distribution of achievement—those for whom special education is needed. My assertions are in an order that makes sense to me, although I admit that many of them are interrelated and that some may have no logical order. I have drawn on much of my own work and my work with colleagues over the past 30 years, but my colleagues should be held blameless for any assertion or explanation in which I do not make sense.

All of my essays address education specifically. You might be able to find examples from some fields in which my assertions do not hold. For example, although I begin with the observation that nothing works all the time, I feel certain that we could find some things outside of education that do work every single time (e.g., some things are invariably lethal, some things invariably render an engine inoperable). The understanding that I am addressing educational issues saves my having to begin each essay with the phrase, "In education." In some cases I refer to *exceptional* children, students, or learners. By *exceptional* I mean not much like the average in particular ways—unusual, atypical, whether because they have disabilities or because they are gifted. These are students who fall under either the far left or the far right tail of the distribution of performance.

By necessity, I have left some things out of this chapter. Early on in this book, I mentioned that too many mindless things about education have been said to recount them all. Likewise, I'm sure there are sensible things about education that I haven't included in this chapter. Some of the ways of thinking about education that I believe are sensible are implicit in my previous discussion of the stupid. But here I try to be more explicit about how to make sense.

I am aware that some readers will think my assertions are witless. However, if my statements seem merely commonsensical to you, I make no apology for that. Too much common sense has been drained out of education by enthusiasm for nonsense. One difference between what may be seen as my banality and the banality of postmodernists is that I intend my comments as an old-fashioned correction to the inane, not a new insight or "paradigm shift." In any case, I rest my case in this chapter: I leave it to you to judge what is silly and what is not.

NOTHING WORKS ALL THE
TIME (I.E., IN EVERY CASE)

By "works" I mean that it accomplishes the stated objective. This is an important point for those interested in education because so much of the popular rhetoric about education includes "all" (e.g., statements that all students will achieve____ or be ____ or learn ____). But failure in some cases is absolutely predictable. Even the very best instructional programs do not work for every single student. Some students are "nonresponders" who do not reach the objective (learning to read at ____ level, for example). *All* should not be and cannot reasonably be taken literally in statements about education. Trouble is, it often is.

Another reason this point is important is that, as I noted in an earlier chapter, perfection is not a reasonable expectation, desirable as a perfect education might be. If people are willing to discard any program that produces a residual—a certain percentage of nonresponders or failures—then they will throw baby out with bathwater. That is, they will not discriminate good from bad programs or best from good. This is why slogans like "success for all" are dangerous. They set up the expectation of zero failures in the program. When people find out they've been sold something through false advertising, they turn against it, even if it's better than the alternative. We need to find and promote programs that produce the lowest percentage of failure but admit that no program produces zero failures.

EVERYTHING APPEARS TO HAVE WORKED AT
SOME TIME (I.E., IN AT LEAST ONE INSTANCE)

"Appears" is an important word here, as people often misattribute an outcome to a cause. In every human service, including medicine, there are what we call "spontaneous recoveries" or unexplained changes. Sometimes people get worse (the treatment is then thought to have failed); sometimes they get better (the treatment is then thought to have been successful); sometimes they stay the same (the treatment is then thought to have had no effect one way or the other). This is true whether the treatment is medicine or education or counseling or anything else.

And sometimes people are fooled into thinking that because X, Y, or Z occurred and ___ effect followed, then the preceding event (X, Y, or Z) *caused* ____. This is the familiar error of logic; post hoc, ergo propter hoc (after the fact, therefore because of it). So many events occur in the universe that virtually anything can be mistaken to have caused a phenomenon. Random connections lead to superstitions, and if these superstitions are not debunked, then they may come to be seen as legitimate knowledge. As Lester Mann noted regarding such errors of logic, "yes, almost every intervention approach has its successes. . . . And so we repeat and repeat and again repeat the outworn, the discredited, the valueless."[2]

People are easily swayed by anecdotal data or personal testimony. Many individuals seem to "buy into" (and may literally buy) programs that are supported by only the flimsiest data, sometimes by observation of change in one or a small number of cases without any evidence of a cause-effect relationship. In short, people often proceed on the basis of superstition or pure hocus-pocus. Astrology is one example.[3] Education has a long history of scams, sham instructional programs, and programs implemented on a large scale but based on little or nothing more than assertions or theories that are never tested. For example, reading or math curricula may be adopted for an entire school system or even a state without evidence that they are effective in helping students learn what is desired. No wonder we get such fiascos as facilitated communication (a pretense of communication),[4] a whole-language-only approach to basic reading instruction, and arithmetic in which precise calculation is unimportant. In all likelihood, many people will agree with Robert L. Fried and others who call for accommodation of students' "learning styles" and recommend "learner-centered" education (or, in Fried's words, "a learner-centered cosmology"[5]) without inquiring much if at all about what the words actually mean or the evidence to support the recommendations. Such gullibility is neither wise nor helpful.

SOME THINGS WORK MUCH BETTER THAN OTHERS

Some things work for more cases or more reliably than do other things. It seems to come as a surprise to some people that we can make discriminations among programs based on the outcomes they produce. However, the data strongly suggest that some instructional approaches are significantly better than others for achieving particular goals.[6]

Here is a misstatement of fact that some people seem to hold: Nothing works in education. Other misstatements of fact that seem to attract adherents, including people who should know better, include these: In education, nothing works much better than anything else; everything works about the same; one approach is about as good as another, so we may as well teach teachers how to use everything, give them exposure to all possible ways of teaching any given thing. What a muddle-headed way of looking at the world, including education! Here's what I think we know: Some instructional approaches are good bets, others are bad bets. We ought to be teaching teachers to make good bets, to know what's likely to work and what isn't.

The fact that nothing works every time and everything appears to work sometimes shouldn't keep us from choosing what's most likely to work most of the time. And when we encounter a nonresponder to our best bet, our tactic should be to go to the *next best* bet, not abandon reason or try things at random. We expect physicians, pilots, mechanics, and every other group of practitioners to try the best-tested, most-likely-to-work things first and to have backup plans if the best bet doesn't work. We expect that they will not try things at random, and we interpret random selection of tools or strategies as incompetence or panic. We should not encourage or tolerate the nonsense of random selection of education strategies by teacher educators, school boards, education administrators, or teachers.

But the idea that we can find no best way to do anything in schooling dies very hard. The idea is alive and well that no way of teaching is better than another.[7] I suppose this idea is a spin-off of the observation that no known method of instruction is foolproof or works every time. But this observation seems then to be taken to mean that we can't find an instructional approach that works best—achieves our objective for the largest number of students. If you can't find a method that always works, then just let educators choose whatever they like, the argument seems to go. I'm glad we don't tolerate this laissez faire attitude in many professions and trades, as it promises continuing but avoidable disasters.

Some things are, actually, impossible—like "all the children above average" or having no low achievers. I suppose it's a good idea to remember that there is nothing less probable than the impossible. Some things are known to be rather unlikely—like producing well-educated children by helping them explore only the topics in which they seem to have an interest and putting education primarily under the control of the students. Why promote them, then?

THE BEST GUIDE TO FINDING OUT WHAT WORKS AND WHAT DOESN'T IS SCIENCE

Our best bet for finding out what works and what doesn't is the objective, replicable, publicly verifiable data that are associated with the Enlightenment and the natural sciences, engineering, and technology. The scientific method involves testing hypotheses that can be disproved or supported by publicly verifiable data to which scientists and philosophers of science have access.[8] If a theory can't possibly be proved false, then it isn't scientific. That's why "creation science" is an oxymoron (a self-contradiction); a creationist's belief "cannot be considered a scientific theory since it cannot be tested and proven wrong." That's also why "true scientists must do everything possible to find the flaws in their own theories, to try to prove them false. Only if they do that and fail can we begin to have confidence in their hypothesis."[9]

The only alternative to science is assertions that are either unsubstantiated or substantiated only by a body of "believers" who require no proof beyond their personal experience and conviction or are willing to accept as fact the pronouncement of a political or religious authority regardless of evidence to the contrary. This nonscientific approach leaves us with one of two situations: (a) a cognitive morass in which the falsity of no statement can be determined, so one idea is as good as another, or (b) an authoritarian state or religion in which truth is assumed to be made by fiat. Neither is compatible with my concept of human dignity.

Doug Carnine has observed that education will become a mature profession only when it rejects idiosyncratic knowledge for a common knowledge based on what can be verified objectively through methods of scientific inquiry.[10] Most of us want and expect those who build or fix cars and airplanes, practice medicine, build houses, and so on to use scientific information in their practices. We should expect no less of educators.

PEOPLE MAY MAKE POLICY BASED ON PHILOSOPHY OR POLITICS RATHER THAN EVIDENCE

To some people, data do not matter much, if at all. In short, people may simply dismiss scientific data about education as trivial or misleading and embrace ideas that have what they consider the right "feel" to them. In an earlier chapter, I discussed why education, at least in the sense of giving people information, is not the answer to getting people to make better decisions. True, people can't make good decisions in the absence of reliable information. But data do not suggest that if people have reliable information they will always use it well. Another way of saying this is that good information doesn't necessarily result in good behavior.

Nonscientific and aggressively *anti*-scientific beliefs are very strong today, and these sentiments or frames of mind pose a significant threat to any real progress in education. *The New Yorker* magazine of April 14, 1997, devoted its entire "Talk of the Town" feature to commentary on the mass suicide of Marshall Applewhite and his Heaven's Gate cult. You may recall that Applewhite and his followers rejected evidence in favor of belief in the supernatural (a spaceship behind a comet was supposed to pick them up and transfer them to, well, someplace where they needed, apparently, to be dead to go). *The New Yorker* concluded, "Though science is stronger today than when Galileo knelt before the Inquisition, it remains a minority habit of mind, and its future is very much in doubt. Blind belief rules the millennial universe, dark and rangy as space itself."[11] At about the same time that *The New Yorker* published its essay on Applewhite, *Life* magazine featured an article on the resurgence of belief in astrology. Its cover read, "ASTROLOGY RISING: Why So Many of Us Now Believe the Stars Reflect the Soul."[12] Belief in astrology has burgeoned in the past 20 years in the absence of any scientific evidence whatever to support its claims and in the face of reliable scientific evidence that its perceived "success" is a function of people's suggestibility and desire for personal validation.[13]

I will never forget my dismay when, in 1998, some of the people in my educator-audience responded to my statement that astrology is pure hokum with protests and expressions of discomfort that I would say such a thing!

E. D. Hirsch, Jr., too, has discussed the lure of philosophical propositions or doctrines, such as those associated with "progressive" education (e.g., child-centered education, learning styles, multiple intelligences, cooperative learning, caring communities in schools; teaching for understanding, developmentally appropriate practice, alternative assessment; discovery-oriented science, whole language reading instruction).[14] Although large-scale comparisons strongly support direct instruction as the most effective approach to teaching, many educators and politicians—especially people in positions of power to disseminate information and make decisions regarding curriculum and instruction—have chosen to ignore the data and proceed on hunch or feeling or philosophical bias.[15] Putting education on a scientific footing will require working against strong antiscientific and anti-intellectual currents in American society.

REAL AND ANTICIPATED CONSEQUENCES OFTEN HAVE PROFOUND EFFECTS ON BEHAVIOR

The great psychologist Albert Bandura has provided what, for me, is the most comprehensive and well-established theory of why people behave as they do. In *Social Foundations of Thought and Action*, he explains how our behavior is built and maintained by both the actual consequences we experience and the consequences we anticipate for behaving in a given manner.[16] Surely, we have overwhelming evidence, as Bandura points out, that the actual social and material consequences of behavior are extremely important in teaching and learning. However, he also shows how and why our thoughts or beliefs about the likely consequences of our behavior—what we think, what we hope for, what we dread, what we anticipate—influence what we do.

A lot of behavior that we call deviant, aberrant, troubled, or unproductive may be the result of real consequences that are perverse or false beliefs about consequences. For example, scientific evidence strongly suggests that much student misbehavior is produced by actual consequences (e.g., lots of attention and increased social status among peers for misconduct, no attention and lower status for desirable behavior).[17] And phobias can be analyzed as false beliefs that terrible consequences are likely to follow certain behavior (e.g., petting a dog, getting on an airplane, riding in a car, entering a hospital, walking under a ladder).

The point is that everyone's conduct—the behavior of students in school, parents of students, school teachers and administrators, school board members, and so on—is profoundly affected by real and anticipated consequences. True, biological factors (e.g., genetics, brain malfunction) affect the way we behave, but the consequence a behavior produces is something we can often control directly and usefully. We can often help people make better predictions about the likely consequences of their behavior, too. So we need to inquire of proposals to change schools or schooling what the consequences will actually be for the people involved and what they believe are the likely consequences. And, if their beliefs are wrong about the likely effects of these consequences, can we change them?

Now, as to the matter of right and wrong beliefs, I realize, as I discussed earlier in this book, that sometimes we cannot ascribe right or wrong to actions, ideas, or preferences. Nevertheless, I think we sometimes can. Sometimes people believe things that are demonstrably wrong; their thinking has gone haywire, and they reach a conclusion that cannot be justified as truth. I will not belabor the issue but merely refer to works on science and pseudoscience.[18] The caution I offer has been tendered by numerous scientists, including Stephen J. Gould in many of his writings: failing to try to discover and acknowledge facts through reason and the methods of Enlightenment science leaves us at the mercy of the most vicious human impulses.

IMPORTANT FACTS AND SKILLS ARE TAUGHT MOST EFFECTIVELY BY DIRECT INSTRUCTION

Any program of education should reveal what it is that students should know and be able to do. If these facts and skills are stated clearly, then we know what the goals of the program are, and we can measure progress toward them with a reasonable degree of precision. If the program does not state what these facts and skills are but only describes a process (e.g., learning through exploration), then watch out! Probably, we will have no way of knowing whether the program is meeting its objectives. But, even if we have evidence that the process included in a program description is being used, the process doesn't tell us whether students are acquiring the knowledge and skills they will need.

Nothing is gained by keeping students guessing about what it is they are supposed to learn. In all or nearly all of the education programs in which the majority of students can be demonstrated to be highly successful in learning the facts and skills they need, these facts and skills are taught directly rather than indirectly. That is, the teacher is in control of instruction, not the student, and information is given to students. Giving information doesn't mean that the instruction is dull, and it doesn't mean that students don't learn to apply their knowledge and skills to everyday problems. Neither does it mean that students have nothing to say about their education. But it does mean that students don't waste time and effort trying to figure out what they're to learn. It also means that students aren't allowed to learn misrules—learn the wrong thing or a faulty application so that their learning can be described as false, misleading, or useless.

Learning facts and skills can be—and it is, actually, for nearly everyone—a self-enhancing, exciting experience. Furthermore, having facts and skills at your disposal enables you to learn more. A point I made earlier in this book, and one made exceedingly clearly by such writers as E. D. Hirsch, Jr., is that a person needs facts to think with. Without factual information, students' futures and learning are foreshortened. Too bad it has become popular to dismiss facts as "factoids" and assume that drill kills learning and interest in it. If drill really kills, I wonder why some of the world's greatest musicians (people like Ray Charles and Stephan Grapelli, for example) practice chords and scales. Actually, I think it's important to "drill to thrill" on some things—learn them to the point that they become automatic and experience the pleasure of having them down pat.

People who know a lot of things can be unpleasant to deal with, but not because they know a lot of stuff. People who don't know important things drive us all nuts when we encounter them in our everyday lives because they can neither help us nor think critically—nor help themselves.

PARTICULAR KNOWLEDGE AND SKILLS
USUALLY HAVE TO BE ACQUIRED IN SEQUENCE

This may seem obvious to a logical thinker, but it is not necessarily a proposition taken to heart in rhetoric about education. For example, except in the most extraordinary cases, a child needs to learn to read in the sense of being able to call the words—say what is written down—before he or she can comprehend what's been written. That is, learning the mechanics of reading—learning the sound-symbol correspondences— almost always precedes learning to comprehend written material. Learning to calculate accurately, including learning the basic number facts, usually precedes learning to make good estimates of quantities resulting from basic arithmetical operations. Becoming scientifically literate requires learning the most important or central ideas on which others hinge.[19] Other writers have explained clearly why you can't be a good thinker without knowing facts to think with. You won't think much with a mind that has no facts, and some facts have to be known before others make sense.

A popular folly is to try to build up a student's self-esteem without improving his or her performance. Another is to instill love of learning while avoiding emphasis on content or facts. Self-esteem that isn't based on improved performance will be false or short-lived or both. And as far as I can figure out, love of learning comes from knowing facts about things and finding it really cool to know those facts and even cooler to be learning more facts all the time. Teaching people to love ignorance or to take pride in not knowing is no gift— a teacher who teaches such is not gifted, nor does he or she give the student a gift. If we want to know whether an educational program is successful, we need to ask what the students learn—the content, the facts, the performances that they master. If the students know or can do little more after going through a program than before, then I don't think it matters that they feel good about themselves. In fact, if they do feel good about themselves for not learning, then I fear we've misled them.

Do children need to feel good about themselves? Absolutely. Feeling good about themselves is really important. But it isn't the only important thing, and it is important that their good feelings be rooted in some realities of their own achievement. And I believe that it is possible and important for all children who can be said to have self-concepts (i.e., whose level of cognitive awareness allows a self-concept to emerge) to learn things about which they can and should feel good.

THE ONLY WAY TO KNOW WHETHER
A PROGRAM IS WORKING IS BY TESTING

Good teachers check frequently to see what their students know or have learned. They measure outcomes. They check on what they are teaching. That is, their testing is curriculum-referenced or curriculum-based. This kind of testing is far more frequent and useful in teaching than the federal- or state-mandated testing that occurs every year or so. In fact, some sort of assessment—a check to see whether the student has the idea or can perform as expected—is built into the lessons of effective teachers. There is no substitute for this kind of nearly continuous checking or testing.

Of course, test results often have been misinterpreted, as Stephen Jay Gould showed in considerable detail in his famous book about the unintelligent uses of intelligence tests, *The Mismeasure of Man*. Sometimes test results have been said to represent things they clearly do not. Sometimes far too much has been made of a test score. But these facts no more make the case against testing than the fact that airplanes can be and have been used for silly or evil purposes makes the case against airplanes.

How people intend to work for social justice and educational equity without measuring what kids have learned beats me. I think measurement is essential, even though we have often seen mismeasurement. All scientists, regardless of their specialty, know the importance of measurement. So do all politically astute nonscientists who want to see social justice achieved. Gould's observations on this issue are succinct:

> My book, by the way, has been commonly portrayed, even (to my chagrin) often praised, as a general attack upon mental testing. *The Mismeasure of Man* is no such thing, and I have an agnostic attitude (born mostly of ignorance) toward mental testing in general. If my critics doubt this, and read these lines as a smoke screen, just consider my expressed opinion about Binet's original IQ test—strongly and entirely positive (for Binet rejected the hereditarian interpretation, and only wanted to use

the test as a device to identify children in need of special help; and for this humane goal, I have nothing but praise). *The Mismeasure of Man* is a critique of a *specific* theory of intelligence often supported by *particular* interpretation of a *certain* style of mental testing: the theory of unitary, genetically based, unchangeable intelligence.[20]

Attacks on the misuse and misinterpretation of tests are sensible. Attacks on testing itself, whether standardized or any other type, seem to me misguided and anti-intellectual. Broadsides against standardized testing seem to me counterproductive, sure to work against the improvement of education by keeping important information from being obtained. If people don't have information, then they can't misuse it, that's true; but, then, neither can they use it well. Ignorance doesn't seem to me to be a good choice.

Standardized testing and only occasional teacher testing have some undeniable limitations. For one thing, by the time a particular student is found to have a learning deficit on a yearly test (or one given by a teacher each grading period), it is way too late to address the problem most effectively. But this doesn't mean the yearly or grading-period check is unimportant. Standardized testing can tell us things that teacher-made, curriculum-based tests can't. It is important to know how a class or school or district or state is doing compared to the average. Damning standardized tests makes about as much sense as damning growth charts that help us understand how a child compares to the average height and weight at a given age. It makes about as much sense as objecting to comparing a child's body temperature or white blood cell count or strength to normal—to a norm. Of course, people can do dumb things with information, including test scores, but that does not make the tests inappropriate. Not wanting to know how a child or group is doing compared to the norm, whether in education or in physiology, is a lapse of common sense and caring that most of us would consider to border on criminal stupidity.

TESTING RESULTS IN A DISTRIBUTION
WITH IMMUTABLE PROPERTIES

I sometimes suspect that many people would like to devise a way of measuring something precisely, yet produce no variance—no detectable differences in measurements. But as far as I can figure out, there are only two ways to avoid variance: (a) measure very imprecisely, so that everything or everyone measured falls into the same category or (b) don't measure at all.

Any reasonably accurate measurement (or test) that has a range of scores, not a single criterion, will produce a distribution that puts some people or things above and some below average on what is measured. You can't produce a distribution in which all the test takers are above average. And if the distribution has more extremely high than extremely low performers, then it is a mathematical certainty that more than half of the test takers will be below the arithmetic average (mean) for that distribution.

To some, ignorance is, indeed, bliss. That is, they are happier not knowing how a child compares to others (or the average) and not knowing what the distribution of outcomes looks like. Some people become very good at ignoring reality and urging others to do so as well.

True, there are "criterion-referenced" tests. The purpose of these tests is to see whether a student has reached a particular criterion or benchmark of performance. The outcome of giving such tests is either "pass" or "fail." As I discussed in chapter 5, criteria or benchmarks are ultimately related to normative distributions. We may be able to avoid considering normative distributions for a while, but not for long.

TESTING IS USEFUL ONLY IF YOU MAKE THE RIGHT COMPARISONS FOR THE RIGHT REASONS

Test scores, like stock prices, are not helpful if you don't know how to interpret them. A lot of people in high places seem to have very low skills in making sense of test information. This gives testing an undeserved bad name.

When you're trying to assess the progress of a student in a curriculum, then perhaps the most important comparison to make is of the student's own performance over time. That is, you'd want to know whether the student is improving, whether his or her performance shows a trend toward increasing competence or fluency in the skill you're teaching. Not only that. You'd also want to know whether a trend line showing improvement was sharp or steep enough that the student would catch up, not just stay behind typical students of the same age. The objective of compensatory and special education is to accelerate kids' learning so that if possible they catch up (remember that some students are nonresponders to the best instruction we can offer, and it is a given that some students will remain below average by any reasonable comparison).

When you're trying to see whether a student is meeting a reasonable expectation, then comparison to others is essential. We have no way of knowing whether an expectation is reasonable—too high, too low, about right—without comparison to other individuals. This seems so commonsensical as not to be a necessary statement, but some comments about education seem based on an alternative assumption. Without norms for growth, temperature, math, reading, and so on we simply don't know whether someone is achieving about what we should expect, way high, or way low.

Making the right comparisons is important, but so is interpreting the results. How much difference is significant or important or should trigger some action, and how much is simply part of the random and predictable error of measurement? What differences should result in our asking, "Who cares?" and what differences are legitimate reasons for elation or concern? Too often, news media, politicians, and educators make something of nothing or miss an important difference. It is not unusual for politicians or news media to make a big deal about a change in ranking or a change of a few points (either test scores or percentiles) that could easily have occurred simply by chance. And whopping differences, such as the marked advantages of direct instruction in very large-scale comparisons, may simply be ignored.[21]

The issue of significant change is critically important for programs designed to reward schools that "improve" or close down schools that "fail." We always need to ask what index of central tendency (average) is the basis for "improvement" or "failure"—mean (arithmetic average), median (the middle score), or mode (the most frequent score)? And what has happened to those at the margins of the distribution— those whose scores are particularly high or low? Could a school be judged to have "improved" by raising its mean and median while neglecting students with exceptionally low scores? It would, of course, be possible to "win" or "succeed" by raising the mean and giving the distribution a positive skew while producing no improvement at all in the scores of the low performers. In fact, this is apparently exactly what some so-called successful schools do.[22]

So, to what population(s) or distribution(s) should we compare ourselves or our schools or students? Just depends on what we want to know and what we want to make of the comparison. I suppose I could compare my bass playing to that of most professional players, and as a consequence I'd look really bad and want to give up. Probably I'd engage in a lot of self-derogatory talk. Or, I could compare my bass playing to that of others who, like me, started playing relatively late in life (age 55). In that case, I might feel pretty good. Or, if I wanted something to make me look really good, I'd compare my bass playing to that of people my age who have never touched a bass in their lives before being given one and told to play. Of course, there's the matter of the test of bass playing, too. Depends on whether it's a test of bowing an open string or playing through a Mahler symphony.

The point here is that in education we often find silly comparisons— apples to oranges, if you will, or something worse. I think it may make sense to judge progress or success by comparison with national norms of achievement on standardized tests, but let's not avoid this reality: Once we get a lot of students above the national norm, the norm will be judged "outdated" and a new norm will take its place. Sometimes I wonder why some of the critics of education don't just compare our current students' performance to old norms, declare the schools "fixed," and stop complaining. I've always wondered how these critics would know that the schools have been "fixed," as their concept of "fixed" seems not to correspond to anything I understand about distributions of outcomes.

COMPARISONS PUT SOMEONE LOWEST OR LAST AND SOMEONE HIGHEST OR FIRST

Obsession with being first, best, highest, #1 any way you choose to say it, may be peculiarly American. Whether it is or not, it's clear that American politicians want American education at all levels to be judged the best in the world (American higher education is almost universally thus judged; it is K–12 education that is depicted in many comparisons as less than best). But here is a hard reality: comparisons of any kind always put someone (or something) lowest or last and someone (or something) else highest or first. And half will be below the median—unless the comparison is to another group's distribution.

Regardless of any obsession with being #1, the fact that comparisons always put someone last means that any program designed to eliminate "failure" defined by being last or lowest is—well, ridiculous. It can't happen. Seems obvious, but that doesn't keep the U.S. Congress or states from trying to do it or secretaries of education from proposing it or politicians and school board members at any level from endorsing it or the general public from buying it.

Is it ok to be last or lowest in a distribution? Well, for me, that depends on the distribution. Being last or lowest should be no cause for alarm in education if one is still doing one's best, and particularly if one's performance is good, though not as good as others'. In my opinion, people often make too much out of being first or last or above or below an average. What it means to be first or last or average depends on the distribution you're comparing to, and it's important to remember than not everyone can be first or even above average and that being lowest isn't always to have failed in life or even to have failed in a meaningful way, depending on one's objectives. However, I'll grant you this: Most of us, most of the time and for good reasons, want to know how we compare to others in the distribution.

SOME INDIVIDUALS ARE ON THE EDGE OF ANY CRITERION WE SET

Anytime we define an acceptable level of performance, some individuals are on the edge of it (i.e., they can be considered "borderline"), and judgments about which side of the line individuals are on will sometimes be wrong. To me, this seems self-evident and something that just needs to be remembered and managed well, but some people make too much of it. Those who object to this observation or to any measurement that produces it (which means to any and all measurement, as every measurement produces this effect) seem to want things to be on or off, black or white, 0 or 1. But most human characteristics are continuously distributed—that is, they have values that range from a little to a lot with really fine gradations of the variable being possible. Height, for example, is continuously distributed, as is weight, age, skin color, reading ability, and intelligence (or stupidity). Some things are discrete (categorical) variables, like citizenship. You are either in or out, a citizen or a noncitizen of a particular country in some legal sense. But, again, most of the things we deal with in education are continuous variables, not categorical (discrete) variables.

For any continuously distributed variable, we set a cutoff value that seems reasonable, although people who come close to it don't quite make it or qualify. "Tall" and "short," for example, are arbitrary distinctions that have value, but if we say a tall person is 6 feet 4 inches in height, then some people are almost tall, but not quite. And we're always making the judgment compared to some arbitrary standard. Sometimes we put people in discrete categories based on a continuously distributed variable that can be measured rather precisely. "Tall" is one. "Voting age" is another. Still, that leaves some people on the "cusp," the almost-but-not-quite. And to the extent that we consider many variables at once and form a judgment based on the general picture—competent or not competent for a particular job, for instance—we will sometimes find different people arriving at different conclusions in the same case (e.g., one interviewer says "competent," another "not competent"; one reviewer saying "publish as is," another "make major revisions"). So, why do some people have such a hard time with "judgmental" disabilities, such as learning disabilities or emotional or behavioral disorders or mental retardation? Why are they upset by the observation that a child might be considered to have an emotional or behavioral disorder in one school district and not in another or be said by one psychologist to have such a disorder and by another not to have it? Beats me.

Now, I do understand that measurement can be faulty, that assessment can be inadequate, that judgment can be way off, and so on. But this is not the same as criticizing a category of performance or ability simply because people may disagree on who belongs in it and who doesn't and some kids are on the border. There is no way to take all of the ambiguity out of teaching or out of categorizing students.

Furthermore, it's important to consider the costs of making particular kinds of mistakes. Suppose we're considering whether to identify a student for special education. If we identify a student we should not, then our mistake is a false positive. If we do not identify a student whom we should, then our mistake is a false negative. Which is worse? All depends on how you view being identified for special education — the personal costs and risks involved if you make one mistake versus another. Of course, there are the clear-cut cases, but that's not the point here. The point is that in some cases we won't know for sure what to do. There is no way around this.

A "FIXED" SCHOOL WILL HAVE SOME "FAILURES"

It's no secret—it's an undeniable and well-known fact—that schools produce some failures. An implicit if not explicit goal of some school reformers is to eliminate failure. Schools without failure cannot be designed, however, unless success and failure are misrepresented. As I've already noted, you can't measure something without producing variance (differences) and a distribution of values (quantities of what you measure), and every distribution has a top and a bottom tier.

Please note that I am not saying that any amount of failure is ok, nor am I saying that we can do no better than we are doing currently as far as helping children learn is concerned. *We can and must improve schools in terms of their outcomes for students.* At the same time, I think it's important to see the misrepresentation in the name of programs like Success for All (SFA) and slogans like "No child left behind." We do know that some instructional programs work better than others, and we have strong evidence that Direct Instruction (DI) and SFA produce far better results than other programs in comparison studies.[23] Does SFA really, actually produce success in reading for *all* children, *no* exceptions? Of course not! It might more honestly be called Success for More, as it does help more students learn to read than learn to read in most alternative programs. The same can be said of DI.

I put "fixed" and "failures" in quotes simply to indicate that their definitions are completely arbitrary. What would be the distribution of outcomes in a "fixed" school? Of course, some reformers will suggest that the distribution isn't important, only the criterion for acceptable performance (success?), but that is an evasion of the issue. If the definition of "fixed" is that all students will reach a particular criterion, what will we say of those who don't meet it? If each and every student in a school reaches the criterion, will that criterion be judged too low?

Some will suggest that "fixed" means everyone does better than before the school was "fixed." But that notion, too, begs the question. How much better? Will those who improved only a tiny bit be judged to have "succeeded?" Others may suggest that in a "fixed" school the mean or median will be higher than before the fix. But that definition ignores issues of the highest and lowest achievers, especially the lowest, who in some distributions may have disabilities.

Bryan Cook and his colleagues at the University of California at Santa Barbara have examined the question of the distribution of outcomes in schools where reforms were said to address the achievement of *all* students.[24] They found—rather predictably, I think—that schools looking better in terms of *average* achievement did not appear to have done much for the lowest achievers. The students at the bottom of the distribution didn't learn much. A more recent study of the effects of reform-based mathematics instruction in five third-grade classrooms found much the same thing. Remember that much of the current reform rhetoric comes from "progressive" ideology in which discovery learning, cooperative learning, and the same high standards for all students are emphasized. Here is the way the researchers described the reform-based instruction they studied in third-grade classrooms:

> In reform-based lessons, low achievers face the challenge of becoming part of a community of learners in which students are to construct their own understanding of mathematical concepts through conversations with peers and the teacher. An underlying assumption is that students can exchange ideas and learn from each other.[25]

The outcome of the research by Baxter and colleagues was, to me, pretty predictable—which does not mean unimportant, merely that a scientific study confirmed what one might expect. The low achievers in the third-grade classrooms they studied didn't seem to get much at all from the instruction the teachers offered. That instruction might have been just fine for typical and high achievers, but just being there with the average and higher achieving kids didn't help those who didn't understand what was going on. What do we adults do in a group when we don't understand what's going on? We remain passive, marginal members of the group. Usually, we're silent or distract ourselves with other things. Little wonder that a substantial body of research shows that kids react the same way to being in a group where they don't get it. As Baxter et al. summarized, "The assumption that all students will flourish with the challenging mathematics curricula and pedagogy that comprise reform needs to be questioned."[26]

Teachers or principals who are expected to raise average achievement would not be smart to give disproportionate effort to instructing low achievers, as the payoff for raising the median or mean achievement is in the average to high achievers. As I noted in chapter 4, if you give adequate attention to high achievers, then the distribution of outcomes shows a positive skew, and that does two things: raises the mean and puts more than half of the individuals in the distribution below it.

Does the observation that failure cannot be eliminated mean that we should give up on improving (or, if you will, "fixing") schools? No, I don't think so. But it does mean three things for me. First, we need to be forthright about the fact that "failure" is arbitrarily defined and unavoidable. Second, we need to take a realistic view of which students are likely to "fail" in a particular classroom or school and what their "failure" really means. Third, we need to provide alternatives that minimize predictable "failure"—different classrooms, schools, and curricula for students who need them so that the maximum number of students experience relative success (all success, as I noted is relative to some standard).

FAILURE OF SOME STUDENTS WITH DISABILITIES TO REACH A STANDARD IS PREDICTABLE

Why is the failure of some exceptional students to profit from standard educational programs utterly predictable? The answer seems obvious to me. It is because they differ significantly from the modal or typical student in instructionally relevant ways. Standard programs are designed for modal (most frequently occurring) students, not those at the extremes of a distribution. These standard educational programs simply cannot, and can't be expected to, accommodate extreme differences in instructionally relevant characteristics, like abilities to read, perceive, organize, store, retrieve, and apply information to the solution of particular problems. Some students with disabilities are going to fail to meet standard educational goals regardless of the instructional strategies a teacher uses.

Some students with disabilities can meet state testing standards, but not with the standard instructional program or in the standard amount of time or by the typical chronological age. And some students who are gifted will be bored out of their minds by having to repeat and by being expected to *appear* to learn things they learned long ago.

Pixie Holbrook described the futility and cruelty of requiring all students with disabilities to take state-mandated examinations that are appropriate for the majority of students. She describes the agony for herself and one of her pupils, Sarah, a fourth-grader with a learning disability. Sarah is a good and diligent student, but because of her learning disability she hasn't the skills required for the test.

> She knows she doesn't know. And she knows that I know she doesn't know. This is so very humiliating.
>
> Her eyes are wet now, but she's silent and stoic. I check in, and she reassures me she's fine. She appears to be on the verge of weeping, but she will not be deterred. I cannot help her in any way; I can only sit nearby and return a false smile. I can offer a break, nothing more. Later, I calculated the reading level of this selection. Sarah reads like a second-grader, and the poem is at the high end of the fifth-grade scale. Her eyes are not just scanning the paragraphs. I know she has stopped reading and is just glancing and gazing. It's meaningless, and it hurts. Yet she attempts to answer every question.
>
> It is now 2½ hours, and my anger is growing. This is immoral and has become intolerable. And it's only the first day.[27]

Requiring all students with disabilities and those for whom the tests are inappropriate for other reasons to take state exams isn't just cruel to students and their teachers, it also makes certain research comparisons impossible. As Eric Hurley and his colleagues noted:

Unfortunately for researchers, the Texas Education Agency changed test procedures in 1999 and began requiring the inclusion of special education students and significantly changing the rules regarding the administration of the English TAAS to children who were just learning English, especially those children who had been taught reading primarily in Spanish. These changes made the data for 1999 and 2000 not comparable with the earlier data.[28]

Teachers and school administrators have, it seems to me, a moral obligation to recognize the fact that many special education students should not be required to take state competency exams.

Moreover, teachers have to be allowed, even encouraged, to recognize the limits of their instructional competence. Teachers should decline to teach students for whom their training is inadequate and decline to teach a curriculum that isn't right for their students. John Goodlad, a leading teacher educator, recognized that neither those who train teachers nor, by implication, those who teach children, should shirk the responsibility of recognizing the limits of their skill:

> Even supposing it could be argued that all traits are amenable to education, teacher education programs possess neither the resources nor the time to redress severe personality disorders; and they appear ill-equipped to perform lesser tasks. Consequently, the moral and ethical imperatives of selection [of teachers to be trained] require that applicants be counseled out if they fall seriously short in characteristics that are deemed important but for which there are no programmatic provisions. Failure to so counsel is morally wrong, and the consequences are costly.[29]

I think Goodlad is quite right about this. But for the life of me I can't figure out how someone who agrees with Goodlad can then turn around and argue that teachers in elementary and secondary schools should just try to teach all students, regardless of students' characteristics. And, so some argue, if a teacher has a student that he or she can't seem to teach and manage or one who seriously interferes with teaching the rest of the class, then that teacher should just suck it up and learn to deal with it, never work to get the student taught in a special class or school. Maybe that teacher could ask for help, so the full-inclusion or merge-general-and-special-education argument goes, but not give up responsibility for the student and turn education of that student over to someone else.

I try to make this add up with any other profession's attitudes toward its clients, and I can't. What would we think of a dentist who said, "Well, no, I don't know what to do here, but I'm not going to refer you to someone else, because I am responsible for treating *all* of my patients? So I'll ask another dentist what to do and then do my best to follow the advice I get." Would we not want to wring the neck, if not sue, a mechanic or plumber or builder or lawyer who was in over his or her head—didn't have the skills demanded of the case and knew it—yet wouldn't give the job over to someone with the necessary skills?

Knowing the limits of one's knowledge and skill and being given the responsibility for refusing clients whose problems don't match one's training and skills are rather basic professional and moral responsibilities, it seems to me. Those who do not want teachers to decline to teach a child for whom they are not prepared believe one of two erroneous things, I think: (a) teachers shouldn't be professionals in any true sense or (b) students don't actually differ much in what's required to teach them. Teaching is teaching, they seem to believe, and if you can teach one student you can teach any student. I find that kind of denial maddening.

STUDENTS WHO FAIL AT CERTAIN THINGS AREN'T TOTAL FAILURES

Some people fail at few things, others at many. We have a tendency to write people off as failures if they fail at anything we think is important, regardless of the values or abilities of the person whose performance we judge to be failing. Much as we are too quick to judge someone who makes a vapid statement a stupid person, we overgeneralize. Surely, there are people whom failure seems to dog, and I believe there are people who could be described as *being* failures or as having failed generally at life. But those cases are, I think, rare. And, although some people may act like test scores are everything, we know that they're not—and we need to act like they're not.

Some people fail at something because of a disability, and their disability is then used against them in an unfair manner.[30] True, we can't eliminate failure, and we can't and shouldn't "protect" people from confronting their own and other people's failures. But keeping failure at a particular thing or things in perspective is also important. Dan Hallahan and I, as well as many of our colleagues in special education, have noted that although people with disabilities can't do certain things (and, thus, could be said to fail in some respect) it is essential that we focus on what they *can* do, which for most people with disabilities is most of the things we consider normal or expected.[31]

Failure at something doesn't make a person bad, nor does success make them a good person. Sometimes I think people misunderstand this and suppose that those who are gifted are better people and those who are disabled are not as good as others. Achievement or success at something doesn't make someone a better person, but it does enhance a person's opportunities. The more you know and are able to do, the more opportunities you have to learn and succeed. We do want to give students the greatest opportunity we can, and that means teaching them things that will open up new opportunities. I tried to make this clear in a previously published essay.

> Clearly, we do not want a human's worth to be measured simply by what he or she can do. That criterion would, for example, result in very little worth being attached to infants and young children. Yet, what someone can do is not a trivial matter. A just and humane society does not value people *for* what they can do, but it does unequivocally value peoples' ability to do certain things. If we do not value what people can do, then we have no reason to teach anyone anything. We value what people can do because of what accomplishment does for them, the additional opportunities it brings them—not because it makes them better people but because it makes them people who are better off.[32]

Certainly, assuming that the test score is all that matters is perverse. It's the kind of perversion and stupidity we would be much better off without. We want kids to be happy and go to school excited about learning. Those objectives aren't incompatible with test scores unless we act as if, and teach kids that, test scores are all that matter. Still, avoiding test scores is just a way of evading reality.

One more thing here: It's important to note that failure once doesn't mean failure always. Most people can and do learn lots of things. Sometimes they have to try again, sometimes many times, before they learn a particular thing. Sometimes things just start to "click," and away they go. Sometimes people just seem to hit a "wall" and don't progress beyond it. Anyone who's practiced a musical instrument or sport knows the phenomenon most people call a learning "plateau," a point at which progress seems to stop. But persistence usually pays off, in that progress resumes with repeated practice—sometimes people experience a "breakthrough" in their progress, but not unless they're persistent. Yes, people differ in aptitudes for particular things and in skill in picking them up, but we have to be really careful not to assume that because a person is progressing only slowly (or rapidly) they'll always continue at that rate.

SCHOOL REFORM IS MEANINGLESS UNLESS IT FOCUSES ON INSTRUCTION AND EVIDENCE

For some reason, school reformers seem hung up on form and tend to forget about function—how and why *instruction* works. What are the big topics? School choice, vouchers, restructuring, annual testing, standards of learning, inclusion. All are doomed to fail to achieve what reformers say they hope to achieve—better outcomes for all students—unless instruction gets better. And instruction doesn't get better automatically, without specific attention to it. Oh, a few students will do better if they're faced with demanding tests. A few parents will choose schools in which instruction is central. But these will tend to be the students and parents who are already doing what we want. Most won't improve or make better choices, primarily because they can't.

Just consider, for example, the publication of *Rethinking Special Education for a New Century*, a tome edited by Chester E. Finn, Jr., Andrew J. Rotherham, and Charles R. Hokanson, Jr. and published by the Fordham Foundation in 2001. Only one of the 15 chapters is about instruction—chapter 12, about learning disabilities. The rest are about rules, compliance, state versus national responsibilities, accountability (without stressing, of course, that it's unconscionable to set standards without considering instruction), choice, administrative structures, eligibility for services, assigning children to categories. In their final chapter on conclusions and principles for reform, Finn, Rotherham, and

Hokanson recommend six principles for reforming special education, which might be summarized as follows:

1. Make standards performance-based when possible.
2. Reduce the number of special education categories.
3. Focus on prevention and intervention, using research-based practices.
4. Encourage flexibility, innovation, and choice, giving parents and children options and fostering integration of general and special education.
5. Provide adequate funding.
6. End double standards whenever possible.

Here, where we supposedly get the big picture, the important stuff distilled, instruction is but a hint or a whisper. It is not made the central issue. It is reduced to a parenthetical comment: "Chapter 12 presents a compelling case for early identification, prevention, and intervention in what will otherwise emerge as learning disabilities. (This should, of course, be rooted in effective and research-based reading instruction.)"[33]

The focus needs to be on instruction, not form or structure, for reasons that seem obvious to me. Instruction fuels learning. Failing to pay attention to it is a lot like failing to pay attention to whether there's fuel in the tank of a car. Instruction is the active ingredient in learning that those who focus on school restructuring, school choice, standards, and so on—the administrative form of education—seem to make secondary, if not ignore completely. Furthermore, good instruction lessens the probability that students will misbehave.[34]

Why instruction receives so little attention in education reform may not be too hard to figure out. For one thing, reformers would have to come out for the use of reliable methods of instruction—those that well-managed field tests (i.e., the best scientific evidence we can get) show produce the best results. This would require working against the popular affection for progressive education that E. D. Hirsch, Jr., and Diane Ravitch have described. And, of course, teachers would have to be trained or retrained, and that would cost a lot of money and cause some teachers and some teacher educators to get their noses out of joint because they want to use instructional methods that they prefer, not necessarily what's been proven most effective. When reformers say they are going to help teachers teach more effectively, it's terribly important to inquire of them what they consider better and on what basis. In chapter 2, I described briefly how federal officials and educators ignored reliable information about effective instruction in favor of "fairness" to those who preferred other methods.[35] If past is prologue, then we might be wary about superintendents' and others' claims that kids are going to be educated better, unless they can show us the data to support their claims.

And it is wise to recall that even with the best instruction we can muster, as I've stated in earlier chapters and above, someone's going to be hindmost in the distribution of outcomes. I think we need to be careful not to take the attitude that the devil may take him (the hindmost).

PARENTS NEED TO BE REASONABLY
SUPPORTIVE OF TEACHERS AND SCHOOLS

A fairly common complaint of teachers and administrators I've talked to is that in too many instances when they try to discipline a student the parents want to know what they did to provoke their child, accusing the educator of being the person at fault. That is, parents seem automatically to assume that the school—teacher, principal, another student or staff member—is at fault. I suppose that exposés of teacher incompetence, brutality, and discrimination have contributed to this attitude on the part of many parents. And, in truth, sometimes educators are at fault, do engage in indefensible behavior. But now it seems that in many instances educators are assumed to be guilty until proven innocent.

With this kind of suspicion and lack of support, it is little wonder that good teachers leave the field or become demoralized and schools become chaotic and ineffective. Allowing parents to choose their school might defuse some of this kind of suspicion and lack of support, but it won't resolve the issue completely. If we really wanted to resolve this problem completely, then I think we'd have to give schools the choice of saying to a child or parent that they have to go elsewhere—give educators the right to refuse to enroll particular students. I suppose another option would be requiring accusers to prove their case, to assume educators' innocence until they're proven guilty of misconduct.

Another important realization is that learning is often somewhat difficult, in that it demands effort and practice. For most of us, learning some facts and skills requires repeated trials and persistence, not to mention giving up something else for the sake of learning. And sometimes we fail. Parents who want to protect their children from all struggles and all failure are doing their children no service, and they make teachers' lives very difficult. True, too much struggle and failure isn't good either. But parents need to be supportive of reasonable demands on their children.

However, if the school is not providing a good educational program for a student, why should we—why *would* we—expect parents to be supportive? True, parents must shoulder some responsibility for supporting the school their child attends, but not, I think, if the school hasn't taken responsibility for offering a good and appropriate instructional program for their child.

IF SCHOOLS AREN'T GOOD PLACES FOR TEACHERS, THEY CAN'T BE GOOD PLACES FOR KIDS

Psychologist and educator Seymour Sarason explained why this is true in *The Predictable Failure of School Reform*. Too often, schools are assumed to be only for students, not for their teachers. But when teachers' needs are ignored for an exclusive focus on conditions for children, the results are counterproductive—in the end, kids are not well served. As Sarason put it,

> *Whatever factors, variables, and ambience are conducive for the growth, development, and self-regard of a school's staff are precisely those that are crucial to obtaining the same consequences for students in a classroom.* To focus on the latter and ignore or gloss over the former is an invitation to disillusionment.[36]

People working under adverse conditions tend to be short-tempered and to perform poorly. This is true of all human beings in all lines of work. It should come as no surprise that teachers don't do what they should for students when their working conditions are not good. Many teachers work under conditions that would not be tolerated in private industry—many hours of continuous work without a break, work without needed materials or other infrastructure (in the case of teachers, such things as telephones, aides, supervisory guidance, sometimes even books or other instructional materials), for pay that on an hourly basis is unconscionably low, low social status and respect, and powerlessness in the face of unreasonable administrative fiat.

Sarason says a lot about the need to alter power relationships in schools, and his words should be heeded. But—and this is the very point of his book, I think—his discussion of power is likely to be misunderstood and misapplied by many so-called reformers, if not most. As I understand his argument, it is that teachers cannot abandon their roles as adults who are in control, but classrooms must be reasonably democratic places if they are to function well. And teachers will not (because they cannot) make their classrooms more benevolent and democratic when they are powerless in the face of administrators and supervisors and parents.

School reform that has any chance of success has to take on a very difficult problem—the feeling that teachers already have it too easy and should have their feet held to the fire. Want to improve schools? Then improve schools as places for teachers to work. Many people don't want to hear this.

SCHOOLS CANNOT BE EXPECTED TO DO EVERYTHING

Schools have as their central mission helping students achieve academic competence, as Siegfried Engelmann pointed out long ago.[37] If schools do not achieve this central mission, then whatever else they might accomplish (or be saddled with) will still leave students unprepared.

The task of helping students acquire basic academic skills or literacy is itself a tall order if all students are to be taught. But many things—too many things, in my judgment—have been added to the agenda for schools. Exactly where should the boundaries be for what schools are expected to do, and what should schools not take on? That is difficult to say, but it is not very difficult to see that schools are overloaded with responsibilities nowadays. And they cannot be the primary vehicle for changing our society in general or for teaching anything and everything that a school board might demand. Again, Seymour Sarason has some words that I think are wise:

> Schools can be a vehicle for social change, but let us not overestimate the strength, actual or potential, of that impact. Far more powerful is the impact of society on schools, an impact that in recent decades has been as fruitless as it has been powerful. . . . Lest I be misunderstood: I am not advocating that the aims of education should include changing society.[38]

A reasonable question that we have to ask today, simply because the mission of schools has been expanded unreasonably, is this: Are schools charged with the task of insuring the success of students in whatever they undertake in life? I'm amazed at what some people have said about this. For example, Dorothy Lipsky and Alan Gartner have listed what they see as schools' responsibilities for children with disabilities, and their list includes the following:

- Educational services provided in an inclusive setting, that is, in the same school available to their nondisabled peers in age-appropriate classes;
- Educational programs that offer effective opportunities for success, in schooling and life; and
- Holding those who govern and manage schools accountable for the achievement of that success.[39]

They can't be serious, I say to myself. Surely, they're joking! But, apparently, they aren't. Not only do they suggest that all children should be taught in the same schools and classes, regardless of their disabilities, but that schools should be held accountable for students' *success in life*! Well, I think to myself, but they only refer to giving students opportunities. But, then, I note that they say educational programs must offer *effective* opportunities, and I suppose that an effective opportunity is one that leads to success; otherwise, it would be an ineffective opportunity, I imagine. What do we do—how do we think about it—when someone, child or adult, does not take an opportunity that's offered? Was it then not, actually, an opportunity? Or was it just an ineffective opportunity, only pretense?

I think concentrating on the academic mission of schools is important. It's not that other things are unimportant, just that if schools don't accomplish their academic mission, then whatever else they try to teach will be beside the point. Don't misunderstand this point. I do not think the academic mission of the schools is restricted to the standard curriculum goals or achievement standards that apply to most students. It includes the basic, everyday living skills that children with mental retardation may need to learn. For some severely cognitively limited students, these include even basic self-care skills.

Children are in school for only a relatively small percentage of their waking hours (only about 30 percent, even if children are assumed to sleep eight hours per day, the school day is seven hours, and children are in school for five days every single week of the year; 10 percent is much closer to the reality for most children). Schools do not control the economy or job opportunities, nor can they be expected to replace all family and community influences. Holding schools responsible for success in life is, in my judgment, a fool's proposition. Holding schools responsible for helping all the children who can to acquire academic skills and helping other children to learn as much as they can of basic self-care and everyday living skills is daunting enough.

EXCEPTIONAL STUDENTS NEED OPTIONS FOR CURRICULUM, INSTRUCTION, AND PLACEMENT

Because public education must serve all children's educational needs, the largest part of general education must be designed for the modal (most frequently occurring) characteristics of students and teachers. Public education is by definition a service designed for the masses. Any product or service intended for the public at large has to be designed around the typical characteristics of consumers. Economies of scale alone require this. The size, shape, and abilities of the typical citizen fall within a fairly narrow band of variability around the mean, and simple economics demand that things be designed with this in mind.

Surely, what some call "universal design" is important, and good design will accommodate a large range of individual characteristics. But, like "all," "universal" has its limits, often unspoken, sometimes not even recognized. If "universal" design can accommodate a larger segment of the population, that is all well and good. But remember that it is neither economically feasible nor necessary to eliminate all stair steps because some people can't use them or to design and equip every car so that a person with quadriplegia can drive it. Neither is it feasible or desirable to design a reading program for most children that will be appropriate for students with severe mental retardation.

Education has to be designed for what the average teacher and the average student can be expected to do, not what the exceptionally able or those with disabilities can accomplish. I'm not suggesting that the performance of the average teacher or student can't be improved, simply that expectations in the general education program can't outstrip what the average teacher can do with appropriate training or what the typical student can do with good instruction.

Because public education must address all children's educational needs, it must include explicit structures ensuring the accommodation of exceptional students. By definition, exceptional students require an extraordinary response from educators — something different from the ordinary, even if the ordinary is good. The standard educational program can serve most students very well, but it can't serve exceptional students without additional, explicit components — special structures that go beyond the normal or routine in such matters as goals, lines of authority, roles and responsibilities of personnel, budgets and purchases, allocation of time and space, modification of curriculum, evaluation of performance, and assignment of students to classes. Failure to create these explicit structures to accommodate students at the extremes of the performance distribution inevitably results in their neglect. They are forgotten. They don't just fail a little. They fail a lot, and their noses are rubbed in their failures.

The requirement of alternative educational goals and programs must be explicit for exceptional students. It's as simple as this, I think: When the interests of students with disabilities or those who are gifted are not explicitly mandated, they get lost in the shuffle. The implicit or explicit assumption that standard educational goals and programs will accommodate the needs of exceptional students is not just logically untenable. It also places the onus of proof that the program is inappropriate wholly on the student when questions arise about his or her performance. However, if there is an explicit requirement of alternative goals and programs for exceptional students, then the burden of proof is at least partly on the school to show that those alternatives are available to students for whom the typical program is unsatisfactory and in which an exceptional student cannot be expected to make satisfactory progress.

Alternative goals and programs must be expressed as alternative curricula and educational methods for exceptional students. It is not enough to have a separate place—a special class or school. Some exceptional learners need to learn something other than the standard curriculum, not just learn the standard curriculum in a different way or in a different place. And they may need instructional or behavior management procedures that are not needed by most students.

People not familiar with instruction may miss the distinctions of method that are important for exceptional students. For example, students with disabilities may require more trials, more examples, a different pace, smaller steps in a sequence, more reinforcement (praise, encouragement, or other rewarding consequence), more careful monitoring, more structure (e.g., higher predictability, more explicit instructions, more immediate consequences) than is desirable for typical students. There may be other distinctions that I have not listed here, but at least all of these are involved in more precise teaching. In short, the instruction of students with disabilities may need to be considerably more precise than the instruction that produces good results for typical students.

In many types of performance, it is the precision with which something is done that makes the difference, not the basic operation. This is true in driving, flying, playing music, shooting guns, and so on. Just consider the differences in level of performance of the same basic operations in the following comparisons: the typical drive to work versus driving in a high-speed race; flying from city A to city B versus flying with a stunt team; playing in a municipal band versus playing in one of the world's virtuoso combos; shooting targets in the backyard versus sharp-shooting for a SWAT team. Highly expert, precision performance requires extensive training. You don't give all soldiers the competence of the Special Forces by giving them a beret. You don't make every teacher a special educator by telling them good teaching of exceptional children is just good teaching because, after all, kids are more alike than they are different and good teachers use the same basic operations regardless who their students are.

NOBODY KNOWS HOW
TO CURE MOST DISABILITIES

In some commentaries on schools and special education, there is a lot of emphasis on the infrequency with which students "escape" from special education. Michelle Cottle describes special education as "a disaster. Poorly defined, poorly run, poorly enforced." She commented further that "Once in the system, a child has only an estimated 5 percent chance of ever escaping."[40] Yet we know that the vast majority of students with disabilities will require special education throughout their school years. In fact, many will require special support services throughout their lives.

Apparently, those who feel that infrequent "escape" is a scandal see disabilities as often or usually temporary, like a broken bone or fever or indigestion. But most disabilities are chronic conditions, more like diabetes, alcoholism, depression, or schizophrenia. Like educational disabilities, these are conditions that can be well managed, but they virtually never go away. The fact that they don't go away doesn't mean that their treatment is inept.

People who complain that too few kids exit special education have an unfortunate view of disabilities that can be characterized by one of two words: (a) ignorant—they lack knowledge about the nature of disability or (b) stupid—they deny disability, holding a warped view of the world and refusing to recognize what we know; they purposefully retreat from knowledge.

Those who see special education as a failure or scandal typically describe it in very negative terms. Kids, they say, are "shunted," "shuttled," "shoved," "funneled," or "segregated" into or "relegated to" special education. Most of the kids who receive special education, they say or seem to assume, are misidentified—they have no real disabilities, but their teachers or parents, for nefarious reasons, want them to be identified and are offered perverse incentives for identification. Probably the Individuals with Disabilities Education Act (IDEA) has put the kibosh on most of the easy and unjustified identification that critics of special education believe is widespread. IDEA requires agreement of educators and parents that the child has a disability and needs special education before he or she can be placed. Before a student can be "decertified" for special education, the parents and educators must agree that the child no longer has a disability or no longer needs special education. The fact that a relatively small percentage of students with disabilities are "decertified" doesn't mean that many individuals are misidentified, nor does it mean that special education has failed. In most cases, it appears that both educators and parents recognize that the child has a disability for educational purposes and that the disability persists even though it has been addressed reasonably well.

SOME KIDS NEED OPTIONS, BUT THAT DOESN'T JUSTIFY SCHOOL CHOICE FOR ALL KIDS

A basic tenet of American justice is fairness. Does fairness consist of treating all individuals exactly alike? For some things, yes, but obviously not always. We make reasonable exceptions and accommodations, depending on a person's abilities and circumstances. This is why we recognize that the death penalty for someone who is mentally retarded is not exactly the same as the death penalty for someone who is not, even though mental retardation may be a somewhat ambiguous condition and even though we might conclude that the death penalty isn't a good idea in any case. This is why killing someone in cold blood is seen as different from killing someone in self-defense. In educating children, too, reasonable people see the need for treating some kids differently, depending on what the difference is, to achieve fairness.

Should *all* students or their parents be able to *choose* where they go to school? I think the answer has to be this: No, not all; it depends on the student. I think the case for options—choices—for exceptional students, those at the margins of the distribution on any relevant variable, is very strong. These options can be provided either by the public schools or, if the public schools don't have what's needed, private schools.

But were all students (parents, usually) given their choice of school, public or private, I'm not sure how it would work out in practical terms, and I'm more than a little skeptical about the outcomes such universal choice would produce. Suppose all students could choose, if they wanted, private schools. Would private schools be required to take any applicant, regardless of the school's enrollment or focus and regardless of the characteristics of the student? Suppose all students could choose any public school they wanted. What if a school is already over-crowded? Does it have to take any student who wants to attend, lack of room or characteristics of the student notwithstanding? What happens to students who want to go to a school that has to close down because too few students want to attend it? This doesn't exhaust the list of questions one could pose.

As I discussed in other parts of this book, market forces are good for lots of things. I'm not convinced they're good for improving schools, given that the goal is to provide a good floor of educational opportunity for every student.

Should we allow students now required to go to school to opt out of schooling altogether? Kids can be schooled at home under certain conditions. Should kids and parents be allowed to simply avoid schooling altogether? If not, then why not? If so, then under what circumstances?

For all the problems that schools have—and some have many more problems than others—I don't know that vouchers and other forms of school choice for all students have been thought through very well, and I doubt that all options are good ones. But it does seem odd to me that there is so much talk about choices of parents and students, yet so little talk about choices for teachers (e.g., what or whom not to teach without giving up their job) or schools (e.g., which students to admit and which to refuse without losing their accreditation or acceptability for a voucher). And I don't think, for reasons I discussed earlier in this book, that turning education over to private enterprise is going to eliminate the problems we see in government-run schools.

My hope is that people making decisions will look before leaping, think things through before changing wholesale the public enterprise of schooling and the choices we allow. We hope kids will be able to think logically about the consequences of their actions, and we ought to expect the same of ourselves.

A TEACHER CAN'T TEACH ALL KINDS OF STUDENTS AT THE SAME TIME AND DO IT WELL

Alternative curricula and methods sometimes require alternative grouping of students. Most teachers can't teach wildly different students in the same group and be highly successful.[41] True, you can't eliminate all heterogeneity (differences) in a group, but unless the group you're teaching is relatively homogeneous (pretty much like each other in level of knowing about what you're teaching), things aren't likely to come out very well. Special classes and special schools have a legitimate place in education because they allow reasonably homogeneous groups to be maintained. This is beneficial to both the exceptional learners and those who are typical.

Homogeneous grouping is important for *instruction*, not for all situations. The homogeneity in classrooms must be based on performance related to instruction only. This means that heterogeneity of ethnicity, gender, social and economic status, and all other factors must not matter *for instruction*. What matters is that homogeneity is limited to performance on the topic of instruction. Heterogeneous grouping is desirable in other school situations in which the objective is not instruction (i.e., in situations that are primarily social).

Some proposed reforms of education might go *part* way in meeting the instructional needs of exceptional students. For example, lowering class size dramatically (to 12 or fewer students—and not fudging the ratio by including administrative or support personnel) or having two competent teachers in every class of 25–30 students would allow schools to accommodate greater variability in student characteristics. But I see two problems here. First of all, any reasonable person has to ask questions like these: Where would we get the extra classrooms, and how would we pay for them? Where would we get the extra teachers, and how would we pay for them? My guess is that the funding for training teachers, teacher salaries, and construction just isn't in the picture, as such changes in teacher-pupil ratios would make the cost of public education about double what it is now. Second, no single teaching arrangement is infinitely flexible, so that even in such an idealized world of education, some children would need even lower teacher-pupil ratios and a classroom environment much more carefully controlled and monitored than is desirable for typical students.

So, a full range of optional placements is needed to accommodate exceptional students. The full range includes regular classrooms in neighborhood schools (including accelerated placement for some gifted students and placement behind age peers for some students with disabilities), resource classes, special self-contained classes, special day schools, special residential schools, hospital schools, and home teaching. The only protection against abuse of these options—actually, the only protection against abuse regardless how education is administered or structured—is good instruction in each placement option.

What happens when options for placement or curriculum are abandoned? It's no mystery; some students are badly served. To the extent that special classes or schools are abandoned in favor of full inclusion, the consequences are predictably negative for some students. Furthermore, as I and my colleagues have suggested, eliminating the option of special classes just results in more kids needing to go to special schools because they clearly can't be taught and managed well in a regular class.[42]

Students aren't exceptional if their needs are met in a standard educational group and standard curriculum without supplementary services. Some students who are exceptional can be included in regular classes with supplementary services, such as a resource teacher who comes into their class from time to time. But many exceptional students simply can't thrive without being educated in a special class or school.

MISMANAGEMENT AND STUPIDITY ARE NOT PECULIAR TO GOVERNMENT OPERATIONS

I was somewhat amused by Cal Thomas's column about Senator Fred Thompson's report that in the federal government he found "'pervasive and continuous mismanagement, waste, fraud and duplication that the average American would find shocking.'"[43] What amused me first was a United States Senator pretending to be shocked by his own revelations—someone who, presumably, is aware of Mark Twain's description of politicians as America's only native criminal class. What amused me more was Cal Thomas's apparent presumption that government is peculiarly prone to such evils. He notes caustically—and I think correctly—that the Clinton-Gore administrations' "reinvention of government" was laughable. But wanting to get rid of government for having problems that are pandemic in human organizations doesn't make much sense to me, especially when the alternative of privatization is proposed as a cure.

Mismanagement, waste, fraud, duplication, and stupidity are found in the private sector, too. Scientist Emilie Rissman, a friend and University of Virginia colleague, pointed out in our local newspaper that a city-county government agency, the Rivanna Solid Waste Authority (RSWA) is self-serving, not serving the community. I think she's right about that. And she makes this revealing statement: "Like a for-profit business the RSWA continues to bury solid waste in [our neighborhood] to keep from shutting down."[44] Yes, at every level we can find government agencies that seek self-perpetuation and forget they exist to serve the public interest. We expect such self-serving, self-perpetuating behavior from private industry. That's why it exists—to serve its bottom line, to make a profit, and if it doesn't then it eventually fails or we (through our government) bail it out. From government we expect more selfless conduct than characterizes private industry, and we should.

The comic strip Dilbert isn't funny because it pokes fun at government agencies alone. It's mostly black humor about private business. The savings and loan debacle of the 1990s was about mismanagement, waste, fraud, and stupidity in private businesses, not government agencies. Chrysler Corporation did not need a government bailout because it had been so expertly managed. The maddening encounters others and I have had with the incompetence and stupidity of banks, cable companies, and phone companies were not encounters with government agencies but private companies.

Yes, mismanagement, waste, fraud, duplication, self-serving decisions, and stupidity can be found in government agencies, including schools and teacher organizations. These are undesirable characteristics, to say the least. We should not just shrug them off. But make no mistake about this: Turning functions over to private industry will not eliminate these evils. These are basic human problems that dog every administrative structure, every organization, private or public.

Facile solutions to the problems of education are frequently offered, with school vouchers being a prime example. One Charlottesvillian provided this advice:

> But there's a simple remedy [to the problems of public schooling]—just what the Bush Department of Justice is now bravely advancing: no longer a state-school, totalitarian, ASHist [atheistic secular humanist]

monopoly, but rather parental school choice, non-racist, backed by no-strings vouchers from our own taxes. And, hey, presto — the aching, long-time school problem in our midst is democratically solved![45]

I wish the solution were so simple. But I fear that vouchers, like many other "solutions," provide an "answer" that is both simple and wrong.

MULTICULTURAL EDUCATION SHOULD EMPHASIZE COMMON ATTRIBUTES OF HUMANITY

This is a contentious point for some people and seems commonsensical to me — and, I'm sure, to many other people. I suppose that my experiences on this matter are like many others'. Several years ago, I gave a speech in which I expressed just this idea — that multicultural education must emphasize common humanity, not to the exclusion of differences among us but in a way that makes differences secondary to commonalities. Following my speech a person of color advised me bluntly not to publish the speech because people of color would find it — well, unacceptable, perhaps threatening. This person was concerned about my ideas because I was not affirming enough of diversity and stated that although there are many commonalities among different racial, cultural, and ethnic groups, we must honor their uniqueness in cultural beliefs and values. I was somewhat taken aback by this advice, and I haven't followed it, not because I want to be offensive to persons of color (or anyone else, for that matter) but because I think it is ultimately incompatible with multiculturalism as I understand it. I think it feeds the victimology described by John McWhorter.[46] I think it suggests a facile and misleading explanation of the achievement discrepancies between black and white students.

After all, how does anyone justify the atrocious treatment of someone else? As far as I can figure out, it is usually impossible for someone to commit an atrocity against someone whom they see as a human being very much like themselves. Atrocities almost always follow dehumanizing the person who is to be attacked, seeing their difference as more important than any similarity, seeing the other person as fundamentally a different creature. Whether it's skin color, tribal affiliation, nation of origin, religion, gender, sexual orientation, or something else is immaterial; the particular difference on which someone focuses really doesn't matter much. What matters is that a particular human difference trumps the universal tie among human beings. It is the focus on difference as more important than commonality that allows folks to talk about mud people, sun people, ice people, infidels, and every other "type" that is subhuman or unworthy of human rights. I think human rights have to trump black rights and white rights and Catholic rights, Protestant rights, well, name the rights of any group you will. Without that assumption, and without our embracing it openly and explicitly, I fear not just for American institutions that try to ensure justice (and usually, not always, come about as close as we can hope). I fear that highlighting cultural (or other) differences more than shared humanity dashes any hope of actual justice.

I feel sure that many people, including many persons of color and those who are minorities in their communities, agree that a focus on common humanity is our only hope of achieving a just and fair multiculturalism. For example, William Raspberry wrote about how common language is getting lost in the obsession with linguistic differences. He noted, "But when we have no common shorthand—worse, when we, black and white, have two separate shorthands—it isn't just our language that gets weaker. So does some of the glue that binds us together and makes us *American*."[47]

I think I have made clear my position in this book and my other writings that differences are to be recognized, and when they are compatible with fairness and human dignity they should be accepted. But what group of people—nation, color, religion, or other minority of the world's population—does not have its shameful history of violating human rights? None, at least none of which I am aware. One's culture doesn't sanctify anything. Multicultural education should emphasize the virtues that apply to all cultures and reject the negative aspects of all cultures. All of us—each and every one—are members of cultures with histories of complicity in the violation of human dignity. Even we Americans, with our history of human slavery and present failures, such as our outrageously high rate of incarceration. This not only is obvious from current news reports from all nations of the world but has been the stuff of literature, both fiction and nonfiction. I think no one can read Annie Proulx's novel *Accordion Crimes* without noticing a significant subtext: Every ethnic group in America has been demeaned by and has demeaned every other.[48]

No one representing either the majority or the minority in a given community should be allowed to lay blame exclusively on the other. Speaking of the tensions raised between Jews and Poles as to who was to blame for the demise of the Polish Jews, Eva Hoffman says:

> If cross-cultural discussions of difficult histories are to be at all fruitful, they need to start with acknowledgement of complexity rather than insistence on reductiveness.
>
> Ideally, in such encounters, both partners would feel enough equality and strength to supplant accusation with self-examination, and to talk fully and openly about their own histories. It is of course necessary in such conversations for the majority culture to admit its history of dominance or injustice; but the dialogue cannot proceed if the minority group continues to hold the majority moral hostage in perpetuity, or if the history of powerlessness is taken as proof of moral superiority. And it is unproductive, always, to counter prejudice by denying facts.[49]

I fear that postmodern philosophies, critical race theory, and the like dash any hope of achieving such communication. These theories assume that the existing order is inherently oppressive (by virtue of "race" or Enlightenment views), claiming that those who hold postmodern views are both powerless and morally superior. They presume that facts do not exist, are unimportant, or can be written into existence.

A fair question is how multiculturalism might work out in practice in the classroom. I think Jeanmarie Bantz, one of the most gifted and talented special education teachers I have ever seen, offers a good illustration. In her class, kids' diverse cultures are respected, but that does not mean that she accepts all of their culture's values, whatever they might be, or that she does not teach her students different, more universal and human-rights-oriented cultural values. She notes that kids' status in school and community is often based on clothes, looks, power (bullying, intimidation), athleticism, noncompliance with authority, or other values that she (and I, and I think many others) feel are inappropriate. She seeks to re-establish status based on desirable behavior—respect, kindness, equity, fairness, compliance with rules and reasonable requests, and what she refers to as a positive mental attitude (PMA, she calls it in teaching kids) toward schoolwork, authority, and peers. This is what I consider to be multicultural in a true and best sense—taking the positive aspects of any culture (or, if you will, a universal culture that focuses on human rights) and applying them to all cultures. This also involves removing or replacing at least some of the negative aspects that are found in any culture.

Another fair question is how one can achieve a basic consensus on human rights or common standards. I think those working in Amnesty International have a good start on this, but it also comes down to more everyday attitudes toward and interactions with people. I think it's important not to assume that ideas or competencies are determined by one's color, ethnic origins, or gender. I think it's important to see those differing from us in cultural features as sharing most of our fundamental concerns and aspirations and to focus on these rather than differences. I think it's important to support public policies that aim to make sure that people aren't neglected or given advantage because of their color, gender, sexual orientation, and so on. I think it's important to admit the mistakes of oneself and others but not to assume responsibility or guilt for acts done by others over which you had no control. I think it's important not to seek and not to justify a rationale of payback that seeks redress for past wrongs. The payback and set-right idea is the stuff of ethnic and religious conflicts that have gone on for millennia. Turn taking in oppression has no place in a truly multicultural society.

In an interview with Studs Terkel, writer Kurt Vonnegut described the negative consequences of payback this way:

> The fact that forgive us our trespasses as we forgive those who trespass against us isn't honored more—I blame that on writers. Because the easy story to tell is the vengeance story, and it's known to satisfy. This guy shot my brother. How's the story gonna wind up? And what does a reader think? OK, that's settled. So it's just the easiest of all stories to tell. So it in fact encourages, makes *reputable* vengeance.[50]

In many ways, America is already an admirable multicultural society. Consider the opinion of Mamoun Fandy, a native of Egypt and an American professor at the National Defense University, as well as a statement of one of his Arab friends:

I came from an old and homogeneous society. Thus questions of multi-culturalism and race relations did not occur to me—until I came here. I saw things in this country that did not match what I had read in the Arab press about the imperialist American view. I saw a society in the making. America sees itself as a human project to which anyone can contribute . . . [and his Arab friend commented] "If there is anything that is close to the idea of what a good Muslim society should look like, America is it. Kind-ness, tolerance, pursuit of knowledge, all the principles that Islam claims, they're all here."[51]

In some sweet bye-and-bye do I see a *perfect* multicultural society in the United States or anywhere else? Nope. As I said early on in this book (end of chapter 1), perfection is something unattainable, although worth approximating. I think we can do much better in working toward a multicultural society and world, and I certainly hope we'll see some improvement in focusing our multicultural education on our common humanity.

ZERO TOLERANCE MINIMIZES JUDGMENT AND MAXIMIZES STUPID DECISIONS

Zero tolerance has become an education policy intended to thwart judg-ment.[52] Like mandatory sentencing in law, zero tolerance grew out of unhappiness with people's judgment. The idea was that to prevent peo-ple from using bad judgment (giving too easy a sentence in law; al-lowing misconduct to go unpunished in schools) we should have a stan-dard way of dealing with a particular offense. Never mind extenuating circumstances or exculpatory explanations, as these are the routes the pushers of zero tolerance felt led to bad judgment and miscarriages of justice. Better, proponents of zero tolerance and closely related ideas suggested, that everyone know the exact consequence for a given of-fense. We should not let unwise administrators decide not to punish an offense of one student but punish another student who (apparently) commits the same type of offense. That would be unfair, discrimina-tory, indefensible, they argued. For a particular category of offense, we need, they said, a standard, predictable consequence; then punishment will be just and also serve as a deterrent because people will know be-yond any shadow of doubt what is permissible and how infractions will be punished. This may seem at first blush like a good idea, but a little thinking will reveal how soon it goes sour or turns idiotic.

Zero tolerance may have started out as a good idea, in which little offenses were taken seriously and law enforcement officers were allowed to use good judgment in selecting consequences. And it's important to note that skillful teachers often step in to stop little things from growing into big problems, a kind of zero tolerance that is not just defensible but necessary to prevention.[53] But as it is practiced in most schools today, zero tolerance is a fool's proposition.

Just how absurd can zero tolerance become? Even worse, I think, than suspending a student for having a tiny toy knife on a key chain. Some can and have taken the idea of zero tolerance for any sign of aggression this far: Prohibiting dodge ball because it teaches students that throwing things at other students is acceptable, allows the strong to prey on the weak, and requires those who have been hit to sit out and watch rather than continue active participation in the game. I think Margorie Williams makes sense in describing the silliness of dodge ball prohibition:

> Of course there are kids for whom gym class is purgatory—just as there are those for whom math class is a bed of nails. Of course we should teach children to treat each other well. Of course we should take seriously the damage that even the best kids can do to each other in the state of nature we call sixth grade. But we can't eliminate social pain from childhood, and we don't do children any favors by suggesting that its every manifestation is unendurable.[54]

No one, I think, can deny that sometimes people use bad judgment. True, sometimes school administrators let things go by when they shouldn't or fail to provide a reasonable consequence for a serious offense. More often, though, their judgment was sound. So, what we got with zero tolerance was a witless policy that made matters worse by prohibiting people from asking questions about motivations or circumstances and from using their judgment. Without zero tolerance, we sometimes see a school administrator use bad judgment, and justice is then not served, although there is always the hope that with help someone will avoid repeated bad judgment. But with zero tolerance we have the absolute certainty that in a substantial number of cases an injustice will be done.

Russell Skiba of Indiana University has reviewed the facts and con-cluded that there is zero evidence to support zero tolerance.[55] In fact, it is a policy that has negative outcomes. Zero tolerance does not make schools safer, and it results in ridiculous decisions regarding many stu-dents. It invites disrespect, as it makes Bozos of those who must carry it out against their better judgment.

In the name of zero tolerance, some students get punished for un-knowingly possessing a weapon, making a simple mistake, being for-getful in ways we all are at times, even for turning in a weapon that they've found or discovered they've brought to school by mistake! Columnist Marc Fisher portrayed the lunacy of zero tolerance in one school system. His comments include the following:

> Zero tolerance, zero sense. Last year, a Loudoun middle schooler was suspended for four months because he took a knife from a classmate who had previously attempted suicide. But the knife was in our hero's locker when authorities found out about it, so off with his head.[56]

Zero tolerance for anything—racism included—is a witless ap-proach that equates trivial or unintentional transgressions (or the mis-takes of those who accuse someone) with the most profoundly serious offenses. In the case of racism, zero tolerance could be used to call someone a racist for having in his or her possession any item carrying a Confederate emblem. It could be used as an excuse for calling a per-son racist because he or she questions someone's qualifications for a job. It *has been used* to accuse someone of racism because he used the word "niggardly," which has only a phonetic similarity to a racial epi-thet (notwithstanding the fact that the word's etymology and meaning have nothing to do with ethnicity, color, or race).[57] Zero tolerance is mindlessness, the gone-craziness of ideology. Yes, violence and racism are grotesque, must be taken seriously, and must be disallowed, but with judgment, not with the loss of judgment that manufactures threat or ignores the proportion of it. Zero tolerance of violence, racism, and other unacceptable behavior merely ensures more grotesquery.

But we are a people of extremes, so I suppose it is not too surprising that this mindless, intentionally nonjudgmental policy called zero tol-erance has become popular. Watch out! My colleague Rick Brigham and I offer this warning: After zero tolerance is exposed for the fool's proposition that it is, we might be in for an opposite extreme—tolerance of virtually anything and everything, which is also a way of avoiding judgment.[58] Tolerance of nearly everything—something that might be labeled *omni-tolerance*—would be no improvement over zero tolerance. It would be harmful to kids regardless of the rhetoric used to justify it. It is seen in embryonic form in schools in which nearly anything goes, in which the attitude is "whatever." It's usually based on a fear of imposing standards of conduct that might be called by some student or parent or other person "overly restrictive" or "culturally oppressive" or something else negative. A helpful and nonoppressive level of tolerance demands careful judgment and won't go to either extreme.

EDUCATION SHOULD CONCENTRATE ON PROVIDING EFFECTIVE INSTRUCTION

Teacher trainers, school administrators, and teachers themselves need to put teaching on a sound scientific footing and provide the effective instruction that the public apparently wants from schools—improved performance. If we educators do not do this, then we deserve the atrophy we will see in our field. I am involved in self-criticism and self-admonition here, as I am a member of what Martin Kozloff refers to as "Edland." I am a faculty member of an education school, involved in training teachers and contributing to education's literature. So it is entirely appropriate for me to use "we" here: We educators need to clean up our act, sift out the anecdotal and personal from the reliable and replicable, teach and recommend the practices that stand up best to rigorous testing of their effects on learning. Kozloff described the situation quite well:

> Edland [the field of education] is an enormous and astonishingly expensive arrangement of schools of education, publishers, and organizations such as the National Council of Teachers of English, the National Council of Teachers of Mathematics, the National Association for the Education of Young Children, and the National Council for the Accreditation of Teacher Education. Edland provides curricula to public schools—curricula which reveal their creators' superficial understanding of logical design. New teachers are trained to deliver these curricula in public schools via "progressive" forms of instruction—which increasingly resemble group therapy. Edland justifies its curricula and instruction with

a so-called research base on "best" and "developmentally appropriate practices"—a research base consisting largely of anecdotes, authors' opinions, and pre-experimental research designs. And Edland maintains an apparatus of conferences and publications that disseminate always innovative—but seldom effective—models of school reform, classroom instruction, and teacher training. The apparatus functions to legitimize Edland's existence and activities, and to hide the failures in Edland's outcomes and the ineptitude of its leaders.

[A variety of writers] all point to the intellectual frivolity, the doctrinal theologicality, and almost compulsive attention to everything but what is important to instruction, that characterize ed school thinking and curricula.[59]

Kozloff and numerous other writers have noted that various training programs can turn out "90-day wonders" who, although trained at a small fraction of the time and cost of an ed school degree, seem to perform just as well as the graduates of most education schools. My own view is that this isn't a compliment to the outfits like Teach for America (TFA) but an indictment of schools of education. To me it seems clear that alternative training programs like TFA don't produce highly competent teachers. The fact that most schools of education don't either, though, is what's troubling to me.

Too much of what passes for teacher education is nonsense or fluff. Actually, too much of what passes for education is nonsense or fluff (as I mentioned in other chapters, schools of education are not alone in teaching and promoting gibberish). But we teacher educators can't shirk our responsibility just because some of our colleagues in higher education babble. We do know some of the things that work—that typically produce much better outcomes than the alternatives that typically get the endorsement of educators and the public.

Ah, here is a problem. It is not just educators nowadays who like "progressive" and ineffective instruction and eschew more direct and more effective practices. As E. D. Hirsch, Jr., Martin Kozloff, and Diane Ravitch have pointed out—and as the popularity of Alfie Kohn's books demonstrates—the general public, including school board members, often prefer tried and failed practices. So, actually changing the schools will require not only that we educators reject popular but failed practices and promote the practices that work best but that we help the public understand the value in doing so.

EDUCATORS SHOULD MAKE AS MUCH SENSE
AS THE MAGLIOZZI BROTHERS' "CAR TALK"

How do we get people to make more sense about education? I'm not sure, and although I'm optimistic about the prospects I'm not boundlessly so. I do look at other endeavors in which people make what seems to me good sense—common sense, but also scientific sense.

One example that comes immediately to mind is a program on National Public Radio called Car Talk. In a speech I gave in Dallas several years ago, later published as an essay, I suggested that special education should be built on a model similar to Car Talk.[60] Actually, I think all of education would benefit from taking the practical and scientific approach to problems of the hosts of Car Talk, Tom and Ray Magliozzi.

By the way, Car Talk is also a feature in some newspapers, and you may want to check out the web site at www.cartalk.org. On the radio show, the Magliozzi brothers, Tom and Ray—two mechanics who call themselves Click and Clack, the tappet brothers—take calls from people who are having car trouble or want advice about cars or car repair. Tom and Ray are consummate problem solvers. They know the science and technology of cars. They know a lot of other things, too, and they are therefore witty teachers of those who listen. They're really into solving puzzles and problems. Their work is applied science. But they're also very funny, full of good humor, including joking with people about their problems and making self-deprecating wisecracks.

Now, I understand that kids aren't cars, that K–12 and so-called higher education involves dealing with people, not machines, and that a totally mechanistic view of education isn't appropriate. But I think there are lessons to be learned from the Magliozzi brothers. We can find some valid parallels between their work and education. A significant part of what educators do—a significant part, not everything—involves helping people find solutions to problems. Without this problem-solving part, education is a flop. And, as I indicated earlier, I think an empirical, scientific approach to problems usually provides the best solution—the one that is most reliable, useful, cost-effective, and satisfying. So, I repeat: I realize that kids aren't cars, but I think Car Talk can be said to represent an ideal of problem solving for which education should strive.

Click and Clack know cars and are able to discriminate problems they can solve from those that are simply preferences on the part of their clients. They are scientific problem solvers who understand the value and limitations of science and its alternatives. Education should be so focused on problem solving through a scientific approach. Postmodern car repair? I can hear Tom and Ray laughing now at the very idea! To me, postmodern education is no less laughable.

Click and Clack do not see themselves as able to function properly only if the car manufacturing industry or the auto sales industry are restructured or reformed. They are in the business of car maintenance and repair, which will always provide a needed function. And they will do it well regardless of what happens in the rest of the auto industry. Teachers should be focused on their mission of helping students become academically competent, regardless how education might be structured or restructured or reformed. What will make a real difference in education is the instruction kids get, not the administrative structure of the education business. "Restructuring" is a diversion, a distraction from the important task of improving instruction through the adoption of scientifically proven methods. I hope reformers come to understand this.

The Magliozzi brothers aren't so serious about themselves or their work that they don't see the humor in what they do, either as individuals or as mechanics. They have a lot of fun because they're so comfortable with who they are and what they do. They're masters of their trade, and they know how to help others. They laugh at nonsense because they can separate it from sense. They know the empirical basis for the discriminations they make between the witless and the smart. Educators could do no better than to strive to be like them in this regard.

Tom and Ray Magliozzi take their business to the public, to the people. Most people understand enough about cars and the way they work to know that they're going to get the straight poop on Car Talk, not some metaphysical, theoretical, postmodern, deconstructivist, culturally relativist mumbo jumbo. What they get will be based on real-world, scientific, reliable knowledge of cars, not "knowledge" created by a script or half-baked, make-biased or make-based epistemology.

Tom and Ray: Gotta hand it to 'em, they know their stuff. They know when they know something and when they don't. They know how to ask for the critical information about a problem and make sense of it.

They know when to refer a caller to someone else. Education badly
needs its Toms and Rays.

NOTES

1. E.g., Brigham & Polsgrove (1998), Sasso (2001), Sugai (1998), Walker,
Forness, Kauffman, Epstein, Gresham, Nelson, & Strain (1998).
2. Mann (1979, pp. 541–542).
3. See Feynman (1999) and Miller (1997) for discussion in the popular literature.
4. See Gould (1997b), Jacobson, Mulick, & Schwartz (1995), Mostert
(2001).
5. Fried (2001, p. 135).
6. E.g., Engelmann (1997), Forness (2001), Forness, Kavale, Blum, &
Lloyd (1997), Hirsch (1996), Lloyd, Forness, & Kavale (1998), Rosenshine
(1997).
7. E.g., Brandt (2001), Glickman (2001).
8. E.g., Diamond (1997), Gould (1997a), Gross (1998), Wilson (1998).
9. Ehrlich (2001, p. B3); see also Gould (2000), Shermer (1997, 2001).
10. Carnine (1998).
11. *Talk of the town*, (1997, April 14, p. 31).
12. Miller (1997).
13. See Feynman (1999), Miller (1997).
14. Hirsch (1996).
15. For elaboration see Engelmann (1997), Becker & Gersten (2001),
Watkins (1996).
16. Bandura (1986).
17. Kauffman (2001) reviews the related research.
18. E.g., Feynman (1998, 1999), Koertge (1998), Shermer (1997, 2001).
19. See Trefil (1996), Mann (1979), Hirsch (1996).
20. Gould (1996b, p. 40, italics in original).
21. See Becker & Gersten (2001), Watkins (1996).
22. See Cook, Gerber, & Semmel (1997).
23. Becker & Gersten (2001), Hurley, Chamberlain, Slavin, & Madden
(2001), Watkins (1996).
24. Cook, Gerber, & Semmel (1997).
25. Baxter, Woodward, & Olson (2001, p. 543).
26. Baxter, Woodward, & Olson (2001, p. 545).
27. Holbrook (2001, p. 783).

28. Hurley, Chamberlain, Slavin, & Madden (2001, p. 752).

29. Goodlad (1990, p. 284).

30. Rohrer (2001).

31. Hallahan & Kauffman (2000).

32. Kauffman (1999d, pp. xi–xii).

33. Finn, Rotherham, & Hokanson (2001, p. 344).

34. See Kauffman, Mostert, Trent, & Hallahan (2002), Walker, Colvin, & Ramsey (1995).

35. See Watkins (1996).

36. Sarason (1990, p. 152, italics in original).

37. Engelmann (1969).

38. Sarason (1990, pp. 36–37).

39. Lipsky & Gartner (1996, p. 153).

40. Cottle (2001, pp. 14–15).

41. Welsh (2001).

42. Hallenbeck, Kauffman, & Lloyd (1993).

43. Thomas (2001, p. A6).

44. Rissman (2001, p. A6).

45. Shaw (2001, p. A6).

46. McWhorter (2000).

47. Raspberry (1999, A23, italics in original).

48. Proulx (1996).

49. Hoffman (1997, pp. 15–16).

50. Terkel (2001, p. 226).

51. Fandy (2002, p. B3).

52. Kauffman & Brigham (2000a).

53. See Kauffman, Bantz, & McCullough (2002), Walker, Colvin, & Ramsey (1995).

54. Williams (2001, p. A31).

55. See www.indiana.edu/~safeschl/publication.html.

56. Fisher (2001d, p. B1); see also Fisher (2002) for additional example.

57. See King (1999).

58. Kauffman & Brigham (2000a).

59. Kozloff (2001, pp. 9–10).

60. Kauffman (1999e).

Epilogue

Education is probably at a turning point in the early twenty-first century. This appears to be especially true of public education. It may continue to bumble along, embracing platitudes and the failed but popular rhetoric of "progressivism," or it may become an evidence-based profession that relies to the greatest extent possible on scientific evidence. Pediatrician Jack Shonkoff has noted that knowledge about children's development and education is often ignored or dismissed, and kids are paying a heavy price for adults' ignorance and decisions to dismiss scientific evidence.[1] We have been on the path of ignoring or dismissing scientific evidence in education for some time, but we don't have to stay on it. We do not have to stay adrift on what Frederick Crews describes as "the choppy, horizonless seas of literary interpretation," nor do we need to remain in what Simon Winchester calls "the fogs of religious dogma."[2] We can help education emerge from the stupors of progressivism, postmodernism, and religious dogma into an enlightened era of rationality, intelligibility, and application of scientific evidence to the problems of teaching.

Alvin Kernan stated in his memoir, *In Plato's Cave*, that although the changes in academe brought by postmodernism are not to his liking, "my argument is not that this radical change is, as many of my contemporaries believe, an educational catastrophe."[3] Yet Kernan suggests metaphorically that literary studies are the Northern Ireland and Bosnia of the culture wars in universities. In the real world, these are two countries where, I think, catastrophes have occurred by nearly any measure. Moreover, I think the current shift of tectonic plates in higher education—again Kernan's metaphor—is essentially different from the other shifts that he describes. The democratization of higher education represented by the GI bill and other policies designed to create wider and more equitable access to colleges and universities was an acknowledgment that people should be given opportunities regardless of their origins. But deconstruction, or postmodernism, represents an attempt either to give ideas equal merit or to make ideas the preserve of race or gender or social class or national origin. This is a shift of a different type, I think. Some tectonic shifts, some earthquakes, destroy whatever rests on the plates. I do not believe that our prime social structures that rest on ideas—political democracy, justice, fairness, and science, for example—can withstand a shift to deconstruction or postmodern ideas. These structures, which we are constantly striving to improve, will be reduced to rubble by a shift to the notions that one idea is as good as another and that an epistemology based on one's personal characteristics of race, gender, sexual orientation, or what have you comprising personal identity is acceptable.

Kernan does, actually, describe the considerable danger in the assumption that all *ideas* are equal. He ends his memoir with the observation that the democratization of education may have gone too far—that democratization cannot make all *interpretations* of literature or physical phenomena equal without very negative, perhaps catastrophic, consequences. Taking democratization—or virtually anything else, for that matter—to an extreme perverts its purpose. He notes that the new democracy is good, "but it has arrived with some very rough edges and a strident ideology, both of which need considerable smoothing against the grindstone of accumulated knowledge from the past and the real, present needs of an effective educational system."[4]

Nevertheless, perhaps postmodern ideas are not a catastrophe for literary studies or other arts and letters. For in these areas, as Nathan Glazer has commented in *We Are All Multiculturalists Now*,

> One gets ahead in academia by developing a new point of view, perhaps indeed an outrageous one. When one promotes this new point of view in literature or some other field of the humanities, or in some parts of the social sciences (such as anthropology), there is little constraint from an external world of experiments and facts and numbers to limit the unleashed mind.[5]

However, for the sciences, both basic and applied, postmodernism does, indeed, promise catastrophe by any reasonable standard.[6] My argument is that education—at least elementary and secondary education, including special education—must be viewed as an applied science with real-world consequences. True, to be done well it must be practiced artfully and ethically, like surgery, dentistry, or engineering in any of its many forms, but education remains at root an applied science. If it is an applied science, then surely postmodernism has about it the smell of education's death.

I'm hopeful that education will embrace reliable scientific evidence, that parents, policymakers, and educators themselves will be roused to the service of kids and our society and turn education onto a new path. This will happen, however, only if more of us speak up for scientific, evidence-based practices and speak out against nonscientific views. We must say clearly what we know, what works, and what makes sense. We must also say clearly what is senseless and what is not supported by evidence. And we must do this knowing that although our knowledge is tentative and partial, it is better than what we are left with if we retreat from knowledge because it is imperfect.

Do Enlightenment notions of science and reason guarantee a better future? Of course not. However, retreating from them does guarantee that brute force, superstition, and myth will rule. Science and reason are necessary but not sufficient for making the future better. We have to care about how we use these tools, too, and use them artfully and ethically.

Stephen Jay Gould stated clearly the catastrophic consequences of giving up the Enlightenment goals of rationality and reliable evidence. He noted first the duality of human nature—our potentials for both good and evil—described by eighteenth-century poet Alexander Pope.

> Only two possible escapes can save us from the organized mayhem of our dark potentialities—the side that has given us crusades, witch hunts, enslavements, and holocausts. Moral decency provides one necessary ingredient, but not nearly enough. The second foundation must come from the rational side of our mentality. For, unless we rigorously use human reason both to discover and acknowledge nature's factuality, and to follow the logical implications for efficacious human action that such knowledge entails, we will lose out to the frightening forces of irrationality, romanticism,

uncompromising "true" belief, and the apparent resulting inevitability of mob action. Reason is not only a large part of our essence; reason is also our potential salvation from the vicious and precipitous mass action that rule by emotionalism always seems to entail. Skepticism is the agent of reason against organized irrationalism—and is therefore one of the keys to human social and civic decency.[7]

All individuals—adults as well as children—take longer to learn concepts if they are told only what is correct, never what is wrong. Telling someone that he or she is wrong doesn't need to be brutal, but it does need to be unambiguous. Neither does telling someone when they've made a mistake mean that focusing on errors is a smart method of teaching. We who want to see education put on a sound footing have not been sufficiently attentive to helping the public understand what makes sense and what doesn't in the light of the most reliable scientific evidence we have.

We know that education can't do everything, but we do know that it can make a huge difference in children's lives. When education is good, when it is effective in helping kids acquire important skills that they can demonstrate, it enhances children's lives enormously, even if it doesn't solve all problems. Good education will not and can't reduce all of the risks for bad life outcomes, but it can contribute to risk reduction. We know and accept this principle in other areas of our lives. We know that when people quit smoking (or don't start), they aren't immune to heart and lung disease, but we know that they have reduced their risk of acquiring them, and that's important. In education, it's time to do what we can—make instruction as effective as possible for all kids.

I have no doubt that some people will argue for a continuation of senseless talk about education—sloganeering and other misleading statements—because they feel it is politically expedient. First, they will argue, we have to capture people's imagination with a catchy phrase, even if it doesn't really make sense. Later, after we've won a political contest or achieved power to do so, we can write policies that actually make sense. Perhaps they are right, but I think probably they're not. Especially in the case of education, which at its most fundamental level is helping people make sense of things, senseless rhetoric runs against the grain of what one is trying to accomplish. "Trust me, I'll make sense later, even though I know I don't now. I don't need to make sense now—actually, I need to say something stupid now because I know people are stupid," they seem to say. This notion recalls for me the Bruce Eric Kaplan cartoon that I mentioned at the beginning of chapter 1: "I was reading somewhere that people are stupid." Few people are pervasively or irredeemably stupid, although many do think very poorly about particular things. As educators, we should be in the business of helping people think more clearly about education.

I'm optimistic that things can and will change because I think more people are starting to pay attention to what is said about education, to think things through, to make sense, to demand reliable data to support educational practices, to argue for putting education on a sound footing. Yes, that describes a minority of the people in our nation, but I think it's a growing number. I agree with Janet Richards that "we need not presume that all the people who seem to have been swept away on the tide of popular irrationality are actually beyond rescue."[8] I'm encouraged by the willingness of many of my colleagues to speak out and speak up for a scientific view—Afredo Artiles, Barbara Bateman, Kelli Beard, Rick Brigham, Martha Coutinho, Jean Crockett, Doug Cullinan, Mike Epstein, Steve Forness, Doug Fuchs, Lynn Fuchs, Charlie Greenwood, Frank Gresham, Mike Gerber, Dan Hallahan, Ann Kaiser, Debbie Kamps, Ken Kavale, Tim Landrum, John Lloyd, Don MacMillan, Rich Mayer, Mark Mostert, Mike Nelson, Ron Nelson, Susan Osborne, Lew Polsgrove, Ed Sabornie, Gary Sasso, Loretta Serna, Phil Strain, George Sugai, Stan Trent, Sharon Vaughn, Hill Walker, Mitch Yell, and Naomi Zigmond, to name only a few. I do not mean to indicate that anybody I've named agrees with everything I've said in this book, but they have spoken up for the view that education is an applied science— for basing education on rationality and reliable evidence. There are many, many more who have, who would, and who will.

I'm sure that people in every area of education and many people who are not educators see the folly of sloganeering, postmodernism, and other nonsense that I have described in this book and the wisdom in careful thinking and scientifically validated practices. The more who do, the better the future looks for our children—and for us, too.

NOTES

1. Shonkoff (2001).
2. Crews (2001, p. xvi), Winchester (2001, p. xvi).

3. Kernan (1999, p. xvii).

4. Kernan (1999, p. 300); see Danforth (2001) for argument that democracy should apply to ideas such that "No knowledge by its very nature or form rises to the top" (p. 357).

5. Glazer (1997, p. 6).

6. Gross & Levitt (1998), Nanda (1998).

7. Gould (1997b, p. x).

8. Richards (1996, p. 405).

References

Artiles, A. J., & Trent, S. C. (1997). Forging a research program on multicultural preservice teacher education in special education: A proposed analytic scheme. In J. W. Lloyd, E. J. Kameenui, & D. Chard (eds.), *Issues in educating students with disabilities* (pp. 275–304). Mahwah, NJ: Erlbaum.

Associated Press. (2000, September 3). Black man dragged to death in S. Africa. *Charlottesville Daily Progress*, A8.

Bain, W. (1995). The loss of innocence: Lyotard, Foucault, and the challenge of postmodern education. In M. Peters (ed.), *Education and the postmodern condition* (pp. 1–20). Westport, CT: Bergin & Garvey.

Bandura, A. (1986). *Social foundations of thought and action: A social cognitive theory*. Upper Saddle River, NJ: Prentice-Hall.

Barry, D. (2001, August 12). North Dakota by any other name would still be up north. *Charlottesville Daily Progress*, E10.

Bartholomew, P. C. (1974). *Summaries of leading cases on the Constitution* (9th ed.). Totowa, NJ: Littlefield, Adams.

Bateman, B. D. (1994). Who, how, and where: Special education's issues in perpetuity. *Journal of Special Education*, *27*, 509–520.

Bateman, B. D., & Linden, M. A. (1998). *Better IEPs: How to develop legally correct and educationally useful programs* (3rd ed.). Longmont, CO: Sopris West.

Baxter, J. A., Woodward, J., & Olson, D. (2001). Effects of reform-based mathematics instruction on low achievers in five third-grade classrooms. *Elementary School Journal*, *101*, 529–547.

Becker, W. C., & Gersten, R. (2001). Follow-up of Follow Through: The later effects of the direct instruction model on children in fifth and sixth grades. *Journal of Direct Instruction*, *1* (1), 57–71.

Berliner, D. C. (2000). A personal response to those who bash teacher education. *Journal of Teacher Education*, *51*, 358–371.

Biancolli, A. (2001, April 27). At least our kids ask questions. *Washington Post*, A23.

Blackman, H. P. (1992). Surmounting the disability of isolation. *School Administrator, 49* (2), 28–29.

Blount, R., Jr. (2001). Mark Twain's reconstruction. *Atlantic Monthly, 288* (1), 67–81.

Brandt, R. (2001). No best way: The case for differentiated schooling. *Phi Delta Kappan, 83*, 153–156.

Brantlinger, E. (1997). Using ideology: Cases of nonrecognition of the politics of research and practice in special education. *Review of Educational Research, 67*, 425–459.

Brigham, F. J., & Kauffman, J. M. (1998). Creating supportive environments for students with emotional or behavioral disorders. *Effective School Practices, 17* (2), 25–35.

Brigham, F. J., & Polsgrove, L. (1998). A rumor of paradigm shift in the field of children's emotional and behavioral disorders. *Behavioral Disorders, 23*, 166–170.

Brigham, F. J., Tochterman, S., & Brigham, M. S. (2000). Students with emotional and behavioral disorders and their teachers in test-linked systems of accountability. *Assessment for Effective Intervention, 26* (1), 19–27.

Britt, D. (2000, January 28). "Their" music is our music. *Washington Post*, B1, B5.

Broder, D. S. (2001a, January 28). Joining hands for school reform. *Washington Post*, B7.

Broder, D. S. (2001b, May 6). Reality check on education reform. *Washington Post*, B7.

Brown v. Board of Education of Topeka, 347 U.S. 483 (1954).

Bush, G. W. (2000). Gov. George W. Bush's plans for education in America. *Phi Delta Kappan, 82*, 122, 125–126.

Carlberg, C., & Kavale, K. (1980). The efficacy of special versus regular class placement for exceptional children: A meta-analysis. *Journal of Special Education, 29*, 155–162.

Carnine, D. (1993). The contributions of a scientific/business perspective to improving American education. *Effective School Practices, 12* (1), 63–65.

Carnine, D. (1998, June). *The metamorphosis of education into a mature profession*. Eugene, OR: National Center to Improve the Tools of Educators.

Carnine, D. (2000). *Why education experts resist effective practices (and what it would take to make education more like medicine)*. Washington, DC: Fordham Foundation.

Carpenter, B., & Bovair, K. (1996). Learning with dignity: Educational opportunities for students with emotional and behavioral difficulties. *Canadian Journal of Special Education, 11* (1), 6–16.

Chase, B. (2000, September 10). Leave no child behind? We need high standards for students—and for politicians. *Washington Post*, B5.

Choate, J. S., Enright, B. E., Miller, L. J., Poteet, J. A., & Rakes, T. A. (1995). *Curriculum-based assessment programming* (3rd ed.). Boston: Allyn & Bacon.

Clemens, S. L. (1897). *Following the equator* (Vol. II). New York: Collier (Ecco Travel).

Clemens, S. L. (1899 [1976]). Christian Science and the book of Mrs. Eddy. In *Mark Twain: Collected tales, sketches, speeches, & essays, 1891–1910* (pp. 371–389). New York: Library of America.

Cohen, R. (2000a, July 25). Life on hold. *Washington Post*, A23.

Cohen, R. (2000b, October 19). Inspirationally challenged. *Washington Post*, A31.

Cohen, R. (2001a, January 23). . . . But in word only? *Washington Post*, A17.

Cohen, R. (2001b, April 17). The wrong kind of closure. *Washington Post*, A17.

Cohen, R. (2001c, June 7). New York madness. *Washington Post*, A31.

Columbia Quotations. Number 22347. www.bartleby.com [accessed 30 November 2001].

Conquest, R. (2000). *Reflections on a ravaged century*. New York: Norton.

Constas, M. A. (1998). Deciphering postmodern educational research. *Educational Researcher, 27* (9), 36–42.

Cook, B. G., Gerber, M. M., & Semmel, M. I. (1997). Are effective schools reforms effective for all students? The implications of joint outcome production for school reform. *Exceptionality, 7*, 77–95.

Coontz, S. (1992). *The way we never were: American families and the nostalgia trap*. New York: Basic Books.

Cottle, M. (2001, June 18). Jeffords kills special ed. reform school. *New Republic*, 14–15.

Crews, F. (2001). *Postmodern Pooh*. New York: North Point.

Crockett, J. B. (ed.). (2001). The meaning of science and empirical rigor in the social sciences. *Behavioral Disorders, 27* (1) [special issue].

Crockett, J. B., & Kauffman, J. M. (1999). *The least restrictive environment: Its origins and interpretations in special education*. Mahwah, NJ: Erlbaum.

Crockett, J. B., & Kauffman, J. M. (2001). The concept of the least restrictive environment and learning disabilities: Least restrictive of what? Reflections on Cruickshank's 1977 guest editorial for the *Journal of Learning Disabilities*. In D. P. Hallahan & B. K. Keogh (eds.), *Research and global perspectives in learning disabilities* (pp. 147–166). Mahwah, NJ: Erlbaum.

Danforth, S. (2001). A pragmatic evaluation of three models of disability in special education. *Journal of Developmental and Physical Disabilities, 13*, 343–359.

Danforth, S., & Navarro, V. (1998). Speech acts: Sampling the social construction of mental retardation in everyday life. *Mental Retardation, 36*, 31–43.

Danforth, S., & Rhodes, W. C. (1997). Deconstructing disability: A philosophy for education. *Remedial and Special Education, 18*, 357–366.

Darling-Hammond, L. (2000). How teacher education matters. *Journal of Teacher Education, 51*, 166–173.

Deno, S. L. (1985). Curriculum-based measurement: The emerging alternative. *Exceptional Children, 52*, 219–232.

Diamond, J. (1997). *Guns, germs, and steel: The fates of human societies.* New York: Norton.

Diamond, J. (1999, February 7). What we don't know, why we don't know it. *Washington Post*, B3.

Dionne, E. J., Jr. (2000, October 20). . . . And the new comeback kid. *Washington Post*, A33.

Dionne, E. J., Jr. (2001a, January 2). What the Senate loses today. *Washington Post*, A15.

Dionne, E. J., Jr. (2001b, May 15). Mr. Fix-it? Got a problem? Solve it with a tax cut. *Washington Post*, A17.

Dixon, B. (2000). A view from askance: Technology in education—much ado about not much. *Effective School Practices, 18* (3), 1–3.

DuPaul, G. J., & Eckert, T. L. (1997). The effects of school-based interventions for attention deficit hyperactivity disorder: A meta-analysis. *School Psychology Review, 26*, 5–27.

Dupre, A. P. (1997). Disability and the public schools: The case against "inclusion." *Washington Law Review, 72* (3), 775–858.

Edelman, P. (2001). *Searching for America's heart: RFK and the renewal of hope.* Boston: Houghton Mifflin.

Elkind, D. (1995). School and family in the postmodern world. *Phi Delta Kappan, 77*, 8–14.

Elkind, D. (1998a). Behavioral disorders: A postmodern perspective. *Behavioral Disorders, 23*, 153–159.

Elkind, D. (1998b). Rejoinder. *Behavioral Disorders, 23*, 178–183.

Eltahawy, M. (2001, November 4). Where were Egypt's best? *Washington Post*, B7.

Emerson, R. W. (1983). *Self-reliance.* Transcribed from: *Essays & lectures.* New York: Literary Classics of the U.S.

Engelmann, S. (1969). *Preventing failure in the primary grades*. Chicago: Science Research Associates.

Engelmann, S. (1997). Theory of mastery and acceleration. In J. W. Lloyd, E. J. Kameenui, & D. Chard (eds.), *Issues in educating students with disabilities* (pp. 177–195). Mahwah, NJ: Erlbaum.

Engelmann, S., & Carnine, D. (1982). *Theory of instruction: Principles and applications*. New York: Irvington.

Ehrlich, R. (2001, May 20). They all laughed at Galileo, too. *Washington Post*, B3.

Ewing, N. J. (2001). Teacher education: Ethics, power, and privilege. *Teacher Education and Special Education, 42*, 13–24.

Fandy, M. (2002, January 20). How I became a recruit for America. *Washington Post*, B3.

Feynman, R. P. (1985). *"Surely you're joking, Mr. Feynman!" Adventures of a curious character*. New York: Norton.

Feynman, R. P. (1998). *The meaning of it all: Thoughts of a citizen scientist*. Cambridge, MA: Helix Books.

Feynman, R. P. (1999). *The pleasure of finding things out*. Cambridge, MA: Helix Books.

Finn, C. E., Jr., Rotherham, A. J., & Hokanson, C. R. Jr. (eds.). (2001). *Rethinking special education for a new century*. New York: Thomas B. Fordham Foundation.

Fisher, M. (2001a, January 30). Lawmakers can't mandate patriotism. *Washington Post*, B1.

Fisher, M. (2001b, May 8). Mountain of tests slowly crushing school quality. *Washington Post*, B1.

Fisher, M. (2001c, December 13). Students still taking the fall for D.C. schools. *Washington Post*, B1, B4.

Fisher, M. (2001d, December 15). It's little wonder a sense of humor can't be learned. *Washington Post*, B1.

Fisher, M. (2002, January 15). Going too far: The case of the nail clipper. *Washington Post*, B1.

Fitzgerald, F. S. (1945). *The crack-up*. Edited by E. Wilson. New York: James Laughlin.

Forness, S. R. (2001). Special education and related services: What have we learned from meta-analysis? *Exceptionality, 9*, 185–197.

Forness, S. R., Kavale, K. A., Blum, I. M., & Lloyd, J. W. (1997). What works in special education and related services: Using meta-analysis to guide practice. *Teaching Exceptional Children, 29* (6), 4–9.

Fowler, C. (2001). What did the Massachusetts Teacher Tests say about American education? *Phi Delta Kappan, 82*, 773–780.

Freire, P. (1993). *Pedagogy of the oppressed*. New York: Continuum.

Freire, P. (1998). *Pedagogy of freedom: Ethics, democracy, and civic courage*. New York: Rowman & Littlefield.

Fried, R. L. (2001). Passionate learners and the challenge of schooling. *Phi Delta Kappan, 83*, 124–136.

Fuchs, L., Deno, S. L., & Mirkin, P. K. (1984). The effects of frequent curriculum-based measurement and evaluation of pedagogy, student achievement and student awareness of learning. *American Educational Research Journal, 24*, 449–460.

Fuchs, D., & Fuchs, L. S. (1988). An evaluation of the Adaptive Learning Environments Model. *Exceptional Children, 55*, 115–127.

Fuchs, D., & Fuchs, L. S. (1995). Special education can work. In J. M. Kauffman, J. W. Lloyd, D. P. Hallahan, & T. A. Astuto (eds.), *Issues in educational placement: Students with emotional and behavioral disorders* (pp. 363–377). Mahwah, NJ: Erlbaum.

Fuchs, D., & Fuchs, L. S. (2001). The benefits and costs of like-mindedness. *Journal of Special Education, 35*, 2–3.

Fuchs, D., Fuchs, L. S., & Fernstrom, P. (1993). A conservative approach to special education reform: Mainstreaming through transenvironmental programming and curriculum-based measurement. *American Educational Research Journal, 30*, 149–177.

Gadamer, H. G. (1959/1988). On the circle of understanding. In J. Connolly & T. Kleutner (eds. & trans.), *Hermeneutics versus science? Three German views: Essays by H. G. Gadamer, E. K. Specht, & W. Stagmuller* (pp. 68–78). Notre Dame, IN: University of Notre Dame Press.

Gallagher, D. J. (1998). The scientific knowledge base of special education: Do we know what we think we know? *Exceptional Children, 64*, 493–502.

Gallagher, J. J. (1993). When ability grouping makes good sense. *Effective School Practices, 12* (1), 42–43.

Gallagher, J. J. (1994). The pull of societal forces on special education. *Journal of Special Education, 27*, 521–530.

Garbeau, J. (2001, July 23). Science's mything links: As the boundaries of reality expand, our thinking seems to be going over the edge. *Washington Post*, C1, C2.

Gartner, A., & Lipsky, D. K. (1987). Beyond special education: Toward a quality system for all students. *Harvard Educational Review, 57*, 367–395.

Gartner, A., & Lipsky, D. K. (1989). *The yoke of special education: How to break it*. Rochester, NY: National Center on Education and the Economy.

Gawande, A. (2002, January 28). Annals of medicine: The learnng curve. *New Yorker*, 52–61.

Gillon, S. M. (2000). *"That's not what we meant to do": Reform and its unintended consequences in twentieth-century America*. New York: Norton.

Giroux, H. (1995). Series foreword. In M. Peters (ed.), *Education and the postmodern condition* (pp. ix–xvii). Westport, CT: Bergin & Garvey.

Glanz, J., & Overbye, D. (2001, August 15). "Laws" of physics may not stand test of time: Team's reported findings cast doubt on one such tenet. *Virginian-Pilot*, A1, A12.

Glazer, N. (1997). *We are all multiculturalists now*. Cambridge, MA: Harvard University Press.

Glickman, C. D. (2001). Dichotomizing education: Why no one wins and America loses. *Phi Delta Kappan, 83*, 147–152.

Golden, F. (2000, October 16). The worst and the brightest: For a century, the Nobel Prizes have recognized achievement—the good, the bad and the crazy. *Time, 156* (16), 100–101.

Goodlad, J. I. (1990). *Teachers for our nation's schools*. San Francisco: Jossey-Bass.

Goodman, E. (2001a, May 15). It doesn't take a psychiatrist to figure out Tim McVeigh. *Charlottesville Daily Progress*, A6.

Goodman, E. (2001b, December 8). From burqas to abayas. *Washington Post*, A25.

Goodman, E. (2002, January 25). Seeking a reduction in human suffering. *Charlottesville Daily Progress*, A6.

Goodwin, T., & Wurzburg, G. (producers and directors). (1987). *Regular lives*. [Video Cassette]. Syracuse, NY: Syracuse University.

Gore, A. (2000). Vice President Al Gore's plans for education in America. *Phi Delta Kappan, 82*, 123, 126–127.

Gould, S. J. (1996a). *Full house: The spread of excellence from Plato to Darwin*. New York: Three Rivers.

Gould, S. J. (1996b). *The mismeasure of man* (revised & expanded ed.). New York: Norton.

Gould, S. J. (1997a). *Questioning the millennium. A rationalist's guide to a precisely arbitrary countdown*. New York: Harmony.

Gould, S. J. (1997b). The positive power of skepticism. Foreword in M. Shermer, *Why people believe weird things: Pseudoscience, superstition, and other confusions of our time*. New York: W. H. Freeman.

Gould, S. J. (2000). *The lying stones of Marrakech: Penultimate reflections on natural history*. New York: Three Rivers.

Gross, P. R. (1998). The Icarian impulse. *Wilson Quarterly, 22*, 39–49.

Gross, P. R., & Levitt, N. (1998). *Higher superstition: The academic left and its quarrels with science*. Baltimore: Johns Hopkins University Press.

Gross, P. R., Levitt, N., & Lewis, M. W. (Eds.). (1996). *The flight from science and reason*. Baltimore: Johns Hopkins University Press.

Grossen, B. (1993a). Child-directed teaching methods: A discriminatory practice of Western education. *Effective School Practices, 12* (2), 9–20.

Grossen, B. (1993b). Focus: Discriminatory educational practices. *Effective School Practices, 12* (2), 1.

Grossen, B. (1993c). Focus: Heterogeneous grouping and curriculum design. *Effective School Practices, 12* (1), 5–8.

Hallahan, D. P., & Kauffman, J. M. (1994). Toward a culture of disability in the aftermath of Deno and Dunn. *Journal of Special Education, 27*, 496–508.

Hallahan, D. P., & Kauffman, J. M. (2000). *Exceptional learners: Introduction to special education* (8th ed.). Boston: Allyn & Bacon

Hallenbeck, B. A., & Kauffman, J. M. (1996). Constructing habilitative environments for students with emotional or behavioral disorders: Conclusion to the special issue. *Canadian Journal of Special Education, 11* (1), 100–108.

Hallenbeck, B. A., Kauffman, J. M., & Lloyd, J. W. (1993). When, how, and why educational placement decisions are made: Two case studies. *Journal of Emotional and Behavioral Disorders, 1*, 109–117.

Hammersley, M. (1998). Telling tales about educational research: A response to John K. Smith. *Educational Researcher, 27* (7), 18–21.

Hertzberg, H. (2000, November 6). Comment: They've got personality. *New Yorker*, 37–38.

Hess, F. M., & Brigham, F. J. (2000). The promise and peril of high-stakes testing. *American School Boards Journal, 187* (1), 26–29.

Hirsch, E. D., Jr. (1987). *Cultural literacy: What every American needs to know*. New York: Houghton Mifflin.

Hirsch, E. D., Jr. (1996). *The schools we need and why we don't have them*. New York: Anchor.

Hirschman, A. O. (1986). *Rival views of market society and other recent essays*. New York: Viking.

Hoffman, E. (1997). *Shtetl: The life and death of a small town and the world of Polish Jews*. Boston, MA: Mariner Books.

Holbrook, P. J. (2001). When bad things happen to good children: A special educator's views of MCAS. *Phi Delta Kappan, 82*, 781–785.

Holton, G. (1996). Science education and the sense of self. In P. R. Gross, N. Levitt, & M. W. Lewis (eds.), *The flight from science and reason* (pp. 551–560). Baltimore: Johns Hopkins University Press.

Howell, K. W., Fox, S. L., & Morehead, M. K. (1993). *Curriculum-based evaluation for teaching and decision making* (2nd ed.). Pacific Grove, CA: Brookes/Cole.

Huefner, D. S. (2000). *Getting comfortable with special education law: A framework for working with children with disabilities.* Norwood, MA: Christopher-Gordon.

Hungerford, R. H. (1950). On locusts. *American Journal of Mental Deficiency, 54,* 415–418.

Hunt, P., Hirose-Hatae, A., Doering, K., Karasoff, P., & Goetz, L. (2000). "Community" is what I think everyone is talking about. *Remedial and Special Education, 21,* 305–317.

Hurley, E. A., Chamberlain, A., Slavin, R. E., & Madden, N. A. (2001). Effects of Success for All on TAAS reading scores: A Texas statewide evaluation. *Phi Delta Kappan, 82,* 750–756.

Ignatius, D. (2001, October 28). The psyche of Bin Laden. *Washington Post,* B7.

Imber, M. (1997). Educational reforms can reproduce societal inequities: A case study. In J. J. Scheurich (ed.), *Research method in the postmodern* (pp. 8–28). Washington, DC: Falmer.

Irving, J. (1989). *A prayer for Owen Meany.* New York: Morrow.

Jacobson, J. W., Mulick, J. A., & Schwartz, A. A. (1995). A history of facilitated communication. Science, pseudoscience, and antiscience silence working group on facilitated communication. *American Psychologist, 50,* 750–765.

Kaplan, B. E. (2000, July 24). Cartoon. *The New Yorker,* p . 35.

Kauffman, J. M. (1981). Introduction: Historical trends and contemporary issues in special education in the United States. In J. M. Kauffman & D. P. Hallahan (eds.), *Handbook of special education* (pp. 3–23). Englewood Cliffs, NJ: Prentice-Hall.

Kauffman, J. M. (1990a, November). President's message. *CCBD Newsletter,* 2.

Kauffman, J. M. (1990b, November). *Purposeful ambiguity: Its value in defining emotional or behavioral disorders.* President's Address, Council for Children with Behavioral Disorders, Tempe, AZ.

Kauffman, J. M. (1992). School reform disorder: Alternative audience responses to nonsense. *Journal of Behavioral Education, 2,* 159–176.

Kauffman, J. M. (1993). How we might achieve the radical reform of special education. *Exceptional Children, 60,* 6–16.

Kauffman, J. M. (1995). Why we must celebrate a diversity of restrictive environments. *Learning Disabilities Research and Practice, 10,* 225–232.

Kauffman, J. M. (1997). Guest editorial: Caricature, science, and exceptionality. *Remedial and Special Education, 18,* 130–132.

Kauffman, J. M. (1998). Are we all postmodernists now? *Behavioral Disorders, 23,* 149–152.

Kauffman, J. M. (1999a). Commentary: Today's special education and its messages for tomorrow. *Journal of Special Education, 32,* 244–254.

Kauffman, J. M. (1999b). How we prevent the prevention of emotional and behavioral disorders. *Exceptional Children, 65*, 448–468.

Kauffman, J. M. (1999c). The role of science in behavioral disorders. *Behavioral Disorders, 24*, 265–272.

Kauffman, J. M. (1999d). What we make of difference and the difference we make. Foreword in V. L. Schwean & D. H. Saklofske (eds.), *Handbook of psychosocial characteristics of exceptional children* (pp. ix–xiii). New York: Plenum.

Kauffman, J. M. (1999e). Educating students with emotional or behavioral disorders: What's over the horizon? In L. M. Bullock & R. A. Gable (eds.), *Educating students with emotional and behavioral disorders: Historical perspectives and future directions* (pp. 39–59). Reston, VA: Council for Children with Behavioral Disorders.

Kauffman, J. M. (1999–2000). The special education story: Obituary, accident report, conversion experience, reincarnation, or none of the above? *Exceptionality, 8* (1), 61–71.

Kauffman, J. M. (2001). *Characteristics of emotional and behavioral disorders of children and youth* (7th ed.). Upper Saddle River, NJ: Prentice-Hall.

Kauffman, J. M., Bantz, J., & McCullough, J. (2002). Separate and better: A special public school class for students with emotional and behavioral disorders. *Exceptionality 10* (3).

Kauffman, J. M., & Brigham, F. J. (1999). Editorial. *Behavioral Disorders, 25*, 5–8.

Kauffman, J. M., & Brigham, F. J. (2000a). Editorial: Zero tolerance and bad judgment in working with students with emotional or behavioral disorders. *Behavioral Disorders, 26*, 5–6.

Kauffman, J. M., & Brigham, F. J. (2000b). Editorial report. *Behavioral Disorders, 26*, 5–6.

Kauffman, J. M., & Burbach, H. J. (1997). On creating a climate of classroom civility. *Phi Delta Kappan, 79*, 320–325.

Kauffman, J. M., & Hallahan, D. P. (1993). Toward a comprehensive delivery system for special education. In J. I. Goodlad & T. C. Lovitt (eds.), *Integrating general and special education* (pp. 73–102). Columbus, OH: Merrill/Macmillan.

Kauffman, J. M., & Hallahan, D. P. (eds.). (1995). *The illusion of full inclusion: A comprehensive critique of a current special education bandwagon.* Austin, TX: PRO-ED.

Kauffman, J. M., & Hallahan, D. P. (1997). A diversity of restrictive environments: Placement as a problem of social ecology. In J. W. Lloyd, E. J. Kameenui, & D. Chard (Eds.), *Issues in educating students with disabilities* (pp. 325–342). Hillsdale, NJ: Erlbaum.

Kauffman, J. M., & Krouse, J. (1981). The cult of educability: Searching for the substance of things hoped for, the evidence of things not seen. *Analysis and Intervention in Developmental Disabilities, 1*, 53–60.

Kauffman, J. M., & Lloyd, J. W. (1995). A sense of place: The importance of placement issues in contemporary special education. In J. M. Kauffman, J. W., Lloyd, D. P. Hallahan, & T. A. Astuto (eds.), *Issues in educational placement: Students with emotional and behavioral disorders* (pp. 3–19). Hillsdale, NJ: Erlbaum.

Kauffman, J. M., Lloyd, J. W., Baker, J., & Riedel, T. M. (1995). Inclusion of all students with emotional or behavioral disorders? Let's think again. *Phi Delta Kappan, 76*, 542–546.

Kauffman, J. M., Mostert, M. P., Trent, S. C., & Hallahan, D. P. (2002). *Managing classroom behavior: A reflective case-based approach* (3rd ed.). Boston: Allyn & Bacon.

Kavale, K. A., & Forness, S. R. (2000). History, rhetoric, and reality: Analysis of the inclusion debate. *Remedial and Special Education, 21*, 279–296.

Kernan, A. (1999). *In Plato's cave*. New Haven, CT: Yale University Press.

King, C. I (1999, January 30). Much ado about an n-word. *Washington Post*, A19.

King, C. I. (2001a, December 15). Condoleezza Rice's oddball critic. *Washington Post*, A29.

King, C. I. (2001b), December 22. Saudi Arabia's apartheid. *Washington Post*, A23.

Kinsley, M. (2000a, September 5). . . . And his wise-fool philosophy. *Washington Post*, A 25.

Kinsley, M. (2000b, October 24). The stupidity issue. *Washington Post*, A27.

Kinsley, M. (2001, June 15). Thinking outside the box. *Washington Post*, A33.

Koertge, N. (1996). Feminist epistemology: Stalking an un-dead horse. In P. R. Gross, N. Levitt, & M. W. Lewis (eds.), *The flight from science and reason* (pp. 413–419). Baltimore: Johns Hopkins University Press.

Koertge, N. (ed.). (1998). *A house built on sand: Exposing postmodernist myths about science*. New York: Oxford University Press.

Kohn, A. (1993). *Punished by rewards*. Boston: Houghton Mifflin.

Kohn, A. (1999). *The schools our children deserve: Moving beyond traditional classrooms and "tougher standards."* Boston: Houghton Mifflin.

Kohn, A. (2000). *The case against standardized testing: Raising the scores, ruining the schools*. Westport, CT: Heinemann.

Kohn, A. (2001). Fighting the tests: A practical guide to rescuing our schools. *Phi Delta Kappan, 82*, 349–357.

Kotlowitz, A. (1998). *The other side of the river: A story of two towns, a death and America's dilemma*. New York: Doubleday.

Kozloff, M. (2001, Spring). Responding to the crisis in education. *Direct Instruction News, 1* (1), 9–13.

Krauthammer, C. (2000, 27 November). No more rule rewrites. *Washington Post*, A21.

Kuhn, T. S. (1996). *The structure of scientific revolutions* (3rd ed.). Chicago: University of Chicago Press.

Landrum. T. J. (1997). Why data don't matter. *Journal of Behavioral Education, 7*, 123–129.

Lemann, N. (2001, July 2). Testing limits: Can the president's education crusade survive Beltway politics? *New Yorker*, 28–34.

Leyner, M. (1997, December 21). Geraldo, eat your avant-pop heart out. *New York Times OP-ED*, 11.

Library of America. (1976). *Mark Twain: Collected tales, sketches, speeches, & essays, 1891–1910*. New York: Author.

Library of America. (1981). *Mark Twain: Collected tales, sketches, speeches, & essays, 1852–1890*. New York: Author.

Lieberman, L. M. (2001, January 17). The death of special education: Having the right to fail in regular education is no entitlement. *Education Week, 20* (18), 40–41, 60.

Lipsky, D. K., & Gartner, A. (1987). Capable of achievement and worthy of respect: Education for handicapped students as if they were full-fledged human beings. *Exceptional Children, 54*, 69–74.

Lipsky, D. K., & Gartner, A. (1996). Equity requires inclusion: The future for all students with disabilities. In C. Christensen & F. Rizvi (eds.), *Disability and the dilemmas of education and justice* (pp. 144–155). Philadelphia: Open University Press.

Lloyd, J. W., Forness, S. R., & Kavale, K. A. (1998). Some methods are more effective. *Intervention in School and Clinic, 33* (1), 195–200.

MacMillan, D. R., Gresham, F. M., & Forness, S. R. (1996). Full inclusion: An empirical perspective. *Behavioral Disorders, 21*, 145–159.

McKerrow, K. K., & McKerrow, J. E. (1991). Naturalistic misunderstanding of the Heisenberg uncertainty principle. *Educational Researcher, 20* (1), 17–20.

Mann, L. (1979). *On the trail of process: A historical perspective on cognitive processes and their training*. New York: Grune & Stratton.

Marston, D. (1987–88). The effectiveness of special education: A time series analysis of reading performance in regular and special education settings. *Journal of Special Education, 21* (4), 13–26.

Mayer, R. E. (2000). What is the place of science in educational research? *Educational Researcher, 29* (6), 38–39.

Mayer, R. E. (2001). Resisting the assault on science: The case for evidence-based reasoning in educational research. *Educational Researcher, 30* (7), 29–30.

McLaren, P. (1999). A pedagogy of possibility: Reflecting upon Paulo Freire's politics of education: In memory of Paulo Freire. *Educational Researcher, 28* (2), 49–54.

McWhorter, J. H. (2000). Explaining the black education gap. *Wilson Quarterly, 24* (3), 73–92.

Miller, K. (1997, July). Star struck: A journey to the new frontiers of the zodiac. *Life*, 39–53.

Milloy, C. (2001, March 7). Students thrive at a supportive special school. *Washington Post*, B1.

Moore, M. (2001, August 8). In Turkey, "honor killing" follows families to cities: Women are victims of village tradition. *Washington Post*, A1, A14.

Mostert, M. P. (2001). Facilitated communication since 1995: A review of published studies. *Journal of Autism and Developmental Disorders, 31*, 287–313.

Myers, B. R. (2001). A reader's manifesto: An attack on the growing pretentiousness of American literary prose. *Atlantic Monthly, 288* (1), 104–122.

Nanda, M. (1998). The epistemic charity of the social constructivist critics of science and why the third world should refuse the offer. In N. Koertge (ed.), *A house built on sand: Exposing postmodernist myths about science* (pp. 286–311). New York: Oxford University Press.

Nash, O. (1957). *Everyone but thee and me*. Boston: Little, Brown.

National Center on Education and the Economy. (1989). *To secure our future*. Rochester, NY: Author.

National Public Radio. (2000, July 12). Renee Montagne reporting. *Transcript of Morning Edition, Hour 2* (pp. 14–17). Livingston, NJ: Burrelle's Information Services.

Neier, A. (2001, October 9). Warring against modernity. *Washington Post*, A29.

Northcutt, W. (2000). *The Darwin Awards: Evolution in action*. New York: Dutton.

Northcutt. W. (2001). *The Darwin Awards II: Unnatural selection*. New York: Dutton.

Nougaret, A. A. (2002). *The impact of licensure status on the pedagogical competence of first year special education teachers*. Unpublished doctoral dissertation, George Mason University, Fairfax, VA.

Oakes, J. (1985). *Keeping track: How schools structure inequality*. New Haven, CT: Yale University Press.

Oakes, J. (1992). Can tracking research inform practice? Technical, normative and political considerations. *Educational Researcher, 21* (4), 12–21.

O'Connor, P. D., Stuck, G. B., & Wyne, M. D. (1979). Effects of a short-term intervention resource-room program on task orientation and achievement. *Journal of Special Education, 13*, 375–385.

Oliphant, T. (2001, June 17). Actually, not just rhetorically, leaving no child behind. *Boston Globe*, C2.

Overholser, G. (2000, September 11). Resistance to school change endemic. *Charlottesville Daily Progress*, A6.

Patterson, O. (1993, February 7). Black like all of us: Celebrating multi-culturalism diminishes blacks' role in American culture. *Washington Post*, C2.

Patton, J. M. (1998). The disproportionate representation of African Americans in special education: Looking behind the curtain for understanding and solutions. *Journal of Special Education, 32*, 25–31.

Peters, M. (ed.). (1995a). *Education and the postmodern condition*. Westport, CT: Bergin & Garvey.

Peters, M. (1995b). Introduction: Lyotard, education, and the postmodern condition. In M. Peters (ed.), *Education and the postmodern condition* (pp. xxiii–xliii). Westport, CT: Bergin & Garvey.

Pfleeger, S. L. (2001, January 14). Can't read, can't count, can't depend on the system to help. *Washington Post*, B8.

Pierce, C. P. (2000, April). The era of big government is over. And, Marcus Stephens is dead. *Esquire*, 146–152, 164.

Pillow, W. S. (2000). Deciphering attempts to decipher postmodern educational research. *Educational Researcher, 29* (5), 21–24.

Popkewitz, T. S. (1998). The culture of redemption and the administration of freedom as research. *Review of Educational Research, 68*, 1–34.

Proulx, A. (1996). *Accordion crimes*. New York: Simon & Schuster.

Raspberry, W. (1999, April 12). An end to our American argot? *Charlottesville Daily Progress*, A23.

Raspberry, W. (2000a, August 22). Tough questions for local educators. *Charlottesville Daily Progress*, A6.

Raspberry, W. (2000b, December 1). Cynicism locks out fair-mindedness. *Charlottesville Daily Progress*, A10.

Raspberry, W. (2000c). Majority justices crossed line of philosophy to partisanship. *Charlottesville Daily Progress*, A10.

Raspberry, W. (2001a, January 26). Bush education plan fundamentally flawed. *Charlottesville Daily Progress*, A6.

Raspberry, W. (2001b, February 5). No-excuses education. *Washington Post*, A19.

Raspberry, W. (2001c, February 26). Woe is all of us. *Washington Post*, A19.

Ravitch, D. (2000). *Left back: A century of failed school reforms*. New York: Simon & Schuster.

Raywid, M. A. (2001). What to do with students who are not succeeding. *Phi Delta Kappan, 82*, 582–584.

Reynolds, D. (2001, July 5). "Good-bye 'retarded,' we won't miss you." www.inclusiondaily.com [accessed 15 August 2001].

Reynolds, M. C. (1989). An historical perspective: The delivery of special education to mildly disabled and at-risk students. *Remedial and Special Education, 10* (6), 7–11.

Rhodes, W. C. (1987). Ecology and the new physics. *Behavioral Disorders, 13*, 58–61.

Richards, J. R. (1996). Why feminist epistemology isn't. In P. R. Gross, N. Levitt, & M. W. Lewis (eds.), *The flight from science and reason* (pp. 385–412). Baltimore: Johns Hopkins University Press.

Rissman, E. (2001, June 18). Big government exists to exist, not to serve. *Charlottesville Daily Progress*, A6.

Rohrer, S. S. (2001, June 7). Disability and human decency. *Washington Post*, A31.

Rosenshine, B. (1997). Advances in research on instruction. In J. W. Lloyd, E. J. Kameenui, & D. Chard (eds.), *Issues in educating students with disabilities* (pp. 197–220). Mahwah, NJ: Erlbaum.

Rosovsky, H. (1996). Science, reason, and education. In P. R. Gross, N. Levitt, & M. W. Lewis (eds.), *The flight from science and reason* (pp. 539–542). Baltimore: Johns Hopkins University Press.

Roth, P. (1997). *American pastoral*. New York: Vintage.

Rotherham, A. (2001, May 29). Asking the wrong test questions: A realistic discussion of the costs of Bush's proposal is essential. *Washington Post*, A15.

Ryan, A. (1992, March 26). Princeton diary. *London Review of Books, 14* (6), 21

Samuelson, R. J. (2001, January 31). It's about goals, not vouchers. *Washington Post*, A21.

Sarason, S. B. (1990). *The predictable failure of school reform: Can we change course before it's too late?* San Francisco: Jossey-Bass.

Sasso, G. M. (2001). The retreat from inquiry and knowledge in special education. *Journal of Special Education, 34*, 178–193.

Satel, S. (2001). The indoctrinologists are coming. *Atlantic Monthly, 287* (1), 59–64.

Scheurich, J. J. (1997). *Research method in the postmodern*. Washington, DC: Falmer Press.

Scheurich, J. J., & Young, M. D. (1997). Coloring epistemologies: Are our research epistemologies racially biased? *Educational Researcher, 26* (4), 4–16.

Scheurich, J. J., & Young, M. D. (1998). Rejoinder: In the United States of America, in both our souls and our sciences, we are avoiding white racism. *Educational Researcher, 27* (9), 27–32.

Schmoke, K. (2001, August 28). The problem with payback. *Washington Post*, A15.

Schwandt, T. A. (1997). *Qualitative inquiry: A dictionary of terms*. Thousand Oaks, CA: Sage.

Semmel, M. I., Gerber, M. M., & MacMillan, D. L. (1994). A legacy of policy analysis research in special education. *Journal of Special Education, 27*, 481–495.

Shattuck, R. (1999). *Candor & perversion: Literature, education, and the arts*. New York: Norton.

Shaw, G. H. (2001, July 3). School vouchers best way to correct omission. *Charlottesville Daily Progress*, A6.

Shermer, M. (1997). *Why people believe weird things: Pseudoscience, superstition, and other confusions of our time*. New York: W. H. Freeman.

Shermer, M. (2001). *The borderlands of science: Where sense meets nonsense*. New York: Oxford University Press.

Shonkoff, J. (2001, July 12). *Neurons to neighborhoods: The science of early childhood development*. Keynote address, 2001 OSEP Research Project Directors' Conference, Washington, DC.

Sibley, D. (1995). *Geographies of exclusion: Society and difference in the West*. New York: Routledge.

Sindelar, P. T., & Rosenberg, M. S. (2000). Serving too many masters: The proliferation of ill-conceived and contradictory policies and practices in teacher education. *Journal of Teacher Education, 51*, 188–193.

Singer, J. D. (1988). Should special education merge with regular education? *Educational Policy, 2*, 409–424.

Skrtic, T. M., & Sailor, W. (1996). School-linked services integration: Crisis and opportunity in the transition to postmodern society. *Remedial and Special Education, 17*, 271–283.

Skrtic, T. M., Sailor, W., & Gee, K. (1996). Voice, collaboration, and inclusion: Democratic themes in educational and social reform. *Remedial and Special Education, 17*, 142–157.

Skube, M. (2001, October 21). Either you are a believer or an infidel. *Washington Post*, B1, B4.

Sleeter, C. E. (2001). Preparing teachers for culturally diverse schools: Research and the overwhelming presence of whiteness. *Journal of Teacher Education, 52*, 94–106.

Slevin, P. (2000, December 30). The name on Bush's signature issue. *Washington Post*, A6, A8.

Smith, P. (1999). Drawing new maps: A radical cartography of developmental disabilities. *Review of Educational Research, 69*, 117–144.

Smith, P. (2001). Inquiry cantos: Poetics of developmental disability. *Mental Retardation, 39*, 379–390.

Snyder, D. (2001, August 17). Potomac gynecologist charged in wife's death. *Washington Post*, A1, A11.

Sokal, A. (1996). Transgressing the boundaries: Toward a transformative hermeneutics of quantum gravity. *Social Text, 14*, 217–252.

Sokal, A., & Bricmont, J. (1998). *Fashionable nonsense: Postmodern intellectuals' abuse of science*. New York: Picador.

Stage, S. A., & Quiroz, D. R. (1997). A meta-analysis of interventions to decrease disruptive classroom behavior in public education settings. *School Psychology Review, 26*, 333–368.

St. Pierre, E. A. (2000). The call for intelligibility in postmodern educational research. *Educational Researcher, 29* (5), 25–28.

Stainback, W., & Stainback, S. (1991). A rationale for integration and restructuring: A synopsis. In J. W. Lloyd, N. N. Singh, & A. C. Repp (eds.), *The regular education initiative: Alternative perspectives on concepts, issues, and models* (pp. 225–239). Sycamore, IL: Sycamore.

Starnes, B. A. (2000). On dark times, parallel universes, and déjà vu. *Phi Delta Kappan, 82*, 108–114.

Sugai, G. (1998). Postmodernism and emotional and behavioral disorders: Distraction or advancement? *Behavioral Disorders, 23*, 171–177.

Talk of the town. (1997, April 14). *The New Yorker*, p. 31.

Tanner, D. (2000). Manufacturing problems and selling solutions: How to succeed in the education business without really educating. *Phi Delta Kappan, 82*, 188–202.

Tashman, B. (1996). Our failure to follow through. *Effective School Practices, 15* (1), 67.

Terkel, S. (2001). *Will the circle be unbroken? Reflections on death, rebirth, and hunger for a faith*. New York: New Press.

Thomas, C. (2001, June 13). Government: Waste much, want much. *Charlottesville Daily Progress*, A6.

Thomas, D., & Bainbridge, W. L. (2001). "All children can learn": Facts and fallacies. *Phi Delta Kappan, 82*, 660–662.

Timberg, C., & Deane, C. (2000, November 4). Personality outshines issues: Suburban married women favor Allen, though they often agree with Robb. *Washington Post*, B1, B4.

Timothy W. v. Rochester, New Hampshire School District, 875 F.2d 954 (1st Cir. 1989), cert. denied, 110 S. Ct. 519 (1989).

Tolson, J. (1998). At issue: The many and the one. *Wilson Quarterly, 22*, 12.

Trefil, J. (1996). Scientific literacy. In P. R. Gross, N. Levitt, & M. W. Lewis (eds.), *The flight from science and reason* (pp. 543–550). Baltimore: Johns Hopkins University Press.

Twain, M. (1894/1969). *Pudd'nhead Wilson*. New York: Penguin.

Usher, R., & Edwards, R. (1994). *Postmodernism and education: Different voices, different words*. London: Routledge.

Walker, H. M., Colvin, G., & Ramsey, E. (1995). *Antisocial behavior in school: Strategies and best practices*. Pacific Grove, CA: Brooks/Cole.

Walker, H. M., Forness, S. R., Kauffman, J. M., Epstein, M. H., Gresham, F. M., Nelson, C. M., & Strain, P. S. (1998). Macro-social validation: Referencing outcomes in behavioral disorders to societal issues and problems. *Behavioral Disorders, 24*, 7–18.

Wassermann, S. (2001). Quantum theory, the uncertainty principle, and the alchemy of standardized testing. *Phi Delta Kappan, 83*, 28–40.

Watkins, C. L. (1996). Follow through: Why didn't we? *Effective School Practices, 15* (1), 57–66.

Weiner, J. (1999). *Time, love, memory: A great biologist and his quest for the origins of behavior*. New York: Knopf.

Welsh, P. (2001, October 21). How far do we go to get students to the top? *Washington Post*, B1, B5.

Wilgoren, D. (2001, August 9). D.C. Board to close 3 charter schools. *Washington Post*, B5.

Wilkins, R. (2001). *Jefferson's pillow: The founding fathers and the dilemma of black patriotism*. Boston: Beacon.

Will, G. F. (2001a, January 25). "Art" unburdened by excellence. *Washington Post*, A19.

Will, G. F. (2001b, February 1). Tall order for a few federal dollars. *Washington Post*, A21.

Will, G. F. (2001c, February 5). "Privileging" postmodernism. *Newsweek, 137* (6), 68.

Will, G. F. (2001d, March 15). The SAT's thankless task. *Washington Post*, A25.

Williams, M. (2001, May 9). The painful playground. *Washington Post*, A31.

Wilson, E. O. (1998). *Consilience: The unity of knowledge*. New York: Vintage.

Wilson, W. J. (1999). Bridging the racial divide: A national multiracial coalition is the best hope for progressive politics. *The Nation, 269* (21), 20–22.

Winchester, S. (2001). *The map that changed the world: William Smith and the birth of modern geography.* New York: HarperCollins.

Wiseman, J. (2001). Camelot in Kentucky: Fantasies about early America. *Archaeology, 45* (1), 10–14.

Wright, H. K. (2000). Nailing Jell-O to the wall: Pinpointing aspects of state-of-the-art curriculum theorizing. *Educational Researcher, 29* (5), 4–13.

Yell, M. L. (1998). *The law and special education.* Upper Saddle River, NJ: Prentice-Hall.

Ysseldyke, J. E., Algozzine, B., & Thurlow, M. L. (1992). *Critical issues in special education* (2nd ed.). Boston: Houghton Mifflin.

Ysseldyke, J. E., Algozzine, B., & Thurlow, M. L. (2000). *Critical issues in special education* (3rd ed.). Boston: Houghton Mifflin.

Zhan, G. (2001, August 26). Out of China's grasp, I fight the fear and silence. *Washington Post*, B1, B4.

Zigmond, N. (1997). Educating students with disabilities: The future of special education. In J. W. Lloyd, E. J. Kameenui, & D. Chard (eds.), *Issues in educating students with disabilities* (pp. 377–390). Mahwah, NJ: Erlbaum.

About the Author

James M. Kauffman is the Charles S. Robb Professor of Education at the University of Virginia, where he has been a faculty member in special education since 1970. A former teacher in both general and special education, Kauffman received his Ed.D. degree in special education from the University of Kansas in 1969. He is a frequent speaker at conferences in the United States and other nations and has taught in Australia, Canada, Norway, and Taiwan.

Kauffman's primary research interests are the emotional or behavioral disorders of children and youth, learning disabilities, and the history of special education. He received the 1994 Research Award of the Council for Exceptional Children. His publications include over 100 articles in refereed journals and leading textbooks in special education. Among his prior books are *Characteristics of Emotional and Behavioral Disorders of Children and Youth* (now in its seventh edition), *Exceptional Learners: Introduction to Special Education* (coauthored with Daniel P. Hallahan, now in ninth edition), *Managing Classroom Behavior: A Reflective Case-Based Approach* (coauthored with Mark P. Mostert, Stanley C. Trent, and Daniel P. Hallahan, now in its third edition), and *The Least Restrictive Environment: Its Origins and Interpretations in Special Education* (coauthored with Jean B. Crockett).

DATE DUE

GAYLORD   #3522PI   Printed in USA